Of
Bears, Wolves and Men:
In Homage to the Wild

Of
Bears, Wolves and Men:
In Homage to the Wild

The North Fork of the Flathead, Montana

Joan F. Lang

Writer's Showcase
San Jose New York Lincoln Shanghai

Of Bears, Wolves and Men: In Homage to the Wild
The North Fork of the Flathead, Montana

Writer's Showcase
an imprint of iUniverse.com, Inc.

For information address:
iUniverse.com, Inc.
5220 S 16th, Ste. 200
Lincoln, NE 68512
www.iuniverse.com

Bear photo credits: Chris Bechtold

ISBN: 0-595-16210-X

Printed in the United States of America

For the wildlife, and those who study and work with them to ensure their survival.
And to Joe, who made all this possible.

EPIGRAPH

"Memorize places. Settle your eyes on a place and learn it. See it under the snow, and when first grass is growing, and as the rain falls on it. Feel it and smell it, walk on it, touch the stones, and it will be with you forever. When you are far away, you can call it back. When you need it, it is there in your mind." (Tony Hillerman, *The Ghostway*, Harper, N.Y. 1984)

PREFACE

An appreciation, respect, and love of nature and wildlife are central to *Of Bears, Wolves and Men.* It is a celebration/love song to the North Fork, adjacent to Glacier National Park and one of the last remaining wild areas in the lower '48. Its story is a paean to an area that was a throwback in time. Left behind from the mainstream, the North Fork was hidden and protected by vast empty areas of public land, with a forbidding climate and road that turned people away.

It was a small pocket of natural beauty, shaped by the forces of nature, kept a close secret by the few who ventured into the place until, during a few short years, it was overwhelmed by human exploitation.

The love for this unique place grew within me during my participation in the adventures, the happenings, the very act of living there. I had it all, the wildlife, the action, the beauty. It was a certain time in a certain place, listening to firsthand accounts from North Forkers who had experienced outrageous events. A daily journal formed the backbone of this telling, while taped interviews brought depth and revealed individual personalities. Tom Reynolds was a ninety-six year old living history of the area. The wildlife study people were kind enough to welcome me into their circle, magnifying my respect and appreciation of every facet of the natural world. The North Fork became a paramount force in my outlook on life. We were all shaped in some manner by the area.

The wildlife was the core of the North Fork: the grizzly, black bears, wolves, mountain lions, coyotes and other predators. All interacted with their prey and competed with man.

The threatened grizzly bear, an indicator species, became my true love, but the procession of wildlife up the North Fork was a long and wondrous one.

But who spoke for them? Who really cared about them, with no strings attached? They were taken for granted, thought of by many only as a resource for man's use.

The key to their survival is knowledge. The information gathered by the scientific study groups proved their worth and provided a telling focus on the big picture: the essence of this special place could evaporate because of overuse and abuse by human encroachment.

The ability to absorb, to become involved in the awe-inspiring wonder that is nature, the cohesive inter-connectedness of it all, must not be overrun and lost in the midst of our so-called progress.

How easily, how rapidly invaluable natural resources are allowed to slip away, to disappear forever. A concentrated effort must be made to wake up the American people, to get them involved in environmental matters.

The grizzly bears that disappeared in the North Fork belonged to us all. If these bears don't thrive because of abuse and loss of habitat, neither is it a fit place for other wildlife, even down to that miniscule creature hidden under a rotted tree snag.

The mystery, the wonder of wilderness will be gone forever.

I want to draw the reader into the very being of the North Fork, surrounding them with the events, stories and people that shaped my feelings about this special place. I want the reader to know the individual animals, their names, their attempts at survival, their deaths.

And to awaken in them a love and appreciation of the natural world around us.

CHAPTER 1

Bright moonlight flooded through the cabin window and reflected off the metal water tank at the side of our bed. Nights in the middle of July here in Montana could be colder than the devil, so it was great to be warm and snug, I thought, drifting off to sleep.

Suddenly, one of the most horrendous murderous sounds I'd ever heard exploded through the quiet.

"Something's attacking the horses! Wake up!" I screamed at Joe. "Maybe a bear—a moose!"

Horrible frantic whinnies, screams, clatters and clomping continued to blast at us. I grabbed the big flashlight, slid into shoes, raced down the stairs and beat Joe out the back door by a few seconds. The entire scene was clearly illuminated by the light cast from the full moon.

Specs and Blaze were fighting, biting, kicking, really going at it. Even though she was twice the size of Blaze, Specs was at a definite disadvantage since she was caught up in the poles of the smaller corral that Joe had to build to keep the two apart. Three sliding poles shut off its entrance and Specs was entangled between the ones she had successfully knocked down and the top one, which we had tied to help prevent what was now happening.

Maggie came racing out and finally, between the three of us, we got the animals separated and halfway calmed down. I was standing by

Specs in the outer, larger corral, shivering in the cold, watching Joe drilling holes in a second set of poles to repair the damage.

I couldn't believe we were here—alone—in the middle of all of this, mountain ranges to the front and back, surrounded by deep dark shadowed wild forests, with the sky overhead pierced by a magnitude of glittering stars.

And with these two damn horses.

Specs took a look at me with her wild white-rimmed eye as if saying, "I'll show you, lady!"—and grabbed up the long flashlight I had dropped during the melee with her very large flashing white teeth. She proceeded to prance around with it in her mouth. It was crazy. And the craziest part of all was we had bought this land and this way of life, sight unseen.

We were a tight-knit family because of many Air Force transfers. Six kids made a camper and then a motorhome the best way to travel. We put on a lot of miles, in the back of our mind always on the lookout for that wondrous place that would fulfill something we yearned for that was lost in our harried modern existence.

We had bought a small lake cabin way south of Omaha, but the area was soon discovered. It took less than five years for the rapid onslaught of people and development to destroy the peace and quiet, and thence the waterfowl, beavers, and even the trees.

The empty spaces of the Nebraska sand hills had beckoned to us, but we kept on going west, always further west to the mountains.

We planned it so we'd leave on our vacations the instant school was out for the summer, to be the very first at park campgrounds, days before others came to scare off the wildlife. Yellowstone was great but once we found Glacier National Park, we never went anywhere else. Why not buy and then retire near here somewhere, we thought? It had it all: the lonely empty spaces, mountains, and vast expanses of forests, and especially wildlife.

We subscribed to the *Hungry Horse News*, the area newspaper, and poured over their real estate ads each week. A realtor in Whitefish sent us monthly real estate booklets. Maggie, the last one at home and still in school, agreed with us: only the listings with wildlife had a chance. A log cabin that sounded particularly good, had been pulled from a realtor, then listed privately in the newspaper.

Joe made long distance calls, composed an extensive list of pertinent questions and requested pictures. We knew the general area since it was near the park. And we knew it was for us when the mail arrived with interior pictures and views from the front of the cabin.

A monstrous snowstorm prevented a quick inspection trip over spring vacation from school. Afraid the property would be gone if we waited, we purchased the cabin and twenty acres sight unseen. Joe had already retired from the Air Force and I was a school librarian with most of the summers off.

No more rushed vacations to the mountains each summer. Now we could spend that entire time at our own place. On my last scheduled day at work, we were packed and ready to go.

We had already put the lake cabin up for sale, so we packed its furnishings in a U-haul and headed up to Big Sky the instant school was out.

Joe drove the truck and U-haul. Second son, Steve, on summer vacation from college, traded off with me driving the motorhome. Maggie was in charge of everything else, particularly Robbie, our Old English Sheepdog, and Felix, the Siamese cat. We were off to our great adventure.

On prior visits to the park, Camas Road became a favorite drive. The roadside had been planted with clover, which drew bears, so a park technician had told us. We had spent many an hour over the years slowly driving up and down its length, rewarded with enough bear sightings to make it worthwhile and always hopeful.

Now, as our caravan reached the end of Camas beyond the park, we turned north onto the North Fork road.

I recognized the intersection from years back when I had tried to convince Joe to drive up to Bowman and Kintla Lakes, into some of the wildest and thickest grizzly bear habitat in the park. My hopes had been dashed when a loaded log truck roared south through the intersection and raced down smack in the middle of the rough road, spewing gravel, large rocks and impenetrable dust in all directions. Joe refused to go anywhere but back the way we had come. Now, we slowly and carefully drove up that very road, Joe in the lead, hauling the trailer that now looked much too inadequate and flimsy.

The motorhome squeaked, shook, and rattled and I was busy picking up things that flew through the air from the cupboards that banged open from the rough passage. Excited and worried, I took only quick glances over at the mountains to our east when they appeared between thick stands of forests. The northward journey stretched on and on, past shot-up signs that warned of narrow sections of road, drop-offs, log trucks and narrow bridges that didn't look too safe.

My Lord, we were at the ends of the earth.

We'd be approaching Canada soon. We strained to see anything that resembled the photos we had received and memorized. The cabin had to be here, somewhere close-by.

We drove over a one lane wooden planked bridge across a rushing mountain stream, continued about two miles through a wilder stretch of road with a couple of sharp curves before breaking out into an open area. A large meadow to the west had a frame cabin buried in the midst of spindly lodgepole. A high old ranch gate, three bleached deer antlers nailed to the top cross bar, framed the entrance to a rutted one lane dirt track. Our log cabin, clearly visible from the road, was easily recognizable. We turned north at the Y and headed up to the end of the track.

We were in an ecstatic blur from the moment of arrival. The log cabin itself was picture perfect, set as it was on a sort of promontory, surrounded by unbelievable views on all sides—mountains, rolling hills and forests.

We were in heaven. After a quick look through the inside, Maggie and I abandoned everyone to take off in search of animals, any animal. The wildness and lonesomeness of the place enveloped us in its totality.

Expecting to find something behind every bush and tree, we finally returned much later to the cabin, disappointed and full of guilt at having left Joe and Steve to start unpacking alone.

"See anything?" Joe asked, an odd half smile on his face.

"Not one thing! Not even a deer!"

"You just missed a mom moose and calf. They were walking right down the middle of the road," he laughed.

For ever after, we did everything with one eye peeled for wildlife passing through.

Nothing was work, not in this Eden with its heart-stopping panoramic views of the Rocky Mountain front as it stretched north into Canada and south to forever in the distance as far as we could see. Glacier Park was our front door neighbor since the North Fork of the Flathead River was the park's western boundary, and the North Fork road followed the river course.

We became intimate friends of the peaks smack in front of us, making up our own names when we weren't sure of the official ones. To our north in Canada, the twin peaks, one shaped somewhat like the Matterhorn, were in reality Starvation Peak and King Edward Peak. Kishenehn Ridge was to the south and bordered Boundary Mountain, which divided Canada and the United States.

Kintla Lake was directly opposite our front door but hidden behind the forested stretch between Boundary and what I nicknamed Avalanche Peak because of a deep natural cut that ran vertically down its rounded face. Rainbow Peak followed, and after that, it was beyond me, there were so many mountains, one after another. I did learn to differentiate Numa after Maggie climbed to its lookout much later. It was only visible to the south when the sun shone on it a certain way, casting a shadow to separate it from the higher surrounding peaks. Beyond, near the end of our view, one always showed white, no matter how hot the summer.

The spectacular lower expanse of Glacier's forested ridges and rolling timbered hills that thrust flush against the bases of these mountains, was called Starvation Ridge. Our views gave a true indication of the vastness and the magnitude of this glorious area, prime wildlife habitat with one of the densest grizzly counts in the lower '48.

The North Fork River, its length fed by mountain streams, was over there somewhere beyond the road, probably a rough three mile hike as the crow flies, through dark, almost impenetrable forest.

The Whitefish Range behind our cabin, to the west, was as beautiful in its own way and perhaps more lonely and wild looking. You knew there were all kinds of wildlife in those uneven thick forests and small, more open areas that spread upward, sometimes to rolling three-crested ridges, or to bare, scrubby rough protrusions of rock formations. Cleft Rock was down to our south, an aptly descriptive name and ideal hiding habitat for mountain lions.

We could see the shine of Thoma Lookout high up to the northwest of us, when the sun hit its distant pinpoint roof. We had so much to explore, to see, to discover, and to learn. My brain was overwhelmed at times, trying to decide where and what to look at first.

The presence of wildlife had been the prime consideration in our purchase. And animals there were. Gophers, actually Columbian Ground squirrels, flooded our open meadows, front and back, chewing grass, scurrying back and forth to their holes, giving shrill warning whistles while watching us intently.

With such a tremendous food supply, of course we had badgers. My first encounter with one was more than memorable. I had just stepped out of the motorhome. This creature, so full of fury and so belligerent that he had raised his entire body up off the ground so it sort of swooped over his squat legs, passed between me and the cabin, defying my presence and daring me to even notice him. I heeded its warning and never moved, so intimidated by him that it took a second for me to identify him by the white stripe down his face. He could have taken on any animal just then with impunity.

Badgers could be fun to watch. Maggie spotted one as it cut across our side yard past the kitchen window with a gopher hanging from his mouth. I caught a glimpse of his tail end as he disappeared under the rail fence and down the slope into our front field. Fifteen minutes later, he passed through again with yet another dangling gopher. Beautiful and huge, he'd have a good feed at home.

Another badger, probably after a gopher that ran under the porch, got confused and climbed up on our back stoop, snarling at his mistake and such a bundle of rage and claws we feared for the screen door before he chose to amble off toward the garage. Never did they seem to hurry during any encounter we had with them, always ready to stand their ground. There were so many badgers around that one came out toward Maggie as she walked down the North Fork road. Two were fighting along Trail Creek on the same day. This was all their territory, badger heaven with a plethora of ready food and few human disturbances.

Deer, by far, were the most numerous in our daily count of animals. They were every where, especially early in the morning, in the evening or after a rain. The fifty pound trace mineral salt blocks we positioned in strategic places, away from the cabin, drew them in immediately. Our back acres, left wild, became a crisscross of animal trails, all leading to our three salt blocks.

We'd check and measure with joy the tongue grooves as they deepened in the blocks. Areas around the salt soon became open bare spaces as the rains spread it and killed small growth. I'd even sprinkle loose trace salt on the stumps and logs nearby the sites so the wildlife could chew on them. We'd position the blocks on tree stumps or bared roots to hold them up from the wet so they'd last longer. Larger animals would knock them over sometimes, in their eagerness. The lick further away and on a slight hill, lasted longer, but the middle one eventually became the animals' favorite, proven by the trampled messes they left. A large natural basin trapped water runoff smack in front of the raised block, making a sort of black bog that lasted into midsummer, or even longer, depending on the rains. Trampled by moose, elk, deer and God knows what else, it was the first place I'd dash up to check immediately upon arrival each season, reveling in the tracks, trying to identify who all had been in the muck. The blocks were always gone, soaked away into disappearance by the heavy snow and rain. We'd hurry to get out the new blocks as fast as we could.

Moose, lots of them, all different sizes, became favorite visitors. Mom moose would bring her calves and, as yearlings, they'd return. They appeared to have regular rounds: from the large water sloughs way behind us in the deep woods, to a stop at our salt licks, then on to Mud Lake, about two miles northeast of us and to the smaller ponds and lakes beyond. They'd make the circle and begin all over again.

I loved them, these huge, long-nosed, dark, majestic discombobulated ugly beasts who would grab a branch of an aspen, halfway pulling the tree down to eat it with relish. Or nibble daintily on shrubs as if out of politeness.

One, with a torn right ear, nubs of a rack appearing on his head, discovered our lower salt, easily seen from the back of the cabin. He thereupon became like a drunken sot, hanging around for hours, raising his head to stare toward the cabin at times, licking his salty lips, looking around to the side and back, bending back down to slather away before—oh joy—stepping forward to the water that had collected nearby in an old stump hole. He drank away thirstily for long minutes before lifting his massive head, letting the water stream from his mouth before returning to the salt. He turned around to walk away, disappearing into the trees in an instant, then in a few minutes, he'd be back at the salt. He couldn't bring himself to leave. Neither could I. I never got much done when he was around. He returned about every three days for long visits.

We watched a mom moose with two calves chase off two yearling moose from the salt. Her new babies came first. One even kneeled down to get closer to his "fix".

Elk were less common but they did come back at times, after passing through to the higher elevations for the summer. It was special excitement to see their white rumps and dark longer necks as they gathered in the upper open area, as big as horses.

Small gray birds fluttered and flew around the salt licks, constantly adding their presence to these centers of animal activity. What we didn't see ourselves, especially in the dark of night, we could imagine.

The hummingbirds were voracious companions from the instant we hung our two feeders, one at the kitchen window and one at the south main room window. They came from all directions, hurtling through the air, attacking one another, taking quick sips between swipes, with constant swift action their life.

We learned to boil the sugar solution as the Canadians did, with no color additive. I could not keep the feeders filled fast enough during the height of their stay. They'd keep close watch and follow as I'd remove their empty bottles, to clean and refill inside the cabin.

They were such pigs that they would gather, waiting, striking closer and closer, like tiny fighter pilots on the attack, reminding me to hurry, that they were starved. As I brought the filled feeders back outside, one even lit on the feeder footrest as I was carrying it. I didn't move fast enough for him. I'd be on the ladder and they'd come at high speed, stop in midair, check me out face to face and then flash away streaking high into the air before coming back like a dive bomber run amok. They were stupendous, tiny bits of supercharged life with their constant whirr and buzz.

Joe was sitting quietly on the front porch, in his red jacket, when one shot by, stopped in midair, then lighted on the tip of his shoe on his crossed leg. There it stayed for an instant, checking him out before racing away to better places.

But it wasn't all fun and games with them. Every once in awhile, one would race into the garage if it was open and end up at the far window, flying repeatedly against the glass. Gently engulfing it in soft toweling against the pane, I'd carry it quickly out into the open and release the bird, scared to death its long bill might be bent. But they'd streak straight up into the sky at full throttle, apparently none the worse for their experience.

The weirdest and worst hummingbird experience we ever had? Maggie and I found the stunned body of one on the front porch, took it tenderly into the cabin so nothing could get at it, and made a soft nest for it on top of the hot water heater. We watched the bird closely and I thought I caught a flicker of movement in its tiny breast. We waited another day, my suspicions growing as a small rippling crossed through the body. When I checked an hour later, it was a mass of maggots.

So much for Bird Doctor.

CHAPTER 2

In such a setting, we spent as much time as we could outside, using the cabin only when we had to, for eating, sleeping or rest when the sun shone too hot. We had more than enough to do if Maggie was to get her dream wish, a horse. Steve had to return to civilization, missing some of the fun.

The front meadow was a rough uneven sloping field of deep gullies, stump holes, and millions and billions of glacier country rocks and boulders, interlaced by metropolitan cities of gopher holes. Long dead, bleached gray tree limbs and roots were scattered evidence of past logging efforts. An aspen grove bordered a more level lower section of the field. Thick willow bushes grew in the northern, rougher ravine that not only marked our property line but housed deep badger excavations. The wood was so easy to clear, it was a pleasure. But we worked on the rocks ad nauseam, throwing and dumping the worst in stump holes.

We divided our labors between the field work and putting together a jack fence from the many long narrow trees that had fallen and were strewn all over the back property. There were more than enough to delineate the northern boundary of our land. Joe set up a sawhorse in back. We all gathered the poles, and he would trim and notch for the cross legs and top rail. Then we hauled them down to the side meadow, holding in place and nailing and watching the fence grow, week by week. We became closer to the land, and continually looked around and up to the sky as we worked, afraid we'd miss something.

We'd catch flashes of startling bright blue when the blue birds flew along the old pole fence going down the lane. Swallows hovered and swooped about the garage and cabin eaves, building nests with their resultant mess of waste below. Red-tailed hawks hunted from above, searching for unwary prey, soaring on the wind currents above us and over Starvation Ridge, all this against the spectacular mountain background. Sometimes the hawks, in pairs at first, would separate to scout individually to the north and south, swooping down into the trees, or away in wide gliding circles, meeting again before disappearing into the distance of the park.

Oh, to have their view! I'd stand still, looking to the sky, head bent backward until I'd lose my balance. When one lighted on a lower fence post, I was astonished at its large size—yet a group of about five small birds succeeded in driving one away once, flying at him in sharp concentrated attacks until he flew off.

Hawks may be the epitome of wild nature but ravens, with their keen eyesight, are the sly, intelligent, raucous communicators. Wheeling around in circles, their loud caws were an indication something was happening; maybe even carrion was available to any interested party. Some say coyotes follow the call of their friend, the raven, as it shows the way to a meal. To catch the beauty of natural sounds against a wilderness backdrop of utter silence is wondrous. A large glistening black raven passed over not more than four feet away, intent on his steady straight course. I could hear the whisper of feathers on its wings, literally, as he flew past with a strong steady beat, the under air making a concentrated whirring lift.

Coyotes passed through the outskirts of the fields, usually going in the direction of the woodpile hidden behind a line of trees to the southwest of the cabin. Wasted space for us, maybe, but not for the smaller creatures that lived and hid there. No wonder coyotes visited it almost daily. Perhaps they even denned nearby. Easy to admire because of their stunning adaptability and intelligence, I liked to think they were safe with us. We'd hear them often across the road to the southeast as they sang us to sleep at night and wake us in the morning. Sometimes their yips and songs sounded so nearby, I'd lay there in the middle of the night, listening, happy with the closeness of "God's dog", old man coyote, our welcome neighbor.

To hear the achingly haunting cries of the loons in the coolness of early morning as they flew between Mud Lake to the north, and Tepee Lake, a few miles to the south, was to begin a day on a special high note of light-hearted happiness. We were directly on their flight path. No matter when they called, I'd stop whatever I was doing, smile, look to the sky and try to catch sight of the special creatures that to me signified the lonesomeness and beauty inherent to the wild.

Maggie and I took long hikes to learn the lay of the land whenever we could be spared from the front field. We became familiar with the many overgrown logging roads that cut through the woods behind us. We discovered a deep dark ravine, bordered on the west by an almost impenetrable stand of forest so spooky we turned back. During these hikes we'd talk quietly, or not at all, for we were on the lookout to see what we could see. It was against all back country reason and rules. We knew better, but we just wanted to **see!**

Maggie, with her great sense of direction, would lead and I'd follow her anywhere, often astounded when, hot, thirsty and exhausted, we'd find the cabin again. Grouse, bird eggs, deer—these were great, but we'd be overjoyed when we'd discover bear scat. We'd poke at it with sticks, to see what the bear had eaten recently, or for hair, worms, or whatever. One had a particularly difficult time with tiny red berries and left a trail of loose poop that extended for yards and yards. Do bears get belly aches?

Our cabin with the Livingston Range

Black bears were great but I was a grizzly bear person from the beginning. We may have been fearless but we weren't totally crazy. We didn't want to get the bears in trouble, so as we tramped further and deeper in back, we became more careful, especially when we'd discover recent bear activity. Newly torn up stumps indicated bear presence. Only a grizzly could have left such evidence of its strength by the way he had tossed around ten and fifteen foot tree trunks while investigating for ants in a wood pile behind the cabin.

Steve couldn't stay away and late summer, brought college room-mate, John, up for a vacation of outside work. We took great delight in showing off bear signs and trying to scare them. In the cool of an early morning, we hiked across the road, trying in vain to reach the river. In the middle of the woods we discovered a "killing field" scattered with piles of bones of various sizes and shapes, most neatly cleaned of meat, gristle and hide, a few bleached to china white from the sun. What predators used this small open meadow, so hidden away from everything?

We tried to identify some of the bones before it struck us all at the same time—eyes were peering at us through the surrounding trees. Our imagination? We never knew, for we took off, back the way we came, talking loudly. No one would walk with me for I couldn't pass up such a neat assembly of bones. Stacking some in my arms, I brought up the rear and no one offered to help carry any either. The bones were clean. Nothing would try to grab 'em from me. Cowardly wretched children. They'd leave me in a minute to be eaten.

Maybe they were just smarter than I was.

We had worked hard, hiked enough, and so decided we needed a respite in the cool waters of the river.

The previous owners of our cabin had earlier introduced us to raft-ing, showing us places to put in and get out. Floating a wild and scenic river would be a fitting send-off for the boys return to college. Joe would drop us off, then meet us at the pickup point with the truck.

The four of us were off on a passage through some of the most beautiful scenery in the United States. Here, more to the north, the river stretched wide, banked on either side with rocky shallows. We stayed to the middle, deeper passage, past a dry-docked ancient log jam as big as our cabin. We were quiet, each reveling in the sparkling water, and on the watch for wildlife. We'd catch quick glimpses of the mountains to the east between openings in the trees. The float cushions lay in the bottom of our six-man raft. Taking turns paddling slowly, we daydreamed in the magnificence of our surroundings, alone in God's perfect place.

The river narrowed as we passed through the last of the route Maggie and I had been on before, then rushed into unknown passages, with swifter and deeper water. The west side of the river, bordered by National Forest Service land and a few private holdings, should have looked more familiar, since it followed the road but the Ford Work Center flashed by us so swiftly we barely caught sight of its small wooden sign. Everything looked totally different. We'd have to really watch for the downstream approach where Joe would be waiting. We had checked it out in the truck before putting in but did not know how it would look from the river. Now, we concentrated on our paddling, keeping to the main channel of darker, faster water. It would be easy to get swept into and hung up in one of the many side channels. Appearing from nowhere, a snag log big enough to worry about kept pace with us astern, adding an extra fillip to our adventure.

There must be an added ingredient in the North Fork air. I felt we could do anything and conquer whatever the river threw at us.

"Remember! If you fall out, go feet first and protect your head!" I shouted above the rushing water.

I was concerned about missing the pickup. Joe would park the truck on the curved promontory so we'd see it from as far off as possible. The next access was about ten miles further down so we'd have to be careful to turn in time.

The white waves and rapids came and went, some a bit more exciting than others. Suddenly, in midstream, in a deeper, more narrow section, we skimmed right over the top of a boulder the size of a Volkswagen bug with about six inches of water to spare. My breathing went into overdrive. Dark, deep green swift water swept us onward. We readied ourselves for the sharp bend that loomed ahead, smooth walls on its west side rising above us about 150 feet, trying to keep to the middle.

We whipped right into the bend, caught by the strong current that dragged us sharply to the right in the direction of the sheer sides. Grunts sounded behind me as we all struggled mightily to stay away from the walls. The raft caught up and scraped against the hard clay cliff as I thrust with all my might, letting go the paddle to use my hands, arm, entire body—to shove us away from the treacherous sides, catching a glimpse of the tree snag as it swept by.

Scraped by an overhanging bush that appeared from nowhere, I used it to lean into, gave a mighty heave away with my lower body and feet, and let the branch go an instant before I'd lose the raft from under me. It was enough, together with the mighty efforts of the crew. We sped out of the curve and into more quiet water.

Exhilarated and relieved, we jabbered away like idiots.

And there, truck parked on the high hill where we couldn't miss it, was Joe who had already seen us and was making his way down the steep dirt bank to help us land at the narrow sandy piece of shore.

The main river continued south as we cut over to the smaller channel. We moved fast for the inner rapid surge of water flowed between large rocks and the landing access. It would be easy to whip right through and past.

John, a quiet sort, made a fast magnanimous decision.

"I'll take you on in!" he called.

His feet were already in the water. Then he slid the rest of his body in, not making a sound as he went into the icy numbing water. His left arm hung over the rounded side of the raft, clutching on to it, pulling us toward the shore. He made his way through the current of water like Poseidon, oblivious to everything but the task at hand. He half turned to us, grinned—then—disappeared completely under water. He had stepped into a hole. Gone in a flash. All six feet of him.

Oh, God! He'd be swept away.

His hand appeared immediately, grasping for the raft and found it. Then he continued walking under the water, guiding us in. His hair, forehead, eyes and nose slowly surfaced, then his silly wide grin as he poked his glasses back up on his nose with his right hand.

We were wet whipped dogs climbing the steep, high loose bank to the grassy meadow above, hauling the raft behind us. John squished, so wet he insisted on riding in the back of the truck with the raft.

His mom would be proud of him.

I was.

I vowed never to make such stupid mistakes again. The river might look placid and easygoing in some places, but rougher spots were always right around the next curve.

That evening, we all watched from the front porch of the cabin, as the dark mass of the Rocky Mountain front changed into gradations of shadows along their escarpments. Black clefts and craggy shapes of projecting rock, bounded by vast uneven slopes thrusting upward, became illuminated by a full moon, so bright and intense I swore I could see some of its larger craters. Wind cut through, sighing in the trees, in this quiet place a distinctive, almost living presence.

Behind the twin peaks a faint glow appeared, as if a city lurked there. Subtly at first, then more intense, the glow spread wider, ever brighter, higher, creating a swath of bands of light, undulating, stretching from the north over the Canadian peaks, spreading to the south behind Avalanche.

There, a splotch of lighter, brighter, thicker bands formed and raced outward in all directions, wavering and streaking upward, bright white fingers of light against the rest of the sky. They grew ever brighter as they tinged green with faint nebulous color.

We watched, transfixed.

The play of lighting enlarged, surged upward and outward, then, in some spots, fell downward into valleys of intense light from which sudden building streaks of light rose again, into sweeping ghostly arms darting across the limitless heavens.

Nature was performing one of the most stupendous shows ever put on for man. The aurora borealis had come to visit.

Displays are caused by magnetic disturbances from the sun, which produce light when they collide with atoms of the upper air. They are so awe-inspiring that fantastic explanations have abounded, especially from the earliest of times when there was no scientific explanation for the wondrous sight. On this night, mentally immersed in the wide engulfing waves of light, I could well understand why fanciful stories surrounded the event. Apparently the northern lights have never been measured closer to the earth than about thirty-five miles. But many believe and swear they have seen it come down to meet earth at mountain top height.

I wished I could float high and up into it, or reach out and meet the aurora on the highest mountain, to become immersed in its ethereal gauze. What might it feel like to be enveloped in this nebulous substance, to fly within or atop the swirling bands at the head of a ghostly arm as it swept across the night sky?

Legends grew around the aurora. There were even ancient reports of sounds accompanying displays. Early Eskimos reported noises, saying the sounds were connected to the spirits that lived within the lights. Others said when the lights swished, they were the spirits of children twisting and whirling in their games and dances. Some believe the northern lights were more noisy in the old days. It would be easy to believe anything about these spectacular displays, even now, as the entire heavens above us swirled and moved.

We rushed to the back of the cabin to watch a strong encompassing sweep of a writhing band of light expand clear across the vault of the sky. How stupendously lucky to be in this particular place, so high up, at this point of time, witness to such a magnificent force of nature.

This display was to be the most powerful we ever observed. I was grateful John and Steve were still there to see it. They would leave the next morning, full of never to be forgotten memories and of events many people are not even aware of, much less lucky enough to participate in.

We were to often watch the aurora that always started in the same place, often appearing many nights in a row, sometimes staying away from us for weeks at a time. I'd look toward the twin peaks each night. And if we'd be weary and go to bed too early, I'd make it a point to try to wake during the night to see if they had appeared. Sometimes the far away hazy glow would lurk back in behind King Edward and Starvation peaks, but glow no further. Other times, I'd watch the aurora play about in the middle of the night until I'd stagger to bed in a stupor, full of fanciful thoughts and utter happiness.

CHAPTER 3

The log cabin was perfect for us. Three years old, and built of logs that had been hand peeled with a draw knife, it could have withstood a battering ram. The metal roof, steep so the snows could slide off in the heat of the winter sun, was also a fire safety precaution, as were the surrounding open land spaces. The larger two front windows brought the panoramic view of the mountains from the front, inside. We quickly added screen doors, front and back so that, as the breeze and winds blew through, it was as if we lived outside but for the roof over our heads.

In bad weather, we'd close up snug, hearing the rain drum on the metal roof, while the blustery storm-driven wind tried to lift it, a wonderful sound to fall asleep under at night. The interior had a light airy quality not always found in log homes. The open staircase of half logs rose to the upstairs bedrooms off a balustraded balcony. Decorative chains, fastened to the ridge log, hung down and connected to other chains that formed the stair railing. Joe added another line of chain under the single ones that surrounded the small upstairs landing since Robbie liked to stick his big hairy head through to peer down onto the main floor below.

The downstairs had a dividing tongue and groove wall, one side an all-purpose room, the other, kitchen and dining area. The fully plumbed bathroom was off the back entrance, as was the open utility area and pantry. The pantry was vital for storage since a round trip to town could easily surpass 165 miles and usually took the better part of an entire day, no matter how highly organized we became. If you ran out, you did without 'til next time.

The builder/owner had heated with the large earth wood stove set between the main room and kitchen. We eventually removed the smaller, ancient wood cooking stove on the other side of the chimney and installed a propane heater, easier to maintain and cleaner for the environment.

In the first years, the back door opened directly to the outside. The cabin fairly cried out for a large back screen porch, which we built one summer a few years later. Maggie was reading there one morning when a large moose clattered up the middle of the lane to the cabin as if he owned the place. Which of course, he really did. We were to find out our cabin had been built in an animal corridor, a stunning location for us, but not for the wildlife.

When I'd feel guilty about being in such a location, I'd try to justify it by telling myself the cabin had already been built, that it had gone from year 'round use to seasonal, and that someone would have eventually purchased it. Better us than a person who wasn't as avid an animal lover.

All this was a different way of living, totally new, and thus everything was high adventure. There were no people that we knew of near us. I had been disappointed with the proximity of the frame cabin to the south of us past the Y. In this wilderness I wanted no reminder of people. Over time, we found that the owners were there only a week or so each year. I could stand that.

Even though the cabin was wired for electricity, with hookup to our generator in the garage, we kept its use to a minimum. A deep cycle battery did great for the radio and I grew to appreciate and even love a good, dependable flashlight.

I used to sit in the dusk and dark a good bit. Not cheap, just unable to easily flick the Bic lighter needed to light the propane lamps. The wicks to these lights were preformed, hung down from a round piece of metal, and were supposedly equivalent to a sixty watt bulb. My thumbs were not quite adept enough to get the lighter on, then stand under the propane wick and turn the handle down allowing the propane to sweep through and light with a whoomp. Propane is great to cook and refrigerate with, but try standing immediately by an explosive and incendiary piece of equipment that could possibly blow up in your face. We were seated at the dining room table one evening when the double propane light between the table and stove began to pulsate and gulp air.

"What's it doing?" I asked, fearing the worst.

At that instant, the round piece of metal blew from the lamp, hit the floor like a bullet and began to burn the carpet. Joe quickly turned the light off, I grabbed a towel and picked up the glowing red piece of metal that had, a few seconds before, been part of the light, and tossed it in the sink. The rug still bears the round burn, and I never turned a light on unless I really had to.

Nothing fazed us though, not inside, or outside. We shoveled and raked seeds of native grass in the front field and along the border of the lane to the cabin, closely watched by elk that seemed to think all this labor was just for them; the bears had dibs on the clover we added.

Transplanting small trees to alongside the lane turned into a job from hell. The dirt was as hard as concrete and the shovel kept hitting immovable rocks. It was even harder to dig up and save the scrawny roots of the tiny trees we wanted to move.

The solitude, the beauty and inner richness of this kind of existence appealed to us, a release from the rush and complexity of modern life. We had found this remote area and it rapidly became part of us.

Monty, the previous owner and builder of our cabin, visited us often, to check how we were doing and to clue us in on the surrounding area. After keeping us enthralled one afternoon with grizzly bear stories, he pointed up toward Thoma lookout just before leaving. It stood deserted and high on a mountain behind us to our west, clearly visible from our back area.

"Bears are all back up in there, too. Prime habitat." He described how to reach the trail.

There is safety in numbers so we waited until second daughter, Becky, and her family visited. We left the car at the trail head, excited and enthused, ready for anything. Obviously we were the first hikers of the season, maybe even longer than that. We had trouble at first even finding the narrow, winding trail. Thick understory in some areas grew over it so completely it was as if we were in a tunnel as we waded through the first of many small streams that would be gone by midsummer.

Mike led and I brought up the rear. After about five minutes of climbing everyone in front stopped. Stretching out before us for about ten feet was a black mucky bog, cut up by hundreds of animal tracks. Impenetrable bushes and trees bordered either side preventing any passage but forward. Our shoes were almost sucked off our feet with each step. Somehow, we got through, covered to our ankles with the black stuff, making jokes about not being able to run from anything—slowed down or stuck by the muck on our feet.

Grizzly bears were on our minds, of course.

Everyone talked, sang and I picked up a stick. The forest was the thickest I had ever been in. We thrust aside fallen limbs and pushed through overgrown bushes and saplings that tried to impede our progress along the barely visible trail.

We hiked onward and upward, keeping a wary eye out for grizzly. The first pile of bear poop we found looked sort of dried and old. We kept on, making even more noise as bear scat appeared with increasing frequency, growing in size and looking even more fresh. The trail grew even rougher. We were about two hours into the climb, perhaps two thirds of the way to the top, I figured, when I sat down. I could go no further.

"Give me a bigger stick and I'll sit here 'till you come back. I'll be alright," I laughed.

Everyone suddenly looked skinny and citified as they trudged up the high switchback hill I felt I couldn't make. Their calls back to me were supposed to be funny. I was busy spitting on my worst bleeding scratches.

"More poop, Mom. Pretty fresh—almost steaming. Hang on to your stick!" Maggie shouted high from afar.

I sat there leaning back against a fir tree for a long while, in utter peace and quiet, inhaling the smells of a wilderness forest, a superb feeling of being one with my surroundings. I was content, deep in bear country, knowing the grizzly were all around, that they were in this deep, dark remote area, and that I loved them and this place.

Too soon, I heard voices come from above me. Becky and son, Nicholas, appeared from around the bend, out of breath and half scared. Maggie brought up their rear.

"We came back so you'd be all right. Mike is going on and try to make it to the top."

Then we heard him call from a switchback high above us.

"There's a gradual ascent here. I'm almost there, I think." In a few minutes he came crashing down the trail, breathing hard and fast and looking like he had met up with some rampaging beast.

"I came back. The top is too far away. It just goes up and up and there was so much fresh bear sign I thought I'd better turn back."

Wise decision. We stuck closer together on the hike down, making a hell of a lot of noise, half scared, high with excitement. We were in bear country, grizzly country, the grand beast we so admired and respected. This was their home. We were the intruders. We had come close, probably too close.

Every day I look at Thoma, way above and behind us, the lookout's roof shining in its open space in the sun, surrounded by forest, so dark, thick and overgrown it's barely passable. I imagine the bears at home, deep in their woods, safe. And I am happy. The hike may have been considered a failure since we didn't make it to the top. But just the thought of following a trail of fresh bear scat for hours in late spring in such a place was more than enough.

The muck never did come off my shoes. I wore them for luck until they fell apart and I had to throw them away. I found out later we had attempted the "back way" trail to Thoma which was fine. Let others go the more traveled path.

We soon learned of other special places, Trail Creek springs being perhaps the finest. It was a short drive south. Maggie and I would carry our big blue speckled enamel cups down the steep, rough, rocky path to boulders worn down from centuries of high rushing spring runoff, looking forward to a period of extraordinary peace.

In the hot days of July or August, the creek, its banks thickly lined by trees and willow bushes, was a haven of coolness and beauty. We'd sit and watch the water as it flowed from the higher country through a dark shadowed gorge to the springs. Ice cold water welled up and out from under a small rocky ledge along the near bank laced by bare tree roots. The creek, its flow strengthened by the additional water, then widened into shallows, bottom-lined by an expanse of smooth rocks, a perfect place for critters to play.

Shadows played back and forth across the surface of the water as the clouds moved overhead. There were usually small birds flitting through. Once we were lucky enough to see a water ouzel fly in, then dive around in the water near the edges of the banks, disappearing, then resurfacing, too busy to notice us. We kept a sharp eye on the dense understory across the creek from where we sat. It would only be a hop and skip through the water for surely the bears came and drank and played.

The delicious cool, clean smell engulfed us as we'd lean over, dip our cups, and drink mightily from the swell of water for maybe an hour or so, then, saturated with both the water and the serenity of the place, fill our small water bottles to carry back. We never got spooked and we never made noise. It was everything a wild creek should be.

We had to investigate Tepee Lake, which lay south of Trail Creek bridge, its dark wooden turnoff sign half hidden by thick trees and understory. We parked in the ditch of the narrow forest service road, then walked up a single track so thickly lined with trees the lake could barely be glimpsed through their branches. A small weathered sign posted on a birch tree alerted us to the presence of the rare loons, and marked the beginning of a tiny path that went down to a sandy spot at water's edge. Two loons, quiet at the moment, floated on the other side of the lake. Small black pieces of what appeared to be flat wood washed toward shore, but I set them into wriggling motion as I picked one up from the cold water to examine it. Leeches! Hundreds of them along the small bit of shoreline in front of us. Most were as wide and long as my thumb, constricting to a small blob when handled. Maybe good eating for the trout that supposedly were so hard to catch in this lake? Fisherman had given up trying because of the natural ample supply of shrimp. No fake lure would tempt such well-fed fish.

Tall grasses and marsh grew at the north and south ends of the lake. The over-shadowing multi-greened firs gave the pond-like area a remarkable spooky and lonely atmosphere. The knowledge of the presence of grizzly enhanced the feeling.

A small lone dock poked out into the lake to the south so we continued to explore further up the dirt lane, climbing over or around three blow-downs blocking the way. We found two cabins off a turn, so far back within the deep woods that they appeared gloomy and dispirited. Maybe the vicious attacks of swarms of mosquitoes colored our attitude, for we rarely went back in there again.

But we loved Tepee and the loons and visited it whenever we could, usually at dusk to take advantage of the heightened mystery of the place. We'd stand on the tiny sand beach, or sit on a stump, listen to the loons and play with the leeches. We felt the lake was safe from humans because of its very personality and wildness. It was actually unpleasant looking in many places, with a haze extending from the wild shores thick with natural growth, not your ordinary lake, for sure. God only knew what the bottom consisted of, way out there in front of us. Its beauty lay in its remoteness and wildness.

Mud Lake, with its companion smaller bodies of water behind it, lay at the end of a diagonal line extending from Tepee Lake to the northeast, as the loons flew. They traveled back and forth between the two lakes, flying over our cabin, giving their cries that grabbed right at my listening heart.

The entire area north of Trail Creek was particularly wild, with only a few cabins in the heavily used wild animal corridor. Prime unspoiled forests stretched to the east and southeast of Mud Lake to the river, and thence over to the remote North Fork area of Glacier Park. It was the grizzlies' home territory. On the west side of the river, the forest was spotted with private parcels of land that no one seemed interested in. At this stage it belonged more to the bears than people. Here, the North Fork road cut through thick understory and trees. Shadows ran deep and dark as soon as I headed north from our main gate. Mud Lake was an easy two mile hike, my favorite. I'd turn up a forested, little used lane to check the rutted tire tracks, usually filled with water from rains or spring runoff; any animal passing through left perfect prints in the mud. It would make my day when I'd find a griz print. One particular large one gave me a focal point for weeks as it lay undisturbed under a layer of water that eventually evaporated, leaving a hard mud cast behind.

Madam Queen's cabin at Mud Lake

It was a twenty minute walk up the lane to the crossroads, to the wreck of an old barn, a caretaker's cabin and Mud Lake itself. An old, old cabin, rarely occupied, and historically known as Madam Queen's, was to the north, immediately on the water. Even though the lane continued onward a mile or so to another cabin, I would turn back at the crossroads. But when I had company during my walks we'd turn off onto the overgrown path that partially encircled Mud and continued toward the smaller unnamed lake behind it, a place much too wild to go alone.

To add to the atmosphere there had been murder done in the dark old cabin of Madam Queen, a woman of somewhat ill-repute, back in the twenties. The back of the famous, small, log two story building faced the lake, less than fifty feet away. Heavy undergrowth and trees ran down to the edge of the water. Mosquitoes, thick and voracious, had their perfect home until the new current owner, Marca, a math teacher from California, who was rarely there, had judiciously cleared an area in front and built a small low wooden deck with cuts from logs as seats.

It was perfect to sit there and watch the telltale wakes of the beavers, to catch the breeze as it came from the northwest, pushing the water plants and floating ducks toward the side end of the lake. A few tips of mountains showed above the thick trees. A place of beauty and serenity, to dream, to think great thoughts and become one with nature. Surely a moose would appear through the trees way off in the distance, across the lake to the north. Hidden back in there was a smaller, even wilder lake, a perfect moose haven. A large dead gray tree, some branches still attached, had fallen out into the water long ago, a resting place for birds and other small life forms. The parent loons sometimes parked their chick within its shadow while they played further out toward the opposite end of the lake. There, they would work up a running start for lift-off, overcoming their apparent clumsiness and weight, rising to circle low over the water, lifting higher, ever higher into the air, letting loose with their stupendous wild cries. It took the entire circle of the lake for them to succeed in their takeoffs.

They'd fly away, sometimes out of sight, perhaps on a quick visit to relatives at Tepee Lake. The chick never moved from its designated safe spot, waiting patiently for the parents' return.

Black bears hung around Mud Lake as did the grizzly. The original heavy front door of Madam Queen's cabin that faced the woods sported a huge scar of a whacked-in grizzly bear paw print to the upper left, as the bear sought entrance years before.

After a short while in the North Fork, knowing what a treasure we had stumbled on, I wished that everyone who lived there had to pass a sort of test. They would have to love and respect wildlife and care for their habitat. The animals' concerns would supersede all else.

We knew our kids loved it as we did, for they visited as often as they could. When third daughter, Mary Chris, and her family came, Russ, a biologist, was in heaven as he'd disappear in early morning from our cabin, to return hours later, full of reports of what he'd discovered. When he described the elk carcass beyond Mud Lake, we set off the next day, taking the grandkids. Maggie led, I brought up the rear, allowing no stragglers because of the possible presence of mountain lions, who favor small, moving targets. We turned behind Mud Lake onto a broad sward of land that rose slightly, trees thick to the east, even denser understory to the west.

Maggie appeared from around the slight curve, turned to me bent over, waving her arms low down, a strange expression of warning on her face.

"Bear! Bear!" she hissed at me in a low voice.

I hurried past her and caught a glimpse of the biggest, broadest rear end of a black bear I had ever seen, as it dove away into a thick bush and out of sight. I jumped up and down in excitement as Maggie explained how all of a sudden, there it was, busy feeding right in front of her.

Oh, happy day. Finding the elk carcass was nothing after seeing the bear. The bones were stripped clean, broken and scattered. Only the hooves had some hair on the skinny broken shaft of bone above them. We hunted in vain for the skull since parts of the skeleton had been dragged over a wide area.

It had probably been killed by a hunter the previous fall and he'd taken the skull for the teeth. Elk have two ivory teeth that everyone wants, a fact I had just learned. The smaller lake beyond was surrounded by a marsh. We went down as close as we could—no critters. But I did take a few bones and hoofs back with me to the cabin.

Granddaughter Sarah learned fast. Age five is a good copycat stage. I had poked at some scat with a stick, breaking it apart for examination earlier in our hike. Now, I stayed behind with her as she stopped at every mound of poop to break it open to see what had been eaten. A child after my own heart.

We soon learned who to relate wildlife sightings to, for we were ridiculed by locals when we reported the gorgeous huge brownish gray wolf that had leaped across the road in front of us on one of our first trips to Kintla Lake.

No wolves were around, we were told. It was a coyote.

One late afternoon Joe and I were working in the lane when a far-away different sort of call made me stop and really listen. Many high piercing, continuous howls sounded from way across on Starvation Ridge, carried to us by the winds.

Wolves.

Shouting to Joe to listen, we stood there, focusing on the marvelous wilderness sound that gradually faded away. An unforgettable moment.

Wolves **were** back in the North Fork.

CHAPTER 4

Our main entrance down by the mail boxes was called Ranch Road Exit over the CBs of the log truckers that, in the early years, regularly ran their loads from the border down the North Fork road. Canadian logs were hauled across the line from British Columbia, restrictions forcing them to unload the logs in the large empty field immediately south of the U.S. customs building. Reloaded onto U.S. logging trucks, the felled timber was transported down the length of the North Fork road, on past Glacier Park's Camas entrance, past Big Creek and on to its final destination. Some drivers made two or three trips in a single day, no mean feat since it was about fifty-six miles one way to Columbia Falls, on what many claimed was the worst road in the lower '48.

Traffic was heavy and dangerous those summers. Mile post markers, small bright orange or yellow signs nailed to trees at intervals all along the road by the drivers' wives, enabled them to report over their CBs their exact position to each other: traveling north empty, or south with a full load. The many narrow small bridges over the creeks that flowed to the river, blind curves, and sharp drop-offs down to the water below constituted the gravel road from hell. Woe betide any unwary tourist or local who was caught in the wrong place or in the dust clouds raised by the behemoths as they raced up and down.

The loaded trucks made safety checks at our entrance, the first place wide enough for them to stop in plain view of other road traffic.

Traveling down, it was frightening to discover the headlights of a huge loaded log truck as it suddenly loomed up behind you in your rear view mirror. If the road happened to be straight and wide enough for it to pass, you'd hold your breath as the monster came ever closer, ran alongside and smothered your vehicle with clouds of gravel and dust— all this punctuated by the ghostly apparition of long stuck-out logs of varying sizes, held in place only by a skinny chain, ready to impale any fool that couldn't see and happened too close. Many a headlight was broken by flung-up gravel.

It was even worse to turn a curve going up the road and come face to face with the dust specter and its two glaring eyes bearing down on you from the middle of the road, backed by a mound of logs that reached to the sky behind the cab, ready to roll off and smash you to a pulp any second. It was so bad a driver had to pull over and come to a complete stop until he could tell where he was in the road. A favorite North Fork bumper sticker read "Eat My Dust".

One afternoon when we reached our lane after a hard trip to town, we discovered a log truck blocking our entrance. The logs had slipped and some were hanging perilously over the edge of the truck, ready to break free and roll any second. Joe parked our truck well away, and we walked down through the meadow, never taking our eyes off the danger. It was a scary thought: the same thing could have happened anywhere along the road. Somehow, the driver was able to turn around and crawl back to the border where the load was transferred to another truck.

We met a helicopter and ambulance at the junction of Camas road and the North Fork road once. Everything was under control so we continued north. The accident was covered in the next issue of the local papers: the driver was making the trip north in his empty truck and pulled over for a loaded truck coming down. His rear wheels went off the road and so did he. Earlier that very day his wife had made two of his trips with him, before his fatal mistake.

The North Fork road gave no quarter. Many a driver lost control and wrecked, some ending upside down in canopies of trees whose trunks were way below. Even a two foot drop-off could flip a car. Wildlife ran out in the road from nowhere, a constant threat to the most vigilant of drivers. Scars from old accidents branded some trees for years.

Most anything could be seen on the road, from emergency units on the way north to rescue rafters in trouble on the river, to convoys of green forest service vehicles, headlights on, ready to turn off into the smaller forest service roads for their daily work. The UPS truck, with doors wide open during hot summer days, and never warm enough in the cold, raced up and down, the driver sometimes so remarkably covered with dust he'd have been a natural for a company ad: "Delivery anywhere under the worst conditions."

The posted thirty-five mph speed limit was a joke. At times, twenty was too fast, but when weather cooperated, many a hellbent driver would hit fifty-five or sixty along the straight stretches.

High winds were the precursor to tree blowdowns. One night, a particularly strong storm whipped over and knocked down more than a hundred trees onto the road, a record count. Woe to the first person trying to get through. Most carried chain saws in their vehicles to cut away the larger trees but old hands became adept at by-passing and avoiding the ones that only partially blocked the way.

The road could become a running river with ice flows during a heavy hail storm. Going back up the North Fork was a dreaded part of any return trip from town. Tempers could run short after a one hundred sixty mile, nine and a half hour round trip to town. The areas of tooth-loosening washboard patterns that grew larger were no help.

The North Fork road from the ranch gate

Maintained by the county, we were lucky if the North Fork road was graded more than twice during a summer season. It could take over a week for the graders to work their way up the entire length, and the weather had to cooperate. It was wise to avoid traveling the road while the graders were doing their thing. Caught once, I had to drive over two miles of sharp rocks the size of small ostrich eggs since the raker hadn't finished smoothing the surface. Many a hapless tourist would fight his way clear to the border, stop, then discover a shredded tire.

If the county's allotted time for the grading expired before reaching the border, those last few miles were left abandoned. The stretch from our gate north seemed as if it had just been cleared of trees and understory, then declared a road. Since it had no base, during each heavy rain, and especially after being graded, it turned into a greasy, slimy, slippery, muddy mess, requiring four-wheel drive and extra caution to even stay on track. One spring, an Austrian couple's car got stuck for a couple of days in a deep, large mucky stretch north of Reynold's Ranch, about three miles south of the border. They swore they'd never return.

The few residents who lived up the North Fork year 'round avowed the road was best during the winter, although it could resemble a bob-sled run. The county was good about winter plowing, clearing it for many years up to the most northerly resident. Eventually they made the wise decision to plow clear to the border. It was easier to keep it clear all winter than have to punch through the mess in the spring.

There were other people up the North Fork but they were few and far between in the early days. Mary Louise and John drove up to introduce themselves. Five miles south of us, they were our closest real neighbors. Originally from Florida, now year 'round residents, they became a font of practical advice about North Fork living and landowners. Mary Louise was the best cook on the North Fork and would offer anyone who appeared at their door, even a perfect stranger, food, drink or shelter. John was well-versed in construction and practical know-how in most everything.

Because there were so few people, everyone took care to bring a listener up-to-date on North Fork current events, from the grizzly that hung around south of Polebridge to the mountain lion that had been observed by Whale Creek. Any conversation always included the state of the road and weather. Everyone knew each other's rig and spotted a stranger instantly. A casual meeting of two vehicles on the road provided new information to each driver, an oral newspaper. Each bit would then be passed on, personally edited and perhaps slightly embroidered upon.

Everyone lived for mail days, Tuesday and Friday. We soon learned to meet Becky, our mail girl, at our mail box, for she was our link to the outside world with her truck laden with containers filled with sorted mail. She was from Texas but upon discovering the North Fork, she stayed in the area, forever captured by the place. Nothing stopped her, not snowstorms, fallen trees, nor forest fires. She timed her returns back down the road so answers to just delivered important mail could go out that very day.

We continually compared wildlife sightings with her, for to travel the road was to be on the lookout for animals. We'd feel smug reporting our special ones: the black bear mom who scooted her twins to safety up a tree alongside the road before she ran off into the understory, the golden-haired grizzly back in the trees who swung his massive head slowly back and forth as if trying to decide whether or not to charge the side of our truck, or the yearling moose who crashed out of the brush at the curve just to the south of our cabin, up alongside the truck, right smack at the left rear view mirror, his head about two feet from mine. I shouted at him "Go home!" since I took it for granted he was the one who hung around our place so much. "You have no sense!" I called after him as he trotted off.

Wildlife are the losers wherever roads are concerned. Early one morning, going south, we came upon a dead fawn in the middle of the road, recently hit and killed by a vehicle. The mom doe sniffed around its tiny body as if willing her baby to stand up and run, a pathetic scene. The dead fawn was gone when we returned. It left such an impression on me I remembered it every time I passed the area.

Rarely, however, did we see road kill, for whoever came upon it first usually took it for their own use. CBs and scanners were useful for those who wanted to beat out the authorities to recently reported kills. Some were hard up for food, others who preferred game to other meats weren't too careful about their source of supply.

On the way to town one morning, as I turned the sharp curve around the gravel pit at Vance Hill, there in the middle of the road was a doe and two spotted fawns. The mom immediately leaped high onto a shelf of brush and trees, leaving her twins to fend for themselves.

The east side was a high bank, much too precipitous for them, while the west fell into a sheer drop-off. I stopped completely while the fawns tossed a frightened look back toward Maggie and me, before they ran down the road, cutting from side to side, looking in vain for an escape.

When a car sped around the curve and came down close behind me, obviously eager to pass, I hogged the middle of the road, moving as the fawns moved, blocking the vehicle. There was no way the driver could see the tiny creatures in front. It was a long way down that hill as I continued maneuvering the Blazer so he couldn't pass. I could imagine the curses and anger directed at us.

Finally, we turned into a sharper bottom curve of Vance Hill, safety at last after this last high-banked bend.

Suddenly, a large black and silver pickup flew around that bend straight at us in a cloud of dust and gravel.

There we all were, sitting ducks in the middle of the road. The fawns split, one over toward our Blazer as if for protection, the other disappearing as the truck sped by, so close a sheet of paper couldn't have fit between us. The other fawn was even safe, trotting down the far side. Joined by his twin, they ran a bit faster and I herded them until they reached a small open lane to the east. At least they were on the same side of the road as their mother.

The absolute worst is to have a deer transfixed by your headlights at night, for they don't move and neither do you.

Snowshoe rabbits were more common to the north of us, a funny spectacle when they leaped and ran from cover, on across the road to the other side. Their giant rear feet, out of proportion to the rest of their body, were laughable, but add to that the uneven winter coloration changes and you'd see this creature that looked as if he had clean white socks pulled up to his knees as he made a run for it. Bunches of gray and white ruffed grouse would congregate along the road edges, picking for the grit they needed for their crops.

The road tied us all together, like it or not. Cursed and damned by everyone, it popped up in every conversation. Most of us wanted it kept exactly as it was, for it helped keep people out. Then there were those who wanted it paved for various reasons, sometimes for their own hidden agenda. If the subject of the road was brought up at an occasional landowner meeting, the roomful of people disintegrated into opposite sides and it became a hotly contested verbal fight of major proportions, at times with lots of hollering. Eventually, most avoided the controversy. We all knew who was on which side. Proponents of the gravel road have threatened a class action suit if paving is ever in the forecast. U.S. Fish and Wildlife has succeeded in keeping the road unpaved over the years because of the threatened grizzly.

Knowing the road, it was amazing to hear the story of Jesse, a Vietnam veteran who reportedly suffered flashbacks. He had once pulled 300 pounds of supplies up the North Fork road on a sled in winter, dressed in poor outerwear and wrapped leggings. It took him two and a half days. His female companion, of stern demeanor, could often be seen waiting at their mail box, with her leather skirt and huge knife strapped to her waist. All this added to the legend of a mountain man, hiding from society.

He lived off the land. We were told that authorities overlooked poaching when it was a necessity for survival.

We had made plans with Elmer, who worked at the old Wurtz ranch, to make an emergency phone call. Jesse happened to be there, a small, slim, intelligent, soft-spoken pleasant man, obviously in pain. Dressed in worn mountain man clothes, he was describing to Elmer how the previous night, he had been getting his horses and was "felled" by a tree. His face had been cut up and he had passed out from the pain in his back.

He caught up with Becky at noon one mail day on the road by our mail box, to have her report to the local Columbia Falls grocery that they had forgotten his fifty pounds of dog food. She, kind soul, would, of course, bring it up to him the next mail day. Becky told us later how he showed her well-made tongs and campfire utensils he had fashioned at his forge, for sale, or barter.

A few years later, we heard he had left on horseback, to make the long journey over into Idaho to escape the influx of people coming into the North Fork.

We happened to be on a side road one day and recognized Jesse's property from people's descriptions. The lay of his land was beautiful, with a Jesse-made bridge crossing a small creek to the front. His log cabin walls rose vertically, giving it the appearance of a block house. The empty windows, now framed by tattered plastic, blowing in the breeze, would never have offered him much protection from the elements, even when they were whole. The forlorn wreck of a place had a garbage pile out back and, of course, it had been scattered by animals.

So ended one person's dreams on the road less traveled.

CHAPTER 5

For use during the winterizing of the cabin, Joe and Maggie built an outhouse the second year. We had selected a spot along the edges of the trees that marked the beginning of the wild back part of our property. It took Joe two days of hard manual labor just to dig the hole in the rocky cement-like ground. The actual construction seemed a snap in comparison. Maggie completed its setting by hunting for the proper sized poles and building a bridge to it over the deep ditch that circled through the rear of the open space behind the cabin. Flat rocks for the small path from the bridge to the outhouse were simple to find.

A ten inch high screened opening split the entire width of both sides of the outhouse at seated eye level. To the northeast, the Canadian mountains were in full view. Described by one user as the most beautiful one he had ever been in, it was also fun.

Any animal that happened through couldn't see us, but we sure could see them. Coyotes cruised around from the salt on their way to the woodpile or front field. Maggie caught sight of a badger on the hunt at extremely close range. I'd tease the gophers by suddenly calling to them as they'd be busy chewing away. They'd stop instantly, rise on the alert, then look puzzled. It was as good as an animal blind. On slow days, a person could swat the flies and watch the ants drag them away along the floor.

The fiberglass roof of the outhouse let in rain sometimes, depending on the direction of the wind, but that added to the return to nature feeling. To winterize the outhouse was a simple matter of unhooking and dropping the side shutters in place from above; it was an immediate invaluable outbuilding for it cut down on water usage.

Water is a vital necessity that can be hard to come by in the North Fork. We discovered two kinds of property owners: those who had water and those who didn't. Woe betide either group. The ones who had it, worried constantly that it would, for whatever reason, disappear. The rest were cursed to backbreaking labor and/or throwing money down dry holes. We were lucky to have belonged to both groups.

When we bought the property, Monty assured us we could continue with their perfected water system, used during their three years of living year 'round in the cabin. We could get a large transportable tank and fill it with water from Trail Creek, pump the water up into the large galvanized tank (actually a horse trough) in an upper bedroom, and let simple gravity flow take it through the pipes and hot water heater, then, eureka! out through the spigots. Perfectly healthy and drinkable, he said with a grin.

I remembered daughter Mary Chris telling me how she and another volunteer student conservation worker had been tempted to drink from a creek in the Colorado mountains, then turned around a curve and found the rotted carcass of an elk in the water. So we bought six five gallon plastic containers and kept them filled with good ice-cold drinking water from a park campground spigot. No giardia for us.

Monty kept our tank filled until we had our own system working. After many trips to town and a wait for some of the items, we were able to get our own water in two weeks and two days, quite an accomplishment, considering we had to order a one hundred and fifty gallon green plastic agricultural tank, safe for drinking water, complete with a black plastic lid covering the twelve inch diameter top opening, an orange water pump and heavy duty water hoses, couplings and a fitted end screen to keep from picking up small rocks and gravel from the creek bed. Joe made a wooden frame from 2 X 4 studs to hold the water tank in position during transport back and forth to the creek and for storage in the garage.

We'd pick the tank up in its frame and slide it into the truck, together with the pump and hoses. It was about an eight minute ride down the North Fork road from our cabin to the creek. A small lane just before the narrow bridge, diverted from the road to the creek, where we'd back the truck up as close as we could to the edge of the steep, rocky bank. Joe would lug out the heavy water pump and hook up the hoses. One was clear, ridged plastic, twenty feet long, with the screened end which we tossed down into the creek to suck up the water. We used the other, a blue fire hose, to pump the water into the tank in the back of the truck. It was my job to stand up inside the bed of the truck, position myself around the huge tank, head bent up against the roof of the topper, and hold the hose in the tank against the pressure of the running water. We had to be careful in the placement of the plastic hoses because the heat from the running pump engine melted a spot once when the blue hose kinked and touched the hot engine.

I'd keep close watch on the water level in the tank as it filled, sometimes seeing bugs and other unknowns flow in with the water. I'd holler to Joe to cut the pump motor when the tank was about three fourths full. We'd screw the plastic cover back onto the tank, load all the paraphernalia back into the truck, then head slowly back up to our cabin, careful not to unduly slosh. There, we'd repeat the process, only backwards, pumping the water from the tank into the outside water outlet of the cabin, shooting it up into the upstairs water tank until the overflow vent would gush out water, signifying the tank was full and we could stop. And so we'd be set with water for another two or three days. We tried the bank on the east side of the creek once, thinking it would be

Trail Creek

easier access for Joe since he had to stand on a precarious perch the entire time on the upper side. Never again. The creek bed was too shallow and we suctioned up gravel from the bottom. We had to empty out the green water tank after removing the tight bottom plug in order to clear it, a dreadful job. Not even a bit of gold to make it more worthwhile!

We followed our Trail Creek system every few days for three solid summers, more frequently after Monty and his brothers left their horses in their lower pastures. We had the use of the horses, so felt it only fair to keep the animals in water. We'd make two or three trips in a day, one for us, the rest for the horse tanks. The water those critters sucked up on a hot, summer day was unbelievable.

Maybe because of this, we discussed having our own well, picking the brains of people who had recently had one drilled or would in the near future. It was scary to hear about the dry holes, or bad water. A week before we had to leave at the end of our summer, a driller who had finished working three miles north of us, agreed to come to our place next. This would cut down on the cost of having him travel all the way up the long North Fork road just for us.

The well to the north had come up dry he said, shaking his head, adding, "We have a lot of those up here. We don't like 'em any more than our clients." This simple matter-of-fact statement raised our anxiety level through the roof. Joe and I had picked what we thought was a likely spot, sort of in line with the successful well about a mile to the north.

Certain memories stay with you forever. We watched the drillers set up their massive and highly complicated rig. Seeing and hearing that drill bit go down at a terrifying rate of speed into the earth at twenty dollars per foot, and remembering the feeling of excitement tempered by fear, of the praying to God and to every Saint whose name I could remember—all this was etched with indelible clarity on my brain. Fists clenched, I tried to appear casual about the wretched scene being played out before us as the well came up dry.

They gave up at one hundred forty feet. They had hit shale.

"Any other place while we're here?" the driller smiled at us. Joe and I decided to go for broke. A dry river bed about twelve feet wide ran clear across the northern adjoining property, through ours and continued southward, almost directly in line with the road. Even though it was further from the cabin it seemed a natural place to try. Surely water lurked beneath it.

Again, the watching, waiting, praying and again the dry hole with shale at one hundred forty feet. The driller charged us half price since he had been unsuccessful.

Later, on the return drive to Nebraska, I drove Joe crazy, "See how high that house is, on that steep hill? How would they get water?" Every lonely cabin or home, I'd ask the same question. Water on the brain.

Gus, a young bachelor who lived year 'round in a rusted old school bus deep in the woods about a mile southwest of us had bought from Monty's brother. We benefited from his savvy. When he purchased his acreage he inserted the clause that water would be provided to his boundary line within an allotted period of time.

So in early summer of 1985 talk of drilling a community well circulated. Monty and his brother, Wayne, made us an offer we couldn't refuse. Since we had suffered two dry holes, they'd let us in on their community well with the understanding we would pay our share if successful but nothing if it would come up dry.

The brothers engaged the services of a water witch from the valley, Marge, who had a good reputation for finding water. She coughed a lot and was bundled up in a snow jacket, her gray hair under a heavy scarf. She explained she had just been dismissed from the hospital after a bout with pneumonia. The chill wind of early summer cut through us as we began our walk around the properties. I feared for her health.

Intent on her mission, Marge used an aspen Y branch, holding the ends of the Y in each hand, the single point being the indicator.

"I've even used pliers and they've pulled so hard it marked my skin," she told us. She also carried with her a wire a little thicker than a coat hanger, about five feet long, with a handle and a slight curve at the end. After finding water, she would count each time the wire dipped over the magic spot and that would be the number of feet down for the water. Marge got a hit in the Y in the lower main lane that separated the properties. But the best was on a slight hill in the meadow, hopefully a wide stream the width of the road and about 400 feet down according to her thin counting wire.

While having tea afterwards, she told us she'd been witching for over twenty years. "I just have the knack for it," she explained. Taking only a token payment since she does not charge, this frail, wrinkled, elderly woman had an excellent track record, according to Monty. We decided to go for the big hit in the meadow, marking it with stobs.

Before Marge left, we played around with the aspen Y. Joe did good. The branch would move for him. It did nothing for me until Marge grabbed hold of each of my wrists. I felt a force literally flow through her hands into my wrists. The aspen stick came alive! This woman was magic.

Again, there was excitement and hope. A different driller came the back way from Eureka, over the rough terrain of Trail Creek, an improbable route for such a huge vehicle since in many places it's one way.

June 25, 1985 was a day of joy and celebration. The well came in at 125 feet, fifteen to twenty gallons a minute. I was a true believer in water witching!

Now the hard back breaking work began, to install the water lines to each of four properties that would each own twenty-five percent of the well. Wayne did the ditching with his back hoe, about four feet deep and 2,600 feet in length, since the line came from the well, out through the meadow, past the back of the inside cabin, to the Y in the lane where one line branched up to the edge of Gus' property. The other line ran along the right side of our lane to our cabin, and then continued over to Monty's adjoining thirty acres.

We developed a regular work routine. Wayne dug the ditch, Joe, Monty and Gus raked the bottom smooth, and Maggie and I took out rocks, including the smallest of pebbles. Especially to the two of us, glacier country earth contained 5,000 rocks per square foot and any one of them could have worn a hole in the water line over the years ahead. A thick layer of wood chips cushioned the bottom before the line itself was laid. Then another layer of wood chips was forked into the ditch on top of the line. We were like prisoners slaving on a rock pile for five days, under a broiling July sun. Maggie and I were released for a trip to town for fittings, a glorious respite. People we had never seen or met before came up to watch us, since word spreads fast up the North Fork. They offered comments but also learned, with us doing all the work.

We took our time and were extra careful: the water line was down deep, cushioned on the bottom and protected on top by extra layers of wood chips at the Y where the line went under the lane and where the snow would not provide extra insulation. We also installed freeze proof outside faucets at the cabins and at the water line endings at Gus' and Monty's land.

It was cause for a celebration and a toast with the clear, cold water from the hose at the faucet when the first water flowed through the line without a hitch or leak. A friend of Monty's then covered the line with his cat, leaving a long scar the entire length of our lane. Joe leveled the torn up ground and we felt like hard-scrabble farmers, raking in the seed that would grow into cover.

We drew up the legal papers covering every possible problem that could arise with a community well. The agreement was then recorded and legally tied to each other's land so the contract would be binding on future owners as well.

Even with easier access, we were frugal with water. Always mindful of weather conditions, we'd begin the routine of pumping water by opening the upstairs tank valve. Then Joe would go off down the lane in the tractor, pulling the red trailer with the generator riding in it. It took about fifteen minutes to travel over to the meadow and start the well pump.

Meanwhile, at the cabin I went berserk: flush the john, clean it, the tub and sink. Make sure dishes were finished, fill the tea kettle, the pet's water dish, and after we got a washer, fill the tub part way to get a leg up on the water supply. I'd listen for the water splashing into the upstairs tank, then check its level by lifting the small lid fitted over an eight inch diameter hole cut into the tank top, a full sheet of thick plywood covering the entire tank.

I had to use a flashlight to see. Feeling and smelling the clean, cold water vapor rise up from the filling tank was always neat, but not as good as it had been at Trail Creek. After checking, then watching for the final level to be reached, ever mindful of the cat who was utterly fascinated by the entire process, I'd close the lid, then the valve and dash downstairs. The dog had to go with me as I grabbed a light colored towel, went to the corner of the front porch facing the well, and wildly wave it as a signal for Joe to cut the pump. We had a full tank again.

All of this, of course, was intermittent, interrupted by looking at the mountains to make sure they were in place, checking to see if any wildlife was wandering through, or trying to identify that rig speeding down the North Fork road in a cloud of dust.

The routine didn't always work smoothly.

Once Joe was at the well, pumping away.

I heard no splash. Filled with dread, I ran all the way down our lane to tell him we had no water. Tearing past the middle cabin, I was elated to discover the problem: water gushed from their overflow pipe in the roof, flooding onto the ground. The owners had taken off and left their tank valve open. We were the highest spot and that cabin was between us and the well. We could get no water.

According to the legal contract no one else was responsible for any water damage caused by a forgotten open valve. These people usually came about twice a year. We were lucky this time. They had gone to town, left an upstairs window open and even had left a ladder in sight. An incident easily solved.

Sometimes I had to use a flashlight as a signal to Joe to cut the pump, if we were later getting water, or if the weather was gloomy or foggy. Once, when I found water dripping onto the downstairs kitchen counter, visions of having to replace the entire tank and system flashed by me. The outlet hole to the overflow pipe had rusted through and the water had leaked down between the tank and wall. Even though we repaired it, we never filled to the overflow level again, instead, stopping at one of the top ridges on the horse trough.

The work and worry were worth it, of course. We had our own water. Drinkable. Pure. No more water jugs, no more trips to Trail Creek.

Actually, I really missed those water runs. Animal sightings near the creek were more fun, especially the moose who stood smack in the middle of the rushing water until he noticed us and crashed off. Even better was the strange looking couple meandering up the North Fork road. From a distance, the pair resembled an old man and boy trudging northward. Loaded down with water, we had slowly and silently crept up on them. Mom moose and calf, apparently day dreaming, walked their route oblivious to everything around them. We stayed behind them, mesmerized by the closeness of that skinny, tall, angular body, accompanied by her light brown big-headed baby. She looked very old. Suddenly she glanced over her shoulder, saw us, kicked up her hoofs and took off straight ahead before cutting off to the side, her calf right behind her, both disappearing into the woods.

We saw Gus maybe two more times. He had worked like a dog with us as we lay the waterline, although he did not have to. Well educated and personable, I figured him to be a sort of modern-day remittance man. He never extended the water line onto his property.

His bid on an old forest service frame cabin would have provided him with somewhat better housing but it stood empty. He appeared at our cabin one morning, excited and full of plans. He was starting a wilderness survival school, he explained proudly, showing us his new expensive radio telephone. He offered to let us use it anytime. Afterwards, for whatever reason, he fell behind in his mortgage payments and lost everything. Weather peeled his name off his mail box and we never saw him again.

Passing seasons had North Forkers come and go, some never to return.

The time for our own leaving each August crept up on us inexorably. No matter how we psyched ourselves up, about two weeks before it was time to return to Nebraska for the winter, a feeling of melancholy enveloped us. We tried not to count down the remaining days, but it was hard not to, since we had to totally winterize the cabin. We packed the excess food and anything that could be damaged by freezing in boxes to take back with us, judging what to eat those remaining days. We let the water level go down in the upstairs water tank, and I'd clean out the propane fridge to defrost. The very last day of our season, Joe would connect the water hose to the hot water tank, draining water out the back door. It left about a two inch water level in the upstairs tank bottom that we had to sponge up, squeeze into buckets, haul down the stairs, out the front door and throw into the yard. It usually took eleven trips back and forth. Leaving the tank spotlessly clean was a necessity, of course, and we'd carefully replace the plywood top and cover it with a blanket.

Joe had to descend through the trap door in the pantry, with a flashlight to open various drains under the cabin. Pouring RV antifreeze down the sinks, tub and drained john completed the task. We turned the propane off at the main tank just before heading down the lane.

As often as we did it, it never got any better, or quicker. No one would talk much for the first 200 miles. Returning to civilization was a total cultural shock.

Coming back the following summer, of course, was pure heaven, making settling in a snap.

Not so, for the family from Florida, new North Forkers who, when they left for the winter after their first summer in the area, walked out the door and locked their cabin up until spring.

Everything that could freeze, did. Their entire water system had to be replaced since the pipes burst.

They became famous instantly.

CHAPTER 6

What a can of worms we opened when we entered wholeheartedly and naively into one of the myths of Montana which featured at least one horse for every family.

Since Maggie was just plain horse crazy, we accepted with joy the presence of the five horses Monty left in their lower meadow for grazing. Ours to ride at any time, we promised to keep them in water, Maggie becoming their instant faithful companion. Horseback riding off into the wilds, with the vast expanse of mountains as background, was a Zane Grey novel come to life. And we were living it!

Alas, reading can get a person into trouble. We became misfits in a dark comedy of errors.

Goldie was a love until she ran off across the field, hell for leather, with Maggie hanging on for dear life. Misty had the great talent of blowing herself up so big that any saddle ended up under her belly. Lucky had been a race horse so no one ever tried to ride her, not even her owners. Chester, the only gentle, dependable one, was old and so put-upon by the other horses, they wouldn't even let him stand in the shade of an outbuilding. His next stop surely would be the glue factory, especially after he fell over a steep trail in the Bob Marshall with Monty.

Ah, Buck. He was the best, a stallion beauty, so gentle that three year old Sara, Monty's niece, could sit on him safely with her mom walking beside him.

We went off riding on Chester and Misty, and Buck had such a fit we had to split up and escape out of the field through the road gate. Misty couldn't breath 'cause I had her chin strap over her nose instead of under, her saddle fell off, and then we had to fight our way back through Buck and Lucky, who wanted in on the fun.

God bless Elmer, Monty's cousin, to us, a true cowboy, who over the next few weeks took the time to educate us in the weird mysterious ways of horses and their accouterments. After his thorough lessons, we felt ready for anything these paranoid, shifty critters could throw at us.

Sara had been sitting on Buck, perfectly content as her mom led the animal around. Maggie then climbed on him and Buck took her maybe three feet to the dip in the meadow, before refusing to move.

"I'll show you how to make him mind," I told Maggie as I climbed tall in the saddle.

The day was perfect, with a gentle breeze, the mountains accentuating this dream come true, to relive the fun of my past riding experiences and pass it on to my daughter.

Buck stopped dead.

Then I was on the ground, sideways, on a ridge of rocks. Through stars and between hellish, hurtful gasps for air, I reached frantically for my sunglasses so the damn horse wouldn't step on them. He had bucked and thrown me clear off and around so I faced at eye level his monstrous front hoofs. I tried to breathe, braced for a probable kick. I couldn't have moved. Ashamed, I let on nothing much had happened, sitting still on a boulder to collect my wits, bitter at the sight of Sara, back on Buck, happily patting his neck as her mom led them away.

My solicitous kids ran a tub full of hot water for me to sit in after I drove us back to the cabin in the truck. Hanging from my shoulders was the least painful position. By dark, I had to admit how bad off I was and we all left for Kalispell and the hospital. Traumatic pneumothorax: two broken ribs and a collapsed lung. For $1,700, the experienced wonderful emergency room staff stuck what seemed to be a garden hose into my right side, then gave me a plastic contraption about the size of a brief case, with tubes of circulating water that sucked and hissed as I carried it around the hospital for four days.

The human brain blocks out horrid memories. Neat ones to remember? The herd of elk that galloped up the dark North Fork road on our way down to the hospital just before midnight, all the pop I could drink in the hospital—only thing I could keep down—and the weight I lost.

Plus Joe's acid comment, "You'll never get me on a horse."

Nevertheless, Joe started work on a horse corral out back of our cabin the next summer. Not even my run-in with Buck stopped us in our eagerness to savor the experiences that this kind of life offered.

The building of the corral was pure hell. Joe had to use a heavy metal black rod, six feet long, to make a pilot hole for each post. The three inch diameter posts, seven feet long and dipped with a preservative on each pointed tip, had to be hand pounded about three feet deep into the rocky ground. Between the twenty-five pound hand pounder that slipped over the top of the post and the sledge hammer in particularly recalcitrant cases, he was lucky to get in fourteen posts on a good day.

We figured it took between fifteen to twenty hefty pounds onto the top of each pole to ram it in place. The many huge rocks had to be turned up and moved out of the way, if possible, or a new hole had to be dug if moving the boulder was impossible. Sometimes the posts split; many had to be shaved down to fit the three inch diameter pounder.

It took sixty-four posts to enclose the back area. The poles, twelve feet long, had to be trimmed and nailed, a hard enough job, but not quite the back-breaking, frustrating manual labor of putting in the posts.

The corral in late fall

The surrounding mountain scenery continually energized Joe, for in no time we were ready for our very own horse, after rounding up the metal gate for the corral, bales of hay, water containers, horse pellets and other necessaries.

Excitedly, we accompanied Monty to the horse auction just outside of Kalispell, in a small, hot and stuffy inside arena. The show rider made every horse a winner. Monty and his brother, supposedly knowledgeable about horses, decided a paint mare was good for Maggie. Monty let on it was for his small son, "since the guy wouldn't sell a rough horse to a small tyke." How wise, we thought.

We named the paint, Mariah. Monty kept her a week to sharpen her training, shod and wormed her, then brought her up to us. Maggie refreshed herself in her knots and everything was set. We thought.

A week of pure unadulterated misery, frustration, worry and unease followed. Mariah was the unridable horse from hell, uncontrollable, bucking, or not moving at all. What sport she had with us!

In pity, Mary Louise and John mentioned a woman down on Moose Creek who knew horses and might be able to help us.

Alcine drove up that very evening in a beat-up old truck, took one look at the pant, saddled her, blew in the mare's nose, clambered up and proceeded to "ride Mariah down", whip held between her teeth, squashed hat clamped down over scraggly gray hair, a female Rooster Cogburn, minus the eye patch. I never saw anything like it. Mariah had more than met her match.

Of unknown vintage, and off a horse, Alcine could have been Ma Kettle, with her rough voice and demeanor.

Master of all horses, she made things right for us, even taking us down to her place for wonderful confidence building rides on her Peruvian Posos, famous for their "feet thrown sideways" gait that is as smooth as a rocking chair. With Maggie on Specs, a three year old half Peruvian, and me on Stampy, Alcine's show horse, we felt we had died and gone to heaven.

Alcine brought up Specs soon after and we three rode across the road, Maggie on Mariah, Alcine on an Appaloosa and me on Specs, using an antique wooden cavalry saddle. We traveled down old logging roads, spied a large black bear back in the trees, sped over streams, passed by coyote cities, one a bank of over ten holes deep in the earth, and found small lakes we never knew existed. What a way to explore. Exhilarated beyond belief, this was how it should have been.

Of course, Mariah was perfect 'cause she was afraid of Alcine. Alcine charged us for everything, the rides, the use of equipment, the advice— which was fine. It was worth it.

We rented Specs through the month. Instant jealousy and hate erupted between her and Mariah. Watching the resultant rough twenty minute horse fight was scary. They kicked, bit, thumped and tried to tear up the fence near the garage until Specs made it to the top of the pecking order. Shaken, we sent Specs back to Alcine immediately.

And just because Alcine could ride Mariah like a frenzied cowboy didn't really help Maggie at all. As soon as Alcine was out of sight, Mariah was impossibly unruly, perhaps even a bit worse, to get back at us for sicking Alcine on her.

Alcine made us a proposition. She would take Mariah off our hands and trade for a two year old gelding she kept with her other horses down at Cimino's open meadow near Red Meadow.

We were putty in her hands as she called and about eight horses came thundering up toward us, nosing around, stomping, all against the gorgeous mountain back drop, with the added knowledge that a real Hollywood western epic had been filmed on this very spot. The famous plow scene with fourteen women on each crosspiece? Alcine pointed out the plow to us, rotting over to the side.

The deal was made: Alcine would give us back Specs to use since she apparently couldn't return the rental money we had given her. We'd keep Blaze, the beautifully marked light brown yearling, and make him a member of the family. He would grow and be ready to ride in a year. She would keep him over the winter and train him for us. Alcine did know horses. Maggie was perfectly happy with the arrangement. And we didn't know any better.

Robbie, our dear Old English Sheep dog, accepted the presence of the horses with aplomb. After all, he had helped build the corral, overseeing the entire operation. He may have seemed an incongruous sort of breed for the North Fork, but he had played nanny to the entire family for over thirteen years and his big heart let him take the wilderness in stride, especially since he loved his creature comforts within the coolness of the cabin.

Maggie with Blaze

The gophers soon learned to have no fear of this large, gentle, hairy creature that apparently couldn't even see in front of his nose, never paying them the slightest bit of attention. His biggest wild adventure consisted of inadvertently stumbling over a grouse as we climbed off to the side of the road to avoid the dust of a passing truck during one of our walks. The bird flew directly up under his chin in a flurry of leaves and large whirring wings. Rob just looked at it, puzzled, as it ran up and down in the brush in its frenzy.

Revealing his town upbringing, he refused to walk across the front porch after we redid it with new plywood, not liking the sound of it under his feet. I thought it was old age when he began to lay around more than usual, but one morning, on investigation, discovered seeping blood alongside his mouth, then throat, masked by his thick hair. The vet shaved the area to reveal a hidden abscess, probably caused by a bur that had worked its way through his coat and cut into his skin.

The insertion of a wick and six stitches, plus numerous salves and pills started his recovery. He was a comic sight, this huge dog, ambling around in white ankle socks hitched up on all legs, to prevent him from digging at the wound, resembling a sort of strange looking jack rabbit.

We had taken the responsibility of removing the drain after five days, to save the long, hot trip to town. I slipped Robbie one of his tranquilizer pills, for thunderstorms, then waited. Joe coaxed him flat on the floor and I succeeded in cutting loose the top stitch, taking hold of the wick. The dog lay perfectly still as I pulled gently to draw it out—and pulled and pulled. The wick was so extraordinarily long that I left it on the rug as I kept drawing it out, relieved when the end finally dropped down.

Instantly, Robbie stretched his neck way out as he rolled his huge eyes toward the wick, grabbed it and ate it before I could reach it, a remarkable and ludicrous effort on his part. Had he thought I had stolen part of his guts? His recovery was swift and complete upon the removal of the rest of the stitches about five days later.

Alcine visited often. She mentioned she had no horse training video tapes and we could give her a VCR in exchange for her training Blaze over the winter. It was a deal. On Alcine's advice, Blaze became a "doll-baby" pet, laying on the ground with Maggie, his head in her lap, a magnificent young animal, very intelligent and inquisitive. He hung around us, investigating anything we did in his own bailiwick, sniffing and biting at the tractor seat as if wondering where we were taking his poop, or checking over our shoulders to see if we were digging a hole right. In three tries, Carroll, our vacationing oldest daughter, taught him to nod his head for treats, but especially grapes. He pranced around like an Arabian, tail out, ruler of his world.

Joe and I had made a quick necessary trip to town when a storm suddenly blew up. On our return, we met Monty along the road who described it, "Biggest hailstones I've ever seen up here!"

Maggie was waiting for us, a wreck.

"I was about ready to bring Blaze into the cabin," she explained, bursting with excitement. "The hailstones were so huge I was afraid he'd get hurt!"

Big hits of lightning had cracked the trees behind us, exploding them into bursts of flames, instantly extinguished by the buckets of rain.

Elmer opened wide a door to one of Maggie's best horse treks ever. He asked her to help him drive seven horses from their winter quarters at Ladenberg's ranch, up the North Fork road to the Wurtz place for summer pasture, a distance of twenty-two miles. Real cowboy stuff.

Elmer and Tom had trouble even catching the hellish seven to separate them from Tom's horses. Horses aren't that dumb. Why give up freedom and an easy life for one of hauling around riders they don't know or even like?

After two and a half hours, the ornery critters were finally gathered, herded into a group into a small corral only to escape immediately through an open gate on the opposite side. None of the willful beasts had been ridden all winter, so it was a wild ride with mounts that didn't want to go anywhere, especially north.

When we came upon them about halfway into their journey they had already passed through drenching downpours, hail, and high winds; one dumb-headed beast had run off down into another ranch road, leading the rest behind him, adding time and miles besides fueling tempers. Maggie whipped them right along with Elmer, sodden with rain, chilled to the bone, but a big grin showing under her cowboy hat. Nine hours of muscling the obstinate critters may have worn her out, but she had done it, come hell or high water.

In celebration of the successful event, Mary Louise and John had prepared a turkey dinner, but Maggie was too worn out to eat.

These two friends down the road had become family. We traded animal sightings and regaled them with our wild horse experiences. Best of all, they could love up and spoil Robbie. He went wild one evening, playing like a puppy with them all during a movie at our cabin. Prancing around with his toys, he put on a better show, by far.

Later during the night, I heard him go thumping in the dark but half asleep, I attributed it to his dreams of running and chasing. The next morning, I was wakened by the strange noise of Rob downstairs as he tried to move about, dragging his hind legs, not able to walk.

Oh, God! Had he been poisoned? Had he hurt himself someway? It was a stroke, of course. We left for the vet's, me in back, holding dear dog's head in my lap, talking to him, loving him, and crying silently the entire hour and a half to town. I welcomed the weight of his head, looking into his eyes, knowing the inevitable outcome.

After a thorough check, the vet confirmed the stroke. Joe had to leave the room as Maggie and I held his head and upper body, comforting him while the vet gave him the injection that ended his dear life. Joe dug a deep grave at the edge of the yard. We wrapped him in a sheet, then a blue satin bedspread, the vet's plastic bag and finally, a large plastic feed bag. We lined the floor of his grave with small rocks, more dirt, then many more rocks so the coyotes couldn't reach him. We laid even more rocks over the site.

Gophers and chipmunks play on his grave in the midst of wild flowers. It is a fitting place for a grave, surrounded now as it is by wild rose bushes, wild strawberries and Indian paintbrush. He lies facing the line of mountains, with trees shading his spot during the day, and an incredible pattern of stars watching over him at night. A good place to rest, Robbie, dear.

CHAPTER 7

The gophers had a rude awakening the next spring.

Brig, our young Chesapeake Bay retriever, rambunctious and delirious with the astounding array of North Fork odors, became their nemesis. Thrusting his head in their holes in our front yard after they eluded him, he gradually enlarged the entrances to some of their tunnels until he'd disappear up to his eyes, sniffing, snorting and trying like the devil to rout 'em out.

Gophers aren't dumb. They'd sit upright, paws folded across their chests, on the lookout for him at just the correct distance from their burrows, teasing, and timing him exactly as he stalked or chased them. Even the chipmunks raced him along the fence rails, chattering just ahead of his nose 'til they flipped into the front field to escape his onslaught. Only once, over many years, did Brig catch one, and then he dropped it in horror when it stopped running.

We kept Brig totally away from Blaze. Alcine had brought him up to us, putting him through some paces with her whip. He was even more gorgeous than we had remembered although we were disappointed he hadn't grown more. His long flaxen mane was in excellent contrast to his light reddish-brown color, a picture perfect example of a sorrel, the white splash marking perfectly placed along his muzzle.

He really hadn't been trained. It was obvious he was terrified of Alcine and her whip. She then offered to rent Specs to us again, which we accepted. We did want Maggie to have a horse she could ride that summer. So there we were with two horses again, who did not get along.

Alcine brought up a farrier she knew from Anoconda, a traveling shoer of horses who hauled around a little black trailer full of his equipment. He marched up to Specs in our corral, looked her straight in the eye, then walked around to her left side and gave her a good swift, hard kick. He went to her other side and let her have it even harder, right in the belly. She behaved beautifully for him as he shod all four feet swiftly and surely.

Blaze was fascinated by the event, hanging over the fence, paying particularly close attention to the hard kicks that had let Specs know immediately who was boss. Blaze had never been shod but he was a quick study and never misbehaved, cooperating fully with the blacksmith. Because his feet were so small and narrow, the shoeing took much longer. Blaze was smart though. He knew exactly who he could buffalo—and what he could get away with.

Specs too, was well-behaved as long as Alcine was around, but in her sly horse brain, was intent on doing in Blaze. She was twice his size and a holy terror, after Blaze continually. Joe finally had to make an addition to the corral, fencing off a section in order to separate the two. We'd rotate the horses so each would have a chance at the larger corral area.

Horses and wildlife were fascinated with each other. Deer regularly visited, gazing at the strange creatures that were content to stay behind a fence. Moose came right up to the corral to stare malevolently at Specs, as if to dare her to step over the line. Blaze would look inquisitively, then race around in excitement, keeping his distance.

Both horses often stood, ears up, bodies stiff at attention, looking to the back, alerting us to wildlife activity in the thick woods just beyond the corral. It was especially exciting to check later and find torn up stumps, or chunks of bark raked off in a bear's search for ants. We often found long fallen tree trunks that had been tossed aside in a jumble so a grizzly could root for the insects more easily, heady evidence, a reminder that the bears were our closest neighbors.

Storms, as they blew in from over the Whitefish range with accompanying wind, rain or hail, whipped Specs and Blaze into a galloping frenzy, "wind under their tails". The kicking up of their heels, their loud whinnying, the thundering of their hoofs—all rose to a crescendo as the bad weather engulfed them. In a steady downpour, both would stand like orphans, abject, stolid creatures, unhappy and forced to wait outside.

We didn't see as much of Alcine. We heard she had to sell off her beloved Peruvian Posos. There were whispers about possible animal abuse. Blaze's fear and her whip gave credence to the rumors. Apparently desperate, she and her husband, who was in poor health and battling one of the agencies for a questionable pension, appeared at our back door, offering to drill a well for us with their obsolete junked equipment, a sorry last attempt to raise money.

Within the month, Alcine came by to pick up Specs. She had two horses in an open truck and two more in the trailer. With her husband driving the beat-up truck, she rode off on Specs in the pouring rain, sodden with the wet and gray of face, headed for Trail Creek, past Tuchuck and on over the Whitefish range to God knows where. She was an unforgettable tough old lady and led a rough life. She even sorted seeds during season, just about anything for money. But she couldn't make it in the North Fork.

Even before Alcine disappeared into the unknown, we realized we needed someone to board Blaze for the winter. Becky came riding to our rescue. On mail days we had kept her up-to-date with our problem horses. A lifetime rider and owner of three Arabians, she had constantly given Maggie good solid advice along with hands on teaching as she'd stop to eat her lunch with us.

Joy of joys. She would board Blaze for us and made arrangements for him to be schooled by Spain, one of the best horse trainers in the valley. When we'd come back next summer Blaze would be ready and willing—the perfect steed. With our worries over, we could devote more time to the wildlife, the walks and Maggie's riding, with a light heart.

We had a few weeks left before leaving the North Fork for civilization. As a sort of farewell, we decided to pick huckleberries at the secret spot we had found the previous year. Maggie and I drove slowly down Trail Creek road, talking about the various wildlife we had seen over the years.

"Wish we'd have seen a cougar," we both said at the same time.

As if on cue, a huge healthy, tawny mountain lion ambled across the road directly in front of us, and disappeared into the tall bushes to our right.

We couldn't even talk at first, we were so excited.

To see the "ghost of the wilderness" like that was a miracle. The huckleberry spot was not three minutes away. Adrenalin flowed. We could handle anything.

"Let's use the umbrellas for protection, in case he hangs around," I decided, remembering the two beat-up ones that had been in the back of the Blazer for ages. We parked off the road and each took a pail and umbrella into the deep, thick brush, warily looking and listening, staying within sight of each other. Careful to make lots of noise and talking loudly, we stuck the sharp, metal points of the umbrellas into the ground and kept them immediately by us as we moved from bush to bush. I got carried away with the eating and picking. Nothing beats a huckleberry, fat, juicy and fresh from the bush. Later, after I had pulled the umbrella out of the ground to move to a new spot a few times, I suddenly became aware of the utter quiet.

"Maggie?" I cried out, holding the umbrella in front of me, point first like a sword. In consternation I realized I had worked my way quite deep into the bushes and woods—no Maggie, no road, no car in sight. Suddenly the area looked dark and forbidding. "Maggie?" I called again, ready for anything, umbrella poised.

"Here I am! Boy, there are some good bushes here! My bucket's almost filled." She appeared from behind a thick clump of head-high understory. We looked at each other and got spooked at the same time. We didn't breathe until we got safely back in the Blazer.

"There could have even been two lions," I said, thinking of the pair previously spotted in this area, headed east. With their furtive and elusive ways, not too many North Forkers had reported sightings. Even Becky had never seen one.

Some cougar stories became instant folklore. The funniest tale involved a woman who lived a bit south and east of the Trail Creek road. She was in their outhouse one morning with the door open, communing with nature. Their cabin was remote so she had no fear of anyone passing through.

A mountain lion stuck his head in the outhouse door and stared at her fixedly. She almost croaked.

"I didn't know whether to try and get down into the hole or not. I wasn't sure I'd fit!" She elected to sit very still. The cat turned and wandered away, seen by her husband before disappearing into the woods.

Mountain lions, like any predator, are opportunistic. One winter a family was cross-country skiing up Whale Creek road, with their dog running close-by. In an instant, a mountain lion appeared from nowhere, grabbed the dog and ran off. The owners could do nothing.

A family who had moved from Alaska to the North Fork, shut up their dog in an outside shed for a short while. When they returned from their meeting, no dog. From the evidence of the few remains, they figured a mountain lion had gotten to it.

Brig was a house dog, as Robbie had been, watched by us in the yard and not allowed out of it without his leash. He usually let us know instantly with his bark when wildlife was near. He'd get frantic inside the cabin every once in a while, hyperventilating, pacing, scared to death at some unknown out there. To hear the coyotes yap, punctuated by sharp, short howls as they sounded off directly next to us, down from our jack fence, sent the cat fleeing upstairs to hide behind the water tank, and Brig into a whining frenzy.

Joan and Brig

It was pandemonium when Joe hollered one evening for me to get to the front window. Two sub-adult grizzly were running flat out, one behind the other, not ten yards away on the other side of our front yard fence. Roly-poly and handsomely marked with blond capes distinguishing their dark bodies, they dashed in an instant into the trees bordering the jack fence.

Most critters seemed to pass through at an angle fairly close to our cabin, to avoid the main front open meadow as they cut across to the trees and draw. Some favored using the tractor-wide slab of one inch treated plywood Joe placed over the road ditch in our upper lane as a short cut to the back woodpile, a tangle of boards and sawdust left over from an old logging operation.

One afternoon, a large griz crossed over and continued casually into the front meadow to graze. He suddenly rose to his full height, stared back over his shoulder, then moved swiftly for the far trees. He stopped twice more to rise and look back behind him during his flight. About six deer tore out of the trees from where he had been staring and raced after the bear, a strange and wonderful sight, for it was as if the deer were chasing the grizzly.

All of them disappeared into the draw. I watched carefully. What had scared off a grizzly and a bunch of deer? Nothing appeared from that direction, and I certainly wasn't going back there to find out.

Of course, the more low-key life we led, the more animal presence. We were an island in the midst of all the wildlife. Many a time a moose would cross our lower pasture, then stand in the middle of the aspen grove to grab a few mouthfuls before continuing his circuitous route around to our back salt. A bull moose who took a more direct route appeared silently from the shadows of the trees going back to the old woodpile a short charge away, just as Brig and I stepped off the cement block step at the back door. I hadn't leashed him yet and he let loose with a growlish bark and ran a few steps toward the great hulking beast.

Brig paid heed to the sharpness in my voice when I ordered him to come back, for the moose could have dispatched him with a flip of his great rack or sharp hooves. The moose had already lowered his head, at ready. The dog stopped and came back to me. The moose majestically walked back into the trees, blending so well he was just another shadow.

We went ahead down to the mail box and back for I was sure the moose would keep to his tree cover. He could have even been a mile away by now but indeed, there he was back in the trees, watching. I spoke softly.

"What a beauty! Go get your salt. We'll leave you alone."

Brig never even barked and kept his head by my thigh on his short leash, ignoring the moose, almost as if pretending it wasn't there. I think at that instant I became Brig's protector rather than the other way around.

Deer were so numerous we scarcely used the binoculars on them unless they were up to something. They really do play, chasing each other in games of tag, going at it with their forefeet in mock attacks, even being "king of the hill".

One large doe we met along the road north of us was totally intrigued by Brig and me as we walked ever closer to her, to within ten feet. The deer stood stock still, staring at us. I hissed to Brig to not bark. The deer studied us for a few minutes before I called to her to run away, mindful that hunting season was around the corner. Was she confused by Brig being joined to me by his leash? Brig never made a sound although he was sorely tempted.

A yearling moose out back at our salt block

Deer were his favorite sighting on any drive along the North Fork road. He'd stand in the back seat like a vulture, eyes watchful for a creature he could bark at, safe as he was within the confines of the car.

A day of reckoning came on a drive one morning to the border in the Blazer. Brig was in his usual stance, in back, intently staring ahead. A deer suddenly crashed out of the woods, racing to cross this narrow treelined part of the road. We braked, hard, for the deer was right on us. Brig, barking furiously, slid into the open space between the front seats of the car, then flew smack into the windshield, so hard he knocked off the metal inside mounted rear view mirror. Shaken, we were relieved we missed the deer and that Brig hadn't gone through the windshield. He seemed unhurt.

Brig had a seizure about six months later, caused by the hard blow to his skull, we were sure, since he had never had one before. He continues to have them, some light, a few scaringly hard, about twice a year, not enough to put him on medication, but enough to keep us worried.

He still barks at the animals on the North Fork road from the car, but a bit more sedately. Guilt-ridden over his invisible wound, I've tried to become ready for anything.

Never could I have been prepared for Brig's voracious appetite, so evident in the North Fork. Always a dog who put food above anything else, he has gobbled horse poop, hay, sticks, grass, pine cones, an entire banana, skin and all, cat poop and a beautiful chocolate pie cooling on the counter. He wolfed down bear poop in back before I could stop him and was obviously in hog heaven when he found a desiccated gopher with which he ran amok. He surreptitiously ate a dozen doughnuts that I had hidden under the seat from him during a trip up from town.

I could kick myself for introducing him to the wonderfully different, juicy taste of wild strawberries. I'd pick them, warmed by the sun, from their hiding places under their low leaves. You can't save them. You have to pop 'em in your mouth with stained strawberry-red fingers and savor them immediately, to be followed by another and then another.

Our climbs up the rough front part of the field grew longer, as we'd stop, pick and eat, over and over. The berries grew thick and soon their small, close-to-the ground white flowers spread even into the yard, where Brig about ruined the entire crop each season, sniffing out and gulping the strawberries before they were even fully formed.

They are a favorite delight of this goofy dog who is known up and down the North Fork for his exceptionally long tongue that hangs out of his mouth a good two to three inches when he sleeps, drying out on the rug, a tongue so long that somehow a huge black ant pinched into it and remained there for minutes before I was able to tear the body off with a tissue. The pincers stayed for awhile until his drool washed them away.

CHAPTER 8

We truly pined for the North Fork over the winters. This time it was even worse. Maggie was anxious to reunite with Blaze, not only to see if he had grown more with Becky's good care, but to see how he behaved, given professional (and expensive) training. Spain spent time with the two, helping them adjust to each other within the confines of his corral down in the valley. It was great to see rider and horse become one, going through the training steps.

But once in the North Fork, Blaze reverted to type—a horse with a stubborn streak that betrayed his healthy strain of Pony of America. He did what he wanted. Sometimes he'd agree with Maggie, other times he'd balk, dance sideways, and refuse to turn or do anything at all. His favorite trick was to back up at odd times, very pleased with himself.

What a turkey.

We remembered he had been trained with spurs, so Maggie used spurs. He was good for maybe a day or so.

Maggie went off him down by the rocks where I had been thrown and Blaze ran off with saddle dangling. Elmer climbed on him and really rode him hard to make him go where he was supposed to, but even he had problems. The hard-head refused to go up to the gate, refused to cross bridges, and fell apart when a woman on a bicycle happened to meet Maggie and him on a ride along the road.

Maggie would get so mad at him after a frustrating ride that she'd go alone into the woods in back until she calmed down. What a tough way to build inner character.

Becky brought up her splendid, perfectly behaved Willie, a beautiful Arabian she had raised from babyhood, to expose Blaze to good company. They rode the front trail to Thoma. Blaze was fine. Their ride to Sperry Chalet in the park was outstanding, for Maggie rode Willie and Becky, Falcon, her other Arabian.

In no time, Blaze grew even more ornery, refusing to go past the Y in our lane, much less ever head north. Becky came by, read the situation, and instead of lunch, tried to ride Blaze up the North Fork road. The battle of wills became so scary, I begged her to get off the stupid beast. He went down into a ditch, trying to scrape her off against the road bank of bushes and trees. Becky won, but it was as heart-stopping a piece of horsemanship as I have ever seen. Then Maggie mounted, and Blaze went north.

It lasted one day. He tossed Maggie and she received a cracked vertebra. That was it.

Becky sold Blaze for us to a rancher south of Kalispell where, last we heard, he was being worked as a cowpony, hard.

The corral looked forlorn, and was empty, yet crowded with memories. And it didn't take long for the gophers to take over. Their body-width trails soon crisscrossed the growing grass.

One morning while I was inside the outhouse, all hell broke loose out front in the corral—squeaking, shrieking, murderous mayhem sounds, so terrible I hurried outside to see. Two animals, one a large gopher, were rolling around in a death struggle. The gopher was easy to identify but the other attacked so furiously and swiftly all I could see was a fur tail of some sort, for its main body was hidden by the gopher's.

The wild battle continued in a cloud of flying dirt and grass.

I happened to look down. About two feet from where I stood, two adult gophers were watching the fight playing out before them, just as I was. We all three stood there in a row, quietly, waiting for the outcome. The gophers' paws were crossed over their chests, mine on my waist.

Suddenly it was as if the attacker realized he was being watched. Whatever it was, a fisher maybe, moved so fast I still could not identify him because of his swiftness as he streaked into the understory by the side corral fence.

To my utter surprise, the gopher ran off, apparently no worse for the vicious attack. I looked down at my two companion gophers. They looked up at me, realization set in, and they ran off like hell.

I treasure the thought of the three of us, standing so close, brought together by the violence so common and ordinary in nature.

Even after the horses were gone, Joe and I would discuss the possibility of another well, something closer to the cabin, and our very own. It was a necessity if we decided to live at the cabin year round, come retirement time. We decided to go for it since Maggie was almost finished with college. We envied John and Mary Louise's water supply, the best source up the North Fork. A steep heavily forested hill directly behind their property that belonged to the forest service, was loaded with springs. These fed into a creek that meandered through their land, south into a beaver bog, then through a culvert under the North Fork road and on across until it reach the Flathead River. It was only a matter of selecting the best spring, and paying a fee to the forest service for its use. Rigging up a closed system with strong gravity flow, John had pure cold water that ran through the pipes in their cabin, with the overflow creating a constant small stream to the side, producing a pond where deer, moose and even bear hung around.

When they would leave for vacation, all John had to do was shut off the flow that went up into the cabin. Whenever we visited, I'd drink glass after glass of their water until sloshed. He could have bottled it, it was so great. The envy of the area, his truck was always clean, the grass green, and he even had a greenhouse.

Some neighbors, one next to John on the same side of the county road, the other across it, eventually received permission from the forest service to tap into the spring. We wondered how the neighbor on the opposite side would get his water line across a county road, a bureaucratic tangle in the making. But low and behold, one morning it just mysteriously appeared on the other side, no fuss, no bother and no county approval. Not even a scar in the dirt and gravel. Amazing what can be done by the light of the moon on a sparsely traveled road.

Sources of water for other North Forkers varied. You'd see long strings of empty, clean, plastic gallon milk jugs looped together and hung by cabin doors ready to be filled. A family, with an awe-inspiring wondrous view of the Livingston Range and Canadian Rockies across from them, looked down onto the river and surrounding forests. The tortuous moose bogs south of Moose City spread out in all directions hundreds of feet directly below their shelf of land.

They had no water, absolutely none. They had talked to a driller once, but he had been honest with them, "I'd just be taking your money." Thus they'd load up the entire back of their truck with plastic jugs and make the short trip to the customs' border station and its outside water spigot about once a week. Their season was tied to the border.

Others who used Trail Creek usually kept a pure or treated water supply separate. People were always stopped at a forest service spring, fitted with a pipe outlet, along the paved lower section of the North Fork road, laying in a supply of drinkable water to haul to their cabins. Some used lakes or the Flathead River itself as a source.

Our total belief in Marge and water witching had gone to our heads. No one had witched our two dry holes. That was obviously the problem. Marge was positive she could find water for us. She immediately had hits in our own back yard, the best near the corral fence and garage. Exuberant, we contacted a driller still at Red Meadow, who had just finished bringing in a successful well. We'd be able to rig up a pressurized system directly from the pump to the cabin!

I really do think the driller wanted to find water as much as we did. While a coyote, face peering intently from bushes, watched the activity, we hit our third dry hole. We had to be satisfied with the community well, and I lost faith with dowsing.

We didn't let anything like a dry well slow down our plans. While Becky was at our cabin one Friday for lunch, Joe made the comment he had to find something to do when we moved full time to the area. Too young to fully retire, he worried there were no jobs in the North Fork. Becky happened to know that the current U.S. Customs inspector at the port five miles to our north wanted to work full time. Then the five month customs position up the North Fork would be vacant. Joe immediately contacted the Custom's Area Director, applied and landed the perfect job. His previous Air Force experience undoubtedly helped. Thus, Joe, after training at a larger port, became the new U.S. Customs Inspector at the Flathead, officially known as the Trail Creek Port of Entry.

That winter flew by as I took early retirement from school and Joe resigned his part time winter employment. We sold out in Nebraska and moved to the Flathead valley to be closer to the North Fork. Maggie, who had graduated mid-year, would be a substitute teacher in the valley schools for the balance of the school year and still spend summers with us after she started her full time teaching.

We became quick studies of the magnificent region that had suddenly been opened wide to us.

Even with the white concrete markers at the cut-line, I had to keep reminding myself the two Flathead ports, in the middle of nowhere, were a formal international crossing point between two sovereign nations. In reality, it was the setting for international relations and mutual aid at the lowest possible level—between two individuals.

Both sides, Canada and U.S., are single inspector ports, open daily June through October each year, to process mainly tourists drawn to the area by Waterton and Glacier Parks.

Each port is set back about two hundred feet from the actual border, easily recognized by the wide empty strip of land that runs as far as the eye can see in either direction along the 49th parallel. To the west, the cut-line passes through low, rough territory, mucky in places, before rising upward and away to foothills, thence to a higher, sheer rocky slab of mountain.

The cut-line passes right along, up and over the granite, an easy pathway for a giant who could stride along and scramble up over the obstacles. It was especially neat to study the cut-line after a light snow had delineated the terrain, for not only did I wonder how it was cleared and constructed right up and over the high mountains, but lordy, you couldn't help but think what a marvelous, exciting, awe-inspiring route it would be to traverse, the hike of a lifetime.

To the east, the green swath again rolled straight along, up and over everything, forests, steep inclines, and on and on. The dark line of it as it cut through the trees, could be seen from miles away when standing on the bluffs to the south in the U.S. Seen from a plane, the cut-line was a remarkable way to show the separateness of Canada and the United States.

Wildlife are the only critters that can legally cross the border just any old place, freely and easily. Humans were expected to cross through the iron gate, open from nine a.m. to five p.m.

Tourists who managed to traverse the length of the rough North Fork road would reach the border, damn the road, haul out their cameras to pose at the "Entering British Columbia" signs, cross into Canada and be dumbfounded when told there were sixty miles of more of the same to the north. No cabins, no people up there. The Crown land was wild once past Joe Bush's. His small bar/restaurant just across the border had a few cabins to rent. His season was tied to the months the border was open.

Joe Bush hill, steep and almost impassable after a heavy rain or snow melt, was the beginning of a road that crossed through some of the most monstrous clear cuts in North America. It was often necessary to stop and clear off the mess of scattered, sharp wet rocks that had washed down, dangerous for tires.

Joe at work

Larger streams crossed at odd places, caused by beavers damming up culverts, which would wash away the road bed.

Canadian loggers had marked some trees with numbered signs for mileage information, but woe to the traveler who forgot he was in Canada, with the metric system kilometers, not miles. Jokers had hapharzardly turned the few directional signs more to their liking. The Canadian inspector made sure to give copies of a detailed, handmade map to any intrepid stranger who wanted to drive to Fernie. Roads, added as required for logging operations over the years, added a multitude of road options for the unknowing traveler.

The wildlife were free to roam as they chose, to cross the border the easy way, even along the road, like the moose that trotted in under the building canopy on the U.S. side, standing there, huge and unperturbed, almost as if he was waiting to be checked through customs. Maybe he liked to hear the clomp of his hoofs on the slab of concrete.

Bears with dusty paws left perfect prints on the port windows that would be discovered the next morning. One bear stood on the Canadian steps by the front door. Another woke Ron, the Canadian inspector, in the middle of the night, creating a fuss after he ambled into the fenced back yard and couldn't find his way out.

Coyotes had a regular run across the incline of the North Fork road immediately south of the U.S. building, usually heading west from Moose City into the deeper woods. Two mountain lions sat in the middle of the road one morning, watching the inspectors as they mowed their lawns.

Trail Creek Port of Entry, United States Customs

For the first time, we were exposed to the unpredictable spring and fall weather, and were glad of our winter home base in the valley.

Bad weather days in early spring or late fall could be lonely and thus the great border cribbage games became Olympian in nature. The Canadians were professionals compared to Joe who had just learned the intricacies of the cards and small pegs. Joe Bush was a born crib player.

"Do you play crib?" was the first sentence he uttered when introduced to Joe.

Joe Bush wasn't his real name, of course. The story was that when his wife didn't know where he was, she'd explain, "He's in the bush." For health reasons, he stayed in the middle of nowhere, on leased Crown land, making a living in his bar/restaurant, becoming a landmark character. His steady customers were Canadian hunters, tourists from Canada and the United States, and regulars from the North Fork population. A gourmet cook, he had been well schooled in Chinese cuisine. The whole idea of a neat place to eat and socialize in such a remote area was an extremely attractive come-on, and he had developed a good business over the years.

The close area around the ports became a sort of community in itself, the key members being the two inspectors. Thrown together day after day as they were, in such close proximity, made for lifelong friendships. Mutual trust cemented the relationships.

The Canadians certainly were not staid characters. Ron's personality enveloped us in fun, close companionship, and often lurid details of his Royal Canadian Mounted Police days. Dave, single, and still in college, alternated with Ron several summers. Moving picture good looks and friendly persuasion belied his cunning antennae that could ferret out drugs or the presence of a hidden hand gun from the most innocuous of border crossers. The Canadians busted so many going north a VISA charge machine was in their small detached office, to enable the transgressors to pay their fines on the spot with a credit card.

The inspectors would cross back and forth during the day, keeping in touch personally, or by small handheld radios, so powerful they could transmit from the border to our cabin. Each would watch from their own offices whenever a vehicle crossed over to either side, a mutual quiet observation, with assistance always at the ready.

Since our cabin was only five miles south of the border, Joe came home each evening, arriving about a half hour after the five p.m. closing, unless held up by late crossers, or a bust on the Canadian side. Then he would stay, with radio assistance if they needed outside contact. If a traveler was denied entry into Canada, he's wait to allow them re-entry into the U.S. Sometimes he'd have to process paperwork for those who crossed at five minutes to five—all sorts of unknowns could arise.

The best side benefit of Joe's customs' job was the access we gained to the wildlife study groups.

I sat up against the wall one evening, on the floor of the Canadian customs' quarters, listening to the bear comments, information and animal stories that flooded through the crowded room, overwhelmed by the fantastic good fortune that had set me down as an observer in this select group of animal study people. It was pure heaven.

I focused on Bruce, "The grizzlies just run the branch through their lips and suck the berries off, like so—." The Canadian honcho, in charge of the grizzly bear study in British Columbia, knew exactly how to make his mouth go like a bear gobbling juicy huckleberries.

There were over fifteen people packed into the living area. Dave had invited Joe, Maggie and me over to the party which had settled down into a session that few are lucky to participate in.

Initially, the studies focused on grizzly bears and wolves. But the wide spectrum of wildlife in the North Fork gave researchers the opportunity to develop ongoing additional programs over the years, resulting in key base information, including documented predator and prey interaction. Declining wildlife and habitat have made the wildlife studies conducted in the North Fork over the years an invaluable source of first class scientific information, even encompassing available food supplies. Human encroachment on habitat and its influence on the wildlife was of prime concern, since the North Fork, and other wilderness, was becoming developed more rapidly.

Gradually, we were learning more about the study people and their backgrounds. This evening, conversations, led by Bruce, rapid and often spilling over with primary scientific information, were authentic and, at times, sprinkled with hilarious stories, for these young people were in the midst of their grand adventure.

Diane, working in British Columbia and Montana, had been in charge of the wolf study for many years, taking students from all over the country under her wing, giving them the practical field work, gathering statistics and information so necessary for the wolf's eventual recovery in the U.S.

The long-term grizzly bear study, centered mostly in British Columbia, was also carried out by students, both Canadian and U.S., many working for graduate degrees. Their primary camp was just across the Canadian border. Bruce McLellan was in charge in Canada. Chris Servheen, U.S. Fish and Wildlife and grizzly bear recovery coordinator, was the U.S. decision-maker. Funds for the various studies came from government agencies, state, school and private grants.

This neat bunch of people knew more hands on information about bears, wolves, ungulates, and later mountain lions and coyotes, than anyone—really hands on, like trapping, collaring and monitoring the great

Flathead Port of Entry, Canadian Customs

symbols of wilderness so abundant in the North Fork, at home in this remote region straddling the border between British Columbia and Montana.

It has been especially exciting to see researchers we have known over the years in the North Fork appear on nationally televised documentaries with their expertise and to congratulate their dedication as so many of them receive their Ph.D.s.

Animals know no boundaries, so of course, the study groups were frequent border crossers as demanded by their work, and became friends with the two customs inspectors. The truly meaningful part of the North Fork, knowledge of its wildlife, opened wide to us, because of our association with these field biologists and students. Just listening to them, being with them, was an education in the entire cross section of the local creatures, great and small.

I could never hear enough about any animal. But the great grizzly bear was my true love. Hearing Bruce brought back memories indelibly imprinted on my brain as a young child for I had been present at a

Yellowstone feeding of the bears. We sat in bleachers as the black bears wandered out into the center clearing to paw through the garbage thrown out for them. When the grizzly approached, the black bears vanished, leaving the field open to the grand magnificent beast.

I remember seeing a ranger as he was carried away from our campground, after he had been ripped up the middle by a griz who had been after an apple that rolled under a car. Back in those days, people didn't have much sense either, for there was a snapshot of me, about age three, standing, smiling, with bears as a close background.

Since reading everything I could about bears became a natural part of my life, I hung onto Bruce's every word, trying to absorb the rest of the background conversation from the others as well. Total immersion in the grizzly bear, a spectacular evening.

It was the natural order of things that I later dragged Maggie to the annual bear conference meeting held down at the meeting hall on a hot July day, eager and excited about how the agencies were going to make bear habitat, especially the North Fork, a safer place for the grizzly, and thus, the other wildlife.

The three day Board of Grizzly and Wolf Technical Committee meeting was open to all, an exchange of research information and wildlife management opinions, organized by longtime bear researcher Dr. Charles Jonkel.

Forest service, park, state officials and wildlife educators were some of the main participants. Just to hear Jonkel give the introductory address to the packed room was thrilling to me, with its promise of ideas that could come forth from this group. But in no time I was appalled at the turn the meeting had taken as a few scientists and agencies were caught up in arguments that went nowhere, bickering over computer programs and how much information should be exchanged, ad nauseam. These were the ones who were going to help the griz?

I was furious at the pettiness and waste of time. I had to speak out, "By the time you look up, all the bears will be gone!"

Simple words, spoken from the heart, that opened up the stultified meeting to others, in particular a young American Indian from the east side of the park who confessed he used to hunt and kill grizzly, but no more. I had my first real argument with an "original" North Forker who thought that he was the authority on everything in the North Fork, including wildlife. He immediately labeled me a backwoods environmentalist, before everyone, a dirty word to him, but a compliment to me, especially coming from him. The meeting became alive and turned into my own personal invigorating watershed.

I would do all that I could for the animals, especially the grizzlies, too often the victim of bureaucratic fumbling, resented and even hated by some who saw no reason for their very being. It all melded together, for Tom was at that meeting, an eager young student from the University of Montana working with Bruce's bear group, who loved bears as much as I did.

Tom offered to take us north one evening into British Columbia to show us some grizzly with cubs. It took over thirty-five minutes for Dave to drive Joe, Maggie, Steve, on a short visit, and me over an even more narrow maze of roads in the middle of nowhere to rendezvous with Tom, and then follow him to the Commerce Creek drainage. Using his tracking antenna to home in on a radio collared griz, we couldn't miss. There, high on the sloping side of a mountain, in the far, far distance, was a large silver tip sow with two cubs, feeding on huckleberries, barely discernible specks to the naked eye, but close enough to read the ear tags with the aid of ten thousand dollars worth of huge Zeiss binoculars which Tom set up for us on a tripod.

He pointed out that Alberta lay right beyond the mountains. After getting our fill of the sow and cubs, Tom led us back into other drainages, driving along ever more faint ruts that were fast disappearing in the waning daylight. The trees turned into shadowy mysterious shapes, highlighted by the rising bright moonlight. Tom's sharp eyes even spotted a black bear before we turned back.

I was filled with an appreciation and respect for those who did much of their work way out here in such utter desolation. Never before had I been so far away from civilization. For the study groups, it was their every day milieu.

Dave had suggested the trip to Crevasse Lookout a few days earlier. Otherwise, I'd have suspected he was trying to outdo Tom. First, he'd cook dinner for Maggie, Joe and me at the Canadian port. The three of us would make the dash to the lookout in his dad's four-wheel drive pickup, then eat dessert when we returned. Joe would baby-sit Brig. We promised to be back before dark.

Crevasse Lookout glints in the sun during the day, so high it can barely be seen from the small front porch of the U.S. customs building. On the edge of a promontory over in Canada, it had apparently been abandoned the last few years, their forest officials deciding to perform fire watch from airplanes.

Setting forth in high excitement, we drove past Joe Bush's place, then up the steep Joe Bush hill.

Dave turned into an overgrown one-lane track. We bumped down into a low-lying black, humped bog, slogging through with difficulty even though we were in four-wheel drive and first gear. Undaunted, we continued to thrust through mud, water, and low thick understory. The high forest cast shadows that heightened our giddy, excited mood. I wondered how Dave could find his way as we jolted and growled onward to higher ground, finally entering a wide open expanse of bear grass in full bloom, hundreds of them. The thick stands of white pinnacled flowers parted before us as we pushed through, so tall they loomed over the truck's hood.

We started a gradual ascent.

"What do we do if we meet someone coming the other way?" Maggie asked, squeezed in the middle between Dave and me.

"You never meet anyone," Dave said.

We crept upward.

"That's where I got my deer last hunting season," Dave bragged, pointing into the trees to the left. We broke out of the lower hills and suddenly could see for miles.

The ascent grew quite steep and the road became rougher. We crept up to a washout that cut deeply across the road.

"Should we get out and walk around it?" I asked.

"No. We'll make it."

We tilted down and then scraped up and over the hard mud gully edges. There was nothing to the right except a straight drop to nowhere. I figured the side edge of the one lane, rutted, dirt road was maybe a half foot beyond the wheels of the pickup.

"Dave, how do I hook this seat belt?" I asked.

"Don't put it on in case we have to bail out," he answered nonchalantly, interrupting his conversation with Maggie.

I had the best view, able to look out into the vast panorama of the valley below us. If we went over, we'd be dashed to pieces onto the tops of the trees far below. But we'd have already been dead from bouncing off the side of the mountain.

"Uh, how many times did you say you've been up here, Dave?" Maggie asked. We were both getting nervous even though he acted like an old hand at this. Dave stopped, then very carefully backed up a bit before turning a ninety degree curve to continue the steep climb. "Oh," he said in his clipped Canadian accent, "this is my first time up this far."

I was so wound up from either the excitement or the salty coating on the chicken he had prepared for us back at the port, I didn't care. If you're gonna go, you're gonna go. Joe could spend my insurance.

And what a place to die!

By that time, we had about reached the summit, having one last dizzingly sharp turn that led to a tiny unstable-looking area barely big enough to hold the truck. Wind grabbed at us as we climbed out, sharp cold gusts, tearing at us, blowing our words away. It was so cold, I was covered with goose bumps. None of us had thought to bring a jacket.

The splendor seen from this lookout, chosen for its location, was inspiring. The entire Flathead Valley spread out below us: British Columbia, a series of rolling hills and mountains that went on forever swept to the north; to the south on the U.S. side, the Flathead Valley spread out, bordered its entire length by the Livingston Range to the east. We were astonished by the unfamiliar spectacular expanse of peaks before us, since we now viewed them from such a different height and direction: from Starvation and King Edward peaks, south past Longknife (Boundary Mountain) and the cut-line, past Kinnerly Peak, stretching its immense head out of the lesser mountains and hills before us, the rest of the range of the Rocky Mountain front disappearing into the vast distance past the park and on and on forever. I couldn't speak for the beauty of it. It was a totally engulfing breathtaking experience, the view, the cold wind snapping and clutching at us hard enough to send us tumbling over the side. I'd have died happy.

I also had to go to the bathroom because of the excitement, the cold and the pop I had guzzled at the port. There was an outhouse, a tiny decrepit building perched on a gigantic rock on the edge of nothing, down about fifteen feet to the east of the main lookout building which was tied down securely with thick steel cables. Even so, it appeared to sway in the high winds. The outhouse was just **there**, with nothing holding it. I had some pride. No way would I die in an outhouse blown off a mountain. Maggie and Dave were on the opposite side of the main building. I found a spot toward British Columbia.

Very much relieved, I inspected the lookout more closely. The wind helped open the door and blew me right inside to an empty, window-lined room with one of the most superb, majestic views in the world. The floor was covered with worn cheap linoleum. Orphaned propane pipes extruded from the holes in the floor, coming from nowhere and going nowhere. The lookout must have been at least thirty years old.

I tried to imagine what it would be like to be the person assigned to such a spectacularly located lookout, to go to sleep under the stars as seen from here, to view the sunrise and sunset, to feel the rain and thunderstorms buffet the tiny building. It had withstood all the elements nature had thrown at it all these years. It was to be congratulated, this tiny bastion of stout metal and timbers, and yes, even linoleum. I could stay in this spot forever. I would keep this view in my heart, to be revisited and remembered.

Boundary Mountain would never be the same for me. From our cabin, it stretched long, uneven and narrow toward the east, slabs of mountain thrusting upward, separating the two countries like a long knife. From here the splendid mountain seemed to float in the haze, a hole at the very summit somewhat like a rough volcano, but in reality, formed by various peaks coming together in a jagged formation.

Maggie and Dave blew in through the door.

"Where's the crevasse?" Maggie finally asked, after long and thoughtful extended viewing.

Going back outside into the cold wind, we found the crevasse back toward the British Columbia side, a deep narrow slit in the ground, the opening lined by old dried gray wood beams, like the entrance to a small mine shaft. Where and how far down did it go? Oh, to be younger and thinner. Or magic. What would be down there? It was tempting, but we didn't even toss a rock down to hear the sound of it drop. We didn't want to spoil anything.

Great boulders lay strewn around the steep rocky trail from the crevasse back to the lookout. The wind grew more fierce as we climbed the uneven incline to the building, each quiet with our own thoughts against the surrounding backdrop of high country wilderness.

We were startled to notice the slant of the sun as it descended. It would soon disappear behind the mountain ranges to the west.

"We'd better get down before dark," we all said at once.

Maggie and I had Dave turn the truck around without us, letting him negotiate the tiny parking space by himself. We waited until the truck was pointed downward in the right direction before we climbed back in.

Going down was a lot more scary than driving up. Not only did we know what to expect, but Dave seemed to be going faster, even though the switchbacks seemed sharper than ever, and the drop-offs steeper. We'd hurtle off into space in the closing darkness and no one would find us. Experience driving up could not be counted as experience going down. Night was at our heels and it was pitch black by the time we reached the marshy section. Dave shouted obscenities out the window as we sped past Joe Bush's place. Joe Bush had beaten him at their daily crib game.

By the time we got to the border it was way past 11 p.m. Poor Joe undoubtedly had us strewn all over the mountains. The three of us babbled like idiots, still high from the exhilarating experience that we related to Joe between mouthfuls of cherries.

*   *   *

Dave liked to be the first to tell us some of the many "Canadian only" tales, the more shocking the better. Supposedly, the incident occurred in the earlier 1940s. The story surely became even more embellished by Dave, crammed as we were in the Blazer on a drive up from the valley one night. Surrounded by total darkness but for the small bit of rough road lit ahead of us, we seemed to be in a time warp.

In earlier days, the R.C.M.P. in the Northwest Territories, answered a call during a dreadful snow storm. A poor Indian woman had frozen to death in her cabin while seated in her rocker. Since she had frozen in a sitting position, they had to place her in the back seat of their police car for transport.

The only traffic along the lonely road was a snowplow clearing the road for them. Yet, they came upon a lone hiker who desperately needed a ride. The R.C.M.P. told him to climb in the back seat.

Which he did.

The two Mounties were too busy to pay any attention to anything but the dangerous, snowy road.

The hitch-hiker turned to the frozen woman and commented on the terrible weather.

No answer.

Next he offered her a cigarette.

By then, one of the guys in front realized what was happening in the back seat.

"Can't you see she's stiff?" the R.C.M.P. exclaimed. "She's stiff! Dead!"

Realizing what was next to him the poor man leaped from the vehicle, eager to take his chances with the snowstorm.

CHAPTER 9

The main bear study camp was over in Canada, just a ten minute walk up from the border, but on the other side of the river. Because their work was concentrated at times in other areas, temporary camps were often set up further north, to save travel time back and forth. Such was Sage Creek, also a temporary home base for the wolf study since their wolf traps were located in the area.

Names, including Howell Creek, Harvey Pass, and the Wigwam, located in some of the most remote regions of British Columbia, became familiar to us, for the study groups frequented them and then related their deeds and adventures.

The picnic held at Sage Creek one summer was my first eye opener to how these researchers lived—outside! Irene's trailer was the centerpiece of the camp, surrounded by tents scattered about in positions that afforded a degree of privacy. Meg, of the moose study, lived in a Volkswagen camper bus. There were a few picnic tables. The forest surrounded them, the creek running through their camp.

All this was made more interesting when Irene, of the original Canadian bear study, told me how Luke was still hanging around. Luke was a male grizzly that had been shot by a hunter. The injury crippled the bear so that he dragged his front leg, the paw sort of folded under him as he walked, a pitiful and bad predicament for a great predator to find himself in. Tom and Chris had repaired some of the worst damage when he was trapped, but the bear was still crippled.

I kept waiting for Luke to appear that entire evening, paw outstretched, looking for help again.

But the help was forthcoming for another animal instead.

Meg's dog had torn up her chest on a barbed wire fence. Sewn up by a vet, the dog ran into something that reopened the half-healed sutures, and the resultant hanging flap was not only distressing to look at, but almost past the point of repair. It had begun to heal along the edges.

As vets don't make house calls in the wilderness, Tom and Harry went to work. They cleared off a picnic table, tranquilized the dog, covered her eyes, trimmed the wound, and sewed her up to perfection. When anyone spoke, it was in a low tone, so as not to disturb the anesthetized dog. Never have I seen such a caring and careful operation. You knew instinctively that this was exactly how they handled their grizzlies as they trapped and collared them for study. To witness the gentleness, together with the expertise was astounding, especially out in this environment, every bit as good as an operating room theater.

When the dog became conscious and alert within a minute of the finish of the operation, it proved how adept these study people were at figuring out the correct dosage needed, not only for the dog, but any other animal they were working with.

The picnic was memorable because of the remoteness, the huckleberry pie that Arlene, Joe Bush's daughter, brought up from their public house, and the overall low-key good will and happiness, evidence of those caught up and happy with their work and surroundings.

Most of all, I remember Luke, and the successful operation performed by two professionals.

We didn't realize the great numbers of animals that made the area to the north of us their vast playground until Joe traveled that five mile stretch between the cabin and the border twice daily. I'd be jealous at his sightings of the wildlife that used this most narrow and desolate section as their own corridor. Since he was usually the first going north in the morning, the critters would often be along the edges or in the road itself. A huge fat black bear sprang right in front of him from the underbrush, hit the road once in a tremendous leap, then dived head-long into the understory on the opposite side, all in a blink of an eye. If the windshield wipers had been going, he might have missed seeing it.

Deer were numerous and, of course, it was moose country because of their routes between the lakes and sloughs. One waited under the canopy at the port one morning as if to say, "Hurry up! I want to cross the border!" Never will I forget glancing out the large front picture window at the port office late one October afternoon. A large female moose had inadvertently run out into the open field on the Canadian side, realized her danger and stood there, paralyzed, fear showing in her frantic eyes. She fled down into the ditch, crossed into the States, and looked around to figure where the nearest safe cover was, before loping right in front of us, just beyond the building, so close I could see her coarse-haired winter coat part and blow in the cold wind.

"Run! Run!" I breathed, "and hide."

For it was hunting season and I wanted her gone, in safety.

I grew to dread hunting season, for anything was fair game.

"Wish we'd see a bear," I remarked, heading north to the border with Joe one morning, for I needed the vehicle for the day. I'd pick him up in the afternoon and double my chance of seeing wildlife.

Low and behold, as we came over a slight rise, there he was, a small young black bear running with all his might, as fast as his short legs could take him, right in the middle of the road, a joy to see.

Trapped grizzly waiting to be collared

"Run, you fool! Get off the road!" I shouted out to him. That inno-cent dumb bear ran in front of us for a good three full minutes before he scooted into the brush.

"He's not going to last," I worried aloud. "He'll be lucky if he makes it. Surely he's too small for anyone to bother with."

That afternoon, on her mail route, Becky came upon a bow hunter skinning the bear in the middle of the road down from the port. I couldn't believe it—didn't want to. The large smeared blood stain in the road seemed to never disappear, a constant reminder of where the bear had met his death, his life cut short so someone could brag about get-ting a bear the macho way, with a bow and arrow.

Scott, the park ranger for the North Fork area, described to Joe how a family of tourists were happily watching and photographing a black bear as it fed to the side of the North Fork road, just outside the park but near Camas road. It was the first day of the fall black bear hunting season.

A pickup truck stopped and the driver asked the tourists if they had enough pictures of the bear. When they said yes, he reached for his gun and **bang**—shot the bear dead right in front of them.

Horrified and outraged, the tourists rushed to complain to a park ranger who could do nothing since it happened outside the park. Perhaps no other event illustrates better the need for a buffer zone around the park boundaries. Wildlife pays no heed to man-made borders and just one step outside the park makes them fair game.

The North Fork, famous for its wildlife, is overrun during hunting season by pickups that creep along the road from early morning to late into the night. Beer cans soon litter the ditches. Bright orange or red rectangles of wood blossom on tree trunks or fence posts of private property owners, the signal of "no hunting". Some owners spray paint directly on trees. One couple even sprayed their two dogs. Everyone knows that most owners are summer residents and the cabins are usually empty by fall so some hunters go where they please. Oh, how hunters can be careless. One bunch left an elk carcass hung low to the ground, in plain view of the road. One of the animal study people clued them in on the facts of life in grizzly country before they cut it down.

Gunfire can erupt from any where and at any time. Brig leaped into the air at the crack of a gun while we walked along the air strip up at Moose City one morning. Even though I was dressed in bright red, we raced for the safety of the port. Another shot followed. It seems a hunter had been successful, shooting a doe on private property along the road, near the rise from the port. Then he explained he had to shoot the fawn because its mom was dead.

It's slightly disconcerting to be walking down the county road and have two bow and arrow hunters in full camouflage suddenly step out of the shadows of the tall undergrowth, ready for action, visibly unhappy with your presence. Especially so, when "no hunting" signs erected high in trees by landowners, sport arrows imbedded in them, shot in defiance by hunters unhappy over the postings of private land.

Killing didn't have to be in season.

Locals from the North Fork were apt to brag or squeal on each other, spreading rumors, true or false, of who down the road was sloppy over gut piles which attracted griz, which then would be killed and skinned. One old hand at the game described an easy way: kill a bunch of gophers, half bury 'em at intervals in a field, let 'em ripen, then sit back and watch the bears come in for them.

When the fire lookout on Numa spied smoke and had a ranger check it out, he caught a local in the act of burning elk bones, evidence of his recent poaching. Another local with an illegal kill asked a friend to say he did it.

The guy agreed!

The worst was a conversation overheard at the local bar. Liquor and bragging to the girls had loosened a Canadian's tongue and he described in detail how they would take a horse into the wilds of British Columbia, chain it to a tree, kill it and wait for a grizzly to come after it. Because of the vastness of the areas involved, and the chronic shortage of law enforcement people in both British Columbia and this side of the border, they knew the odds of getting caught were slim.

It was a sad day for the bear study group working in Canada when they discovered a pile of bear bones, the buried remains of a poaching spree. At least six or seven animals had been taken illegally, never to be discovered but for Meg's dog, who dashed off the beaten path to uncover the evidence.

I had such a vivid picture of Luke in my mind, I always asked the bear study how he was getting along with his crippled front paw.

Luke was sighted the next season, thin but alive. He had made it through the winter. The bad thing—he stayed in the area of roads. That very year, a Canadian hunter shot him dead.

The study groups, always ready to help anyone, were a tremendously positive force in the North Fork. They would often unobtrusively check on Tom Reynold's wood supply and keep the elderly gentleman well supplied.

What a wonderful man was Tom, our direct link to the North Fork of the past.

During our early days in the area, his name would usually emerge and be bandied about during any conversation we had with the few people we saw.

"He hates people. Keeps a shotgun handy," one told us. "He's the reason why we don't have the idiots from town coming up here, raising Cain. They know he'd get 'em.'"

A hermit. A recluse, perhaps because of a shady past or a lost love, so the stories went. He had been in the North Fork forever, it seemed, but not many knew him. And apparently he liked it that way.

Of course, I was dying to meet him, especially when I heard he was an avid reader.

Joe's new job as customs inspector at the border is what did it. I just happened to be at the port one day when Sue brought Tom with her while she filled her water bottles at the outside faucet.

I liked him instantly, this fine-looking elderly figure out of the past with his ramrod straight posture, dressed in a large, heavy blue and black flannel jacket, chinos, woodsman high boots, and an ancient brown fedora. Tom was hard-of-hearing and Sue did most of the talking.

In bits and pieces we learned Sue and Don had recently purchased Tom's property, about three miles north of us, by luck and the grace of God since it had sort of been sold out from under him by a relative he had signed it over to. With their purchase, Tom was safe, for he could live in his own cabin as he always had, for as long as he lived. It was a tremendous bargain for Don and Sue for within this wonderful gentleman of the old school was a living history of the North Fork.

Tom never spoke to the new owners, not until they happened to meet down at the road one day while Don and Sue were nailing up a sign on a wooden post, "Reynolds Ranch." With that, they soon became more than fast friends. Tom in no time was beloved as family. Over the ensuing years Don and Sue made sure Tom lacked nothing. If they thought he needed it, he got it, from glasses, hearing aids and clothes, to trying to keep his snowmobile in running condition. Fretting over him being alone winters, they even tried to get him to spend winter time with them in Illinois. He considered himself their caretaker since Don and Sue were only there a few weeks out of the year.

Tom was always at his mail box on Tuesday and Friday, waiting for Becky. It was a perfect relationship for them both, Tom, in his early nineties when we first met him, proud, not wanting to ask for help, and Becky, so good and giving and understanding of this old gentleman's needs.

Tom would send grocery lists of basics by way of Becky, to the mercantile at Polebridge. Then she would bring his supplies up the next mail day. She was his life line to the outside world. He would be waiting at his mail box for her, regardless of the weather, put the load in his back pack, and head to his cabin.

Up to his cabin from the road meant a hard, steep walk for about fifteen minutes to a level bench of land on which Tom's original tiny log cabin had been built.

Then the climb really began.

There were two possible routes up to the alpine-looking house Tom had later built for himself, larger, higher, deeper into the woods, and close to a small spring. The lower single lane, at about a thirty degree angle, took longer but the other more direct route went straight up. Four-wheel drive in second gear, to me, was a necessity, since the road consisted of rocks, gullies, and some understory that needed cleared away. Tree branches threatened any passing vehicle's paint job.

Tom hiked down and up twice a week for his mail during his entire North Fork life, snowshoeing in and out in the winters. He did have close friends that lived year round in the North Fork, especially Diane, for over fifteen years with her wolf study. John, who had been a customs inspector for years before Joe, had become fast friends with Tom Reynolds although now he only got up the North Fork for river rafting, canoeing, fishing or short visits.

Becky had mentioned once how the Montana Historical Society had tried to interview Tom over the years, but he had wanted none of it. We even talked about secretly taping Tom and his wonderful stories, a gold mine of history and early North Fork life. But we couldn't do that. It wouldn't have been right.

Becky would pick Tom up at his mail box for lunch at Joe's Place every once in awhile and then drop him back off, on her way down to the post office at Polebridge. It was an easy transition to get Tom to eat lunch sometimes at the border station. We'd send notes via Becky, always a week or more in advance, and set it up. I always made sure lunch was a good warm meal with dessert. Tom had an excellent reputation as a cook, but I couldn't imagine him making an angel food cake in his old wood stove. He loved it. Ron, the Canadian customs inspector, would always join us. We'd make an occasion of it, and sometimes Maggie and I would take him home. He could stay later then since he wasn't tied to Becky's timetable. Eventually we enticed him for dinner at our place.

I wanted the meal to be special. From past conversations, I knew Tom loved his "spuds". Because of his English background I figured I couldn't go wrong with a menu of boiled potatoes, Brussels sprouts and a roast. It was a tremendous success. There were leftovers, of course, since I had no sense and wanted to smother this marvelous old gentleman with food. As I cleared the table, I watched Tom out of the corner of my eye. I sure didn't want to upset him. He had a strange look on his face and a shine in his eye.

"Tom, would you like to take these leftovers home with you? I don't have room in the refrigerator and I sure don't want to throw them out."

His entire face lit up.

From then on, when he was down for dinner, I'd purposely cook extra so he'd have something different to take home with him. Our relationship became firm.

It solidified, according to Sue, when we drove him up to his cabin once and I tossed aside into the bushes a mouse that had the audacity to die on his door step. He especially took a shine to Maggie since she was young and obviously thought the world of him.

We were having lunch at the border sometime later. Ron, Becky, Tom and Joe and I had been quite giddy. Ron had told some of his wild R.C.M.P. police stories over coffee and Tom was not to be bested.

I happened to have our video camera nearby. I was at the opposite end of the table from Tom. As he started in on a story, I surreptitiously turned the camera on.

I worried. Perhaps our relationship was not strong enough. But I had to try it. I'd stop immediately if I sensed he didn't like it.

Quietly, I focused on Tom, watching him from the edge of the eyepiece, so I could see his reaction. Everyone sort of held their breath.

He peered at me, kept right on talking, and an expression came over his face that was delightful.

He liked it!

In fact, he played to the camera, as if he had done it all his life.

This became a usual practice: we'd eat, either at the port or our cabin and after dessert, over coffee, Tom would begin to talk and I would tape. He had enlisted in the British Army at age thirteen, weighing in at seventy-five pounds.

"I was in the British Army, first in Ireland. In those days we wore red tunics and black belts when we had to go out on Sunday. Everything had to be polished up. One Saturday, we went to Belfast. Went on the train, and if we weren't late, we'd catch the same train back. We were just kids. Went to a novelty store and we bought this and that and some stink bombs.

"Coming home we were in the English coach, fitted with compartments off a long corridor. A man came into ours. I think he was a fisherman from one of the towns.

"One of us dropped a stink bomb. Pretty soon, the man said, 'Which of you little bastards shit himself?'"

Tom waited for our reaction.

Of course, we all roared with laughter. I think Tom could have said anything and none of us would have taken offense. And we got him to continue with careful leading questions.

Taken prisoner in 1917 during World War I, he eventually was put in a battalion that went to India. He told us in bits and pieces and at different times, how he came to the North Fork. At first, he came illegally through Canada, went to Chinook, Montana as a sheep worker and met Bill Cruise, his friend.

Eventually deported, he went to Alberta and put his name in for immigration, coming back down legally in 1928.

"I intended to settle down. I bought this place in 1931. Bill Cruise had invited me to stay the winter with him. We roamed over the country. He called McAfee's the North Star Ranch. McAfee had killed himself over on the Kishenehn Patrol Cabin and this place had gone to his father in Texas. So that's how I got hold of it."

The price was $200 plus owed taxes for 160 acres. When Tom retired in 1960 from the forest service, he turned his property over to his nephew in Australia and sold it for him. The deal fell through so Don and Sue were able to buy it.

We invited Tom down to our cabin for one dinner with trepidation. I had dragged my feet when he asked when he could see himself on video, for I was scared to death he wouldn't like the way he looked and that would be the end of it.

We had taped every chance we had, as much as we could. But the time of reckoning had arrived.

The old gentleman was quite taken with the concept of a TV and VCR. He dragged his chair close to the TV screen after Joe's quick explanation of how it worked. We started the tape.

Tom sat there, intent, never moving, keeping his eyes fixed on his image on the screen, listening hard. He never said a word.

"Do you like it?" I asked.

"Yes," was all he said.

He must have been satisfied for we continued video taping Tom over the next three years, off and on. I'd have to always be ready for some times he'd start a story right in the middle of dinner.

"I saw this elk on the side hill and he had two big horns with not one branch on 'em. Like bare sticks and it was staying there week after week. One day he was standing no longer. I was scouting around up on top of the bench just about where he had been and found the elk dead. Every bit of his hide had a tick on it. There wasn't an inch on that hide that didn't have a tick. He was just eaten alive. I burned the body."

Tom loved to tell a funny story, especially to the border audience.

"There was a homesteader not more than a half mile south from Polebridge. He was a moonshiner and he was getting a pension, I believe. He was drunk one day when a couple of neighbors from the park came over to maybe get some moonshine. No one took up with him otherwise. He was dead drunk to the world. One of the visitors, Gene, was a good friend of a senator. They used to come up and stay with Sullivan, and Sullivan brought them up to this homestead. We called him Hoolie Stein, Hoolie for the hooligan. They found Hoolie just dead to the world on his bed.

"So Sullivan undid Hoolie's pants, went outside to get some dried horse manure and stuck it in the moonshiner's pants, and then buttoned them up again and they left."

Everyone at the table laughed uproariously, no doubt thinking of someone they'd like to do it to.

His matter-of-fact stories of some of the old timers described best how life really was back then.

"Shorty was a neighbor. I don't think I'd say he was one of the best. There was a nice cabin around, built with big larch logs. Inside there was a kitchen bench with quite a number of drawers in it. And this took the fancy of Dell Waters, wife of Shorty. She nagged and nagged over the months so she finally got to go down and break into the cabin and steal this kitchen cabinet. They had a Model-T Ford in those days. I was coming down the road and here I see Shorty and Dell and they had this kitchen cabinet on their Ford. He was sitting down on one end to keep it from being over-balanced, because it stuck out the rear end quite a bit. It must have been more than six feet long, that kitchen cabinet, coming out onto the road. When they saw me they said, 'Give us a hand.'

"I didn't think anything about it. I thought I'd help them down to their cabin with the kitchen cabinet, about another mile. Then they said, 'Help me in the cabin with this kitchen cabinet.'

"All the time, I was myself a criminal accomplice. I never gave it another thought until a couple of months after that when I began to think of it. Then I came down the road one day, shortly after this, walking, going down to the mail. The mail was at the other side of Trail Creek, about a five mile walk. And I saw a big smoke coming out from just about where this nice cabin was.

"So I dropped into the Water's place. 'I see you touched off the cabin, Shorty,' I said.

'Yes,' he replied.

"And he told me how he did it. He took some kerosene and he trailed across the floor from one corner to the other and then set fire to the center of it, and touched it off. So that was, although it was a criminal thing, it was a very good thing that cabin was burned down. 'Cause that cabin, they were people from Whitefish who used to come up there in the summer time. The old man and his family from Whitefish would bring up a lot of glass jars and he'd bring 'em to this cabin and he'd put salt outside and wait by one of the windows, day after day, until a deer came to the salt and he'd shoot it, can it, and take the jars to Whitefish to the family. So when Shorty touched off the cabin and it went up in smoke, I think it was a good thing, although it was a criminal act."

"Tell the story of Pegleg, Tom. Who was he?" Joe asked one day.

"Pegleg wasn't a North Forker. He and his woman were just drifters. They came up on the North Fork and parked themselves in an empty cabin just north of Trail Creek and that's where I got acquainted with him."

He paused, looked around at his audience, then laughed, "This is not a Sunday School story.

"One day Pegleg was taking his neighbor's Model-T back to him, and he was mad about it. I met him this side of Trail Creek road. He said he had gone to the cabin there.

'There's nobody home,' Pegleg said. 'And the coffee was percolating away. I pissed in it. Don't tell them. Don't drink any of it!'

"Well, I wasn't going to and I didn't tell.

"So anyway," Tom continued. "They were a tough couple, especially the woman, Alice.

"Shorty and I went up to pay them a visit. By this time, they'd moved out of the cabin they'd been in to an empty cabin on Trail Creek. It was a nasty cabin. Of course, whoever owns it now renovated it and fixed it up.

"I knocked on the door, then just opened it. Pegleg was dead to the world. He'd poured some moonshine and he was lying on the bed with just a shirt on and way up to here. (Tom pointed toward his neck).

"Alice was on the bed along side of him with nothing on. She sat up and reached over for his penis and wiggled it back and forth and said, 'What ya think of this, eh?'

"She got up and said, 'I'll make you a cup of coffee.' Her back was to us while she was putting the kindling in the stove.

"Shorty said, 'What the hell happened to you, Alice?'

"She said, 'You mean my ass?'

"Shorty said, 'Yes.'

'Well, when I was small, somebody picked me up and put me on a hot stove.'

"She had a massive scar tissue on her bottom and halfway down her thighs.

"While I didn't stay for coffee, I took a bit more BS and then I left. But I think I went into the CCC and that was the last I saw of them on the North Fork.

"Pegleg and Alice went on down to Badrock Canyon. There was an old cabin there and he'd been abusing her. So Alice ran out of the cabin to the neighbors. He took a rifle and took a shot at her. I don't know if he really meant to hit her or just scare her. The neighbors called the police and they hauled Pegleg into Kalispell and threw him into jail. He was tried and the judge gave him ten years in Deerlodge prison. We never saw Pegleg again after that.

"Except for a couple of years after that, I saw the woman, Alice. She was on the North Fork with a man I got acquainted with in the CCC.

"There was a fire on their property one day and the CCCs were fighting it. The supervisor came up with the ranger to see how they were making out with this fire. As he was looking at it, he said to the ranger, 'Do you think we can get any money out of them?'

"The ranger said, 'I doubt it. You'll have to take it out in trade.'

"The supervisor said, 'What do you mean, Frank?'

'Well, she's a madam,' Frank answered."

The hardship of living on the North Fork was apparent in many of Tom's stories.

"In the summer time, Charlie Wise would go over into Canada to prospect. He called at this cabin on Sage Creek because it had no windows in it. He opened the door and the stink really knocked him down. There was a dead man there. Must have been there a couple of weeks. Charlie said he was sick for a week afterwards. They called the authorities, (the Redcaps, R.C.M.P.s) and because of his condition, they couldn't take him out. They had to bury him somewhere near the cabin. Nobody knew who it was. Another drifter. He was acting strange around town, they said. The police were going to pick him up, but then he was gone. He found a trail and came down the North Fork and landed in that cabin. He must have been half starved. There was nothing to eat in there. He just died of starvation."

Looking at Tom when he was in his early nineties made me wonder what he must have looked like in his younger days. Quite handsome even now, he had undoubtedly been a heartbreaker. Fine featured and with an intelligent light in his eyes, his remarkable spirit never let him admit to any aches or pains. His speech, refined and with a trace of an English accent, captivated any listener.

Keeping current through his many magazine subscriptions and book clubs, Tom kindly shared *Playboy* with Joe Bush and the customs' staff. We reciprocated with *People* magazine.

Tom's small cabin didn't have propane. He read by kerosene lantern, and cooked on a wood stove. Although Tom always gathered and chopped his own wood throughout his entire life, Joe Bush and the bear study groups would take a few truck loads of firewood to him each fall during his later years. There was also a cadre of North Forkers that made sure Tom always had sufficient wood, but they had to be careful, for the proud old man wanted no charity in any shape or form. He was always afraid some of the officialdom would take him away from his beloved North Fork and put him in an old people's home.

He allowed himself no quarter because of his age. One time Becky found him standing on his kitchen table, trying to fix a ceiling panel. She made him promise "no more".

Bears sometimes got into Tom's beer as it cooled outside so he didn't especially care for them. He had lived around them for over sixty-five years thus his bear stories could be rather matter-of-fact.

One day, talk turned to the famous Giefer bear who had been first trapped in the Giefer Creek drainage near Fielding on the Flathead's Middle Fork August 3, 1975. A year later, he was trapped again and released in the Tuchuck drainage of the North Fork, near the Canadian border. Called the "Bear of the Century", he created havoc up the North Fork and was probably responsible for nineteen break-ins. At 500 pounds, he could pretty much do what he wanted. He simply broke down outside doors and windows, yet was adept at opening cupboard doors. He was especially fond of crackers and jello and could smell them out from any hiding place.

"Did he ever bother you at your place?" Joe asked Tom one day.

Tom answered, "Oh, yeah. At first he didn't bother the house much. He tried to get in. I had shutters on the windows. With his paw, he'd try to go in under one of the shutters and then the next day somebody told Jonkel, the bear man, that the bear had been around my place. He came up, looked very busy, measuring here and measuring there," this in a disparaging voice and going every which way with his hands.

"Anyway, the bear went off. But the next thing I know, during the night, about a week after that, he came and he busted in the kitchen door. I thought it was a black bear. I picked up my flashlight and ran outside and there he was. He'd been trapped a couple of times and was afraid of men and women. They weren't able to trap him any more. The next spring he was shot over in Canada."

A cabin down the road from Tom's boasted a Giefer paw print on the sturdy front door, marked forever in the wood by the hell of a whack. From the height of the paw print, he would have towered over all of us.

And Tom had gone outside with him, at night, with only a flashlight.

CHAPTER 10

Entertainment was home-grown up the North Fork, a forced condition because of the isolation and blessed lack of canned outside interference.

It was a natural thing for the two customs inspectors to reciprocate any festivities of the study groups. Moe, Dave's replacement at the Canadian Customs port when he returned to school, had gorged Joe on the previously unknown delicacy of home-made peroggies. Easy to pig out on, they were boiled dough squares, stuffed with anything from onions and cheese, to potatoes or saukerkraut.

The following year, it was no problem to talk Dave into sharing an introductory and most successful feast of the doughy, delicious things for the entire group of study kids. Many more feasts followed over the years. The term kids came easily 'cause they were the ages of my own.

Ron was especially prone to act the fatherly figure to them. His mechanical knowledge made him invaluable to have around, for many an old beat-up government vehicle barely made it to the Canadian customs parking area before conking out. He'd fix them with spit and odd parts, enough to get them back to a garage for more authentic repairs. Both U.S. and Canadian port fridges stored wolf blood for Diane. And Ron's freezers, with excess space in them, contained everything from the study kids' food to assorted animal parts or samples until they could be taken back to civilization for study and lab work.

Anyone else who happened to store food, was extremely careful to mark and identify their packages properly. Wolf blood in the soup might bring on hirsute howling!

In other words, the study groups and the border inspectors became a close company of people who liked, respected and at times depended on each other.

The gatherings themselves, sometimes on the U.S. side, other times over in Canada, became a bright event to look forward to, a chance to socialize, to exchange information and hear the famous stories everyone looked forward to.

A larger party at the end of October to which other North Forkers were invited, was a double celebration: the closing of the border after another season, and a birthday party to honor the grand old gentleman of the North Fork, Tom Reynolds. An especially outstanding one resulted in packed living quarters in the U.S. Customs building for his ninety-third, during which Tom presented a plaque, made up by my Joe, to Becky, who was dubbed an "honorary North Forker". Tom's spontaneous, and hilarious remarks during the presentation were as great an any stand-up comic.

His close and longstanding friendship with Diane was obvious during these events, as the two would sit in a quiet corner bringing each other up to date. During the long cold winters she and Tom were the only ones north of Trail Creek.

At another event, Diane had a readily available, interested but critical audience for some of her wolf slides. Ron taped an old sheet on the quarters area wall while Diane set up her equipment. We had just finished dinner and were anxious to see her program.

"Usually I charge $300 for this," she quipped.

She and Ron had a lively go-round on the subject of wolves as she presented some outstanding pictures taken in the field.

Ron didn't like wolves. He took pleasure in quantifying some of Diane's remarks with his own.

"When I was an R.C.M.P. out in the boonies, this man drove up to the station in a small Volkswagon. Said the car had been attacked by a large dog or wolf. We checked the man's vehicle and found patches of black hair stuck to the front so we went out in a police car with him, eh? To the spot where it happened? This huge wolf was in the area, standing in the middle of the road. He started toward us as we put the spotlight on him. He kept coming—picking up speed, so I shot it. The head, a monstrous thing, is on display."

Diane countered with the facts that there were only a few documented cases of wolves attacking people, regardless of the fairy tale myths that are so rampant: a hunter wrapped himself in a bloody fresh deer skin and went out to hunt. When the wolf jumped him, the animal was pretty amazed that a human was inside the deer. In another instance, a woman was with a group of friends around a campfire. A wolf leaped over her shoulder from behind, grazed her cheek and ran off.

Neat true stories, but I carry in my mind the slide of Diane's student, posed, holding a wolverine up against him, cradling it like you would a child, head looking straight ahead, the animal's back up against the student's chest, the legs cupped in his arms in an outward hold. The wolverine had been caught in a wolf trap, anesthetized and then released, a slide taken to record the event.

The animal was totally out of it, of course, but it was a large wolverine, with a look on its face I can still see, the facial coat giving the animal a distinct unforgettable malevolent stare.

Even unconscious and just from a slide, it gave off the vibrations of "don't mess with me".

I never spotted a wolverine, but we were lucky with wolves. Brig barked so furiously one early spring evening, I looked out the front window. A mangy looking dog, intent only on quick passage, crossed through our front yard, quite close to the porch, shedding thick clumps of blackish brown hair that hung down from his skinny body in ugly disarray. He broke into a loping stride as he reached the upper lane and disappeared from view.

It was a wolf, of course.

With wolf sightings multiplying as the years went on, the rumors circulated that someone had trapped wolves in Canada and set them free in the U.S. It was all a plot. One person even told Joe that the government was killing deer and dropping them from helicopters to feed "those" wolves. Some could not accept the natural dispersal from Canada.

After returning to the cabin late one evening, I stepped outside onto the front porch with Brig. The full moon had just begun to rise over the mountains' jagged profiles across from us. Shadowy shapes materialized from the darkness in the front yard, seemed to mill about for a few seconds, then disappeared. It was as if we had been visited by ghosts.

In less than a minute, wolves howled from down in the draw, filling the night air with their piercing, indescribable calls and howls, a perfect accompaniment to the shimmering slabs of mountain and fast-moving moon that threw the surrounding forests into patterns of mysterious light and dark.

Scalp-raising. Over ten minutes of wilderness calling, right on our doorstep. Beautiful.

More cautions after this incident, I made it a rule to always take the flashlight to check when I let Brig out at night.

Would he have run off with them?

I doubt it, but I might have.

*   *   *

The lodgepole stand across the road from us, diagonally southeast of our ravine, was a favorite wolf corridor where Brig and I could always find fresh wolf scat along the old logging road.

The abandoned track way to the north of our cabin led to an even wilder area, the ground boggy in a low-lying crossing marked with moose and deer prints. There I once spotted the biggest, freshest pile of bear poop I had ever seen. Black, about eighteen inches in diameter and heaped high, the scat was full of red berries and masses of writhing white roundworms. I immediately made a lot of noise, while singing and calling out loud.

Waist high grasses hid access to an old hunter's camper, famous as the scene for many of Maggie's black bear encounters while scouting around on good old Chester during our horse days. Further along, a small hunter's cabin stood in the open, a salt lick in the field beyond. Hopefully, the critters were smart enough to stay away during hunting season, and not be drawn into a possible trap.

The dark forest to the west of the open sea of grasses looked too forbidding to explore. Returning along the same route, there were the roundworms in the bear scat, now quite dead. If the poop had been scared out of him, it was good for his digestive tract.

Being outside like that, every day, drew me into the North Fork weather, making it a part of me. Thus, my time was measured by the length of my walks, the intensity of a rain and how wet I got, or how quickly the snow filled my tracks. Brig accepted all of it, even when the wind blew his ears away from his head.

It usually engulfed us, a constant companion and bearer of sounds, smells and intimations of our surroundings. Walking in the chill, an orphan layer of warm air from nowhere would touch my face, strong and distinct enough to make me stop and wonder how it had survived in the midst of the cold. And of course, in the warmth of a summer breeze, a chill undercurrent would remind me of the swiftness of the weather changes.

I have gone back alone toward the salt licks and smelled "wildness" carried along on these currents. I know of no better way to describe the musk, pungent odor. I would not move, sniffing the air like any other animal, wondering what was out there and how far away. A few times, the smells were so strong, they triggered a cautious response so that I went no further back into the trees.

Often the wind whipped though the forest so hard the sound was almost like the background noise of highway traffic, a constant encircling muted, low swishing roar.

Only once do I remember complete, utter silence. Brig and I were walking south one morning when I couldn't pinpoint what was wrong. Then it dawned on me. There was no wind, no breeze. None at all. And no sound, not even the birds. Nothing. An oppressive feeling almost overwhelmed me as we walked faster to escape the unusual void.

Rain could be delicious.

It was elemental to walk with fast, long strides along the North Fork road, trying to gauge the swiftness, the ferocity of the approaching black storm clouds from over the Whitefish range in back. To judge the length of time it would take us to beat the main onslaught. Tearing up our lane, pelted in the face with huge raindrops as the wind picked up in intensity. Hurrying to keep up with Brig who ran at the end of his leash, a water dog who hated getting wet. Racing under the ranch gate, breathlessly uphill the rest of the way, just beating the heavy downpour. Excitedly slamming into the screen door in my hurry, hollering at Brig to get in. Then standing on the back porch, sucking in the suddenly chilly air, sniffing at the cleanness of it, unable to see to the corral because of the driving, almost solid rain. Watching it gather on the screen before sliding down in rivulets.

Brig shook, engulfing me in a spray of water, wet dog smell and coldness.

The warmth of the cabin was welcome as I hurried over to the large front windows. Heavy winds gusted over, blowing at the metal roof, trying to lift it away. I checked for any chimney leaks. None.

The buckshot sounds of pea, then bean-sized hail roared through the cabin as it hit and bounced off the metal roof and porch, scattered and joined the white mounds building up on the ground outside.

The sudden drop in temperature, the roughness, the swiftness of it—the raw entity of it. I shivered from the damp, happy.

Deer crossed the field in front, through the gray, like a line of school children, racing for the protection of the trees.

Alone most of the day, I was never lonely. Our radio was always tuned to CBC, the Canadian Broadcasting Corporation station. The beauty of the North Fork was enhanced by their splendid, enriching music. A CBC transmitter was located in Lethbridge, beyond the ranges to the northeast. Our cabin was in perfect alignment through a break in the mountains.

Very few North Forkers could receive this station, to me, one of the best ever. Ron was furious he couldn't pick it up at the border. I hated it when I was away from it, working in the garage, or up at the port.

It became my constant companion and I even scheduled our walks according to some of the CBC program schedules. Some were too special to miss.

Old favorites, Mendelssohn, Dvorak, Sibelius, Vivaldi—all fitted perfectly into the setting, their inspiration before my very eyes.

The CBC news was extraordinarily succinct. It was fun to listen to what was going on in the world, from another point of view, one that did not consider the United States to be the center of the world. Refreshing, with no editorializing, their news programs became our main source of information, a far cry from the local broadcasts from the valley that were so slanted at times, they were absurd. We learned to depend on the Canadian weather forecasts since they were usually correct. We were introduced to Canadian singers—the Rankin Family, Custer LaRue, groups we had never heard of before, some not making it to prominence in the States, but deserving of world-wide recognition.

*   *   *

I pestered Joe to be sure and go up to Crevasse Lookout if he ever had a chance. So it was good news that Ron was rearing to go one evening after the ports closed. He had successfully taken Joe Bush black bear hunting three days previously. It was obvious he wanted to check out the skinned bear carcass, left about two thirds of the way up to the lookout.

He could also show off to Joe the capabilities of the love of his life, Tojo, an old four-wheel drive gray Toyoto jeep. Ron had driven it onto thin ice the year before while ice fishing and the poor vehicle had drowned in cold Canadian waters. Retrieved, and now all gussied up, it could go anywhere with impunity. It had already been to hell and back.

From Joe's reports of the event, it was even wilder than our trip with Dave earlier that summer.

Tojo's engine overheated three times before Ron pulled out his spotting scope to check the side of the road.

Our cabin with the Whitefish Range, looking west

"This is where Joe got his bear," Ron said, searching the area with his scope. "We cut off the bear's head and then skinned it down. He had a good coat. It'll make him a good rug."

"There it is!" Ron called out, pointing. "I thought a grizzly would be on it by now."

Joe found the right spot with his binoculars in time to see a large adult grizzly get up, go over to the black bear carcass and start eating it.

"He's claimed it," Ron explained. "He's telling us it's his and we're not going to take it away from him."

The two watched the feeding griz through the scope and binoculars for quite a while before continuing up to the lookout.

Ron broke the news to Joe at the top. The Canadian government intended to man the fire lookout again. The old building would be torn down and replaced and the parking area would be enlarged for helicopter landings.

On the way back down, they checked to see if the griz was still there. He had been lying down a few feet from the carcass, but then walked over and started eating from it again.

"I bet nothing can made that bear retreat from his meal," Ron said matter-of-factly as he pulled out his homemade elk caller. "Let's see what he does with this. I need practice anyway."

A God-awful noise blasted out of the device that resembled a water hose from an auto radiator.

Instantly, the griz stood up on his hind legs and looked in the direction of Tojo.

Joe, through his binoculars, could see the bear's ears were laid back and the hair on the back of his neck stood high.

The poor bear might not have recognized the bugling noise Ron was making, but if he had only known, he could have come running, and swatted Tojo over on its side, easily tearing it up and finding a much tastier meal, a double serving at that.

Everyone passed on good bear stories. Canadians and Americans both delighted in describing any wildlife sightings that were beyond the normal. Joe and Ron heard many, as did the animal study people.

A group of Canadians had recounted to Diane how they had watched an eagle attack a moose calf, again and again, until the calf followed its running mom into the safety of the forests. On one of their overflights, checking for collared wolf signals, Diane witnessed a grizzly running for cover with a full grown elk in its jaws.

After listening to these events I didn't think much could surprise me, and I was ready when a hawk once circled over Brig and me as we walked up the lane, sweeping ever lower and lower, as if sizing up Brig. I rushed our full grown seventy-five pound dog toward the cabin, all the time shouting and waving my hat and arms like a wild thing.

Even the ravens could appear sinister. They stalked and waddled around as if they owned everything. Their loud and raucous caws were part of the overall North Fork background as they searched for food, be it decayed remains somewhere in back of our cabin, or a road kill. They investigated anything out of place or different.

Common sights, they are easy to ignore in the vast array of other, more appealing birds and animals. Joe Bush had tamed one so it hung around his bar/restaurant across the border, a steady customer for the supply of bits of food.

A flock of extra huge ravens had started to stay around our entrance ranch gate in a count ranging from eight to over a dozen. The horizontal top cross log was their perch, as they sat in a row, or flew about checking, always checking. I measured their perfect undisturbed claw marks in the dust on the road under the gate once when they were elsewhere and was astonished at their size—three inches or more from the back end of the rear claw to the tip of the front ones. Big birds with big feet, black, inquisitive, smart—and always at the ready. I remembered watching two ravens attack and drive off a smallish red-tailed hawk in the air over the corral.

Aerial view of our cabin and surrounding area

Now, as Brig and I approached the *Y*, there was the line of ravens, all in a row on their perch, as if waiting for us. Two of them, the biggest I'd ever seen, flew off the gate and began to circle us, coming lower, ever lower in large sweeping circles. Then the rest of the ravens, each appearing even bigger, lifted to the sky, swooping, circling, looking us over, coming lower and closer.

I shouted at them, flailing my arms, shouting at the top of my lungs. Some broke off but one landed on the old original jack fence down from the entrance. It sat there, staring balefully at us with its small red eyes, ready for who knows what?

I grabbed up a rock by my feet, then more, for two other ravens joined him, sitting on the fence, waiting for us to pass by them.

Too close.

I threw the rock straight at Redeyes, missing him. He never moved, but just sat there, staring.

Brig sat patiently at the end of his leash which I held under my foot so I could take better aim using both hands, throwing bunches of rocks in a cluster, stooping swiftly to grab some more. I could **feel** the one was ready to come at us. I grabbed a larger rock and screamed at the top of my lungs, threw it, then lunged right at them, dragging poor Brig along.

The ravens flew upward and gradually rose higher and higher, but still circled us as a group, watching. Eventually they disappeared.

All but one. Redeyes.

He continued to hang around and followed us at a safe distance while we finished our walk down the road and back. He sat on the crossbar of the gate as we returned back up our lane.

Could they have attacked us? I sure believed they would have. I'd never ever thrown rocks at anything, much less a bird. But I did then, with all my might, for I could picture them going after Brig's head and eyes.

Joe had his own stories to tell, of a different nature, memorable events that had occurred during port hours.

He had started another day at the border. The office was open, radio on, and he was outside raising the flags. Then he noticed the elderly man who had been waiting at the gate, get out of his pickup and come over to salute the flags as they were going up.

He confided to Joe, "I'm a secret agent, going into Canada on a special mission."

"Okay," Joe replied, wondering where this guy came from.

"I can't prove it, 'cause it's a secret and I can't have any identification," the old man explained.

"Okay with me," Joe answered. "I have to finish opening up. There's still a few minutes before we open the gate." Then he went into the customs building and radioed the Canadian inspector on the other side.

"Dave, you have someone coming over who reports he's on some sort of secret mission. He's got a couple of dogs in the back of his truck."

"Keep him over there," Dave called back. "We don't need another one of those."

Joe went outside to unlock and swing open the gate. The old man climbed into his pickup which pulled a camping trailer of ancient vintage. Both vehicles sported Montana plates. After the rig crossed into Canada, Dave went through his routine of checking the man, the vehicle and trailer, before radioing, "He's coming back. Has no papers on his dogs."

The man came back to the U.S. side, asked and got permission to drop his trailer and leave it while he went down to civilization for his dogs' papers, which he said he had left at home.

He and the two soaked dogs in the back of the pickup were waiting in the rain the next morning. He proudly showed Joe the animals' shot papers, one day old, that he needed for Canadian entrance.

Dave let him into Canada, and left for his scheduled break when the border closed that afternoon. Ron drove in early the next morning before the gate opened, listened to Joe's story, and vowed to research Canadian customs regulations for grounds to deny entry to the obviously mentally impaired man.

Soon after, some of the animal study people, returning from British Columbia, reported an old camping trailer on the side of the road a few miles north, with two dogs running around it. They had no food or water.

Concerned, Ron drove north for a look after the border closed for the day. He told Joe the next morning the man was not around and it looked like he hadn't been there for some time.

The R.C.M.P. came out and checked the license plate number on the trailer. The missing man now had a name. Mac.

During the next few days, Joe Bush and the animal study people stopped by the trailer daily to feed and water the dogs, but there was no sign of Mac.

One morning, early, Ron heard a vehicle drive up to the locked gate on the Canadian side. It was Mac.

"Where have you been?" Ron asked. "We've had the R.C.M.P. out looking for you!"

"I've been captured!" Mac cried out. "I was their prisoner but I escaped! They're looking for me! Go get your gun and help!"

"I don't have a gun," Ron answered. "We don't carry guns on this side."

"You don't carry a gun? I have to write to your president about that."

Ron later told Joe that Mac intended to rest after he reentered the States, and promised to be back.

"I'll be damned if he's coming back into this country!" Ron added.

Mac reappeared a few days later, but, true to his word, Ron refused him entry. Mac had to go south to get two U.S. acquaintances to drive into Canada and retrieve his trailer.

Later, we saw his rig parked at Ford access, with other public campers.

Just goes to show you, that camper next to you could be secret agent man.

Of course, we kept Mary Louise and John up-to-date with all the news. Dave especially appreciated Mary Louise's cooking, and he opened the window wide to things Canadian. Joe Bush's name would pop up often, in sometimes hilarious stories he'd relate.

Joe Bush had been to town and imbibed a bit too much. He had to leave his truck on the American side of the border, then cross by the gate and walk about ten minutes to reach his bar/restaurant in British Columbia.

They said he was pretty far out of it.

Walking back to his place, Joe kept reaching in back, feeling fur brushing against his body. He knew it was his dog, coming to greet him. He continued to stagger on home, still feeling the fur behind him.

To his consternation, his dog was locked inside his cabin, waiting for him.

He never really knew what the animal was, but with all the bear activity at the time, everyone presumed it had to be a bear.

Even to those who knew him, Joe Bush could be a mixture of contradictions. An expert crib player, he liked his liquor and women, and hated wolves. He got into a lot of trouble with his "I could care less" attitude, by not living up to his agreement to let U.S. Customs know when he was crossing the borders in the off-season.

Yet, he often gave or loaned money to those that needed it, and made sure Mac's abandoned dogs were fed after the man disappeared into the Canadian woods.

He had been a welder and made the move to the Flathead partially out of necessity after he tried to rescue other workers trapped inside a tank of chlorine gas fumes. The only survivor, he was left with one lung, thus the marvelous clear fresh air of extreme southern British Columbia was perfect for him.

Stranger than fiction, Ron was the R.C.M.P. that investigated the chlorine gas accident. Meeting again years later in the Flathead, they spent many an hour together.

Joe Bush's health, poor at best, seemed to go down hill rapidly in the summer of 1991. Both he and Tom Reynolds, close friends after all the years in the North Fork, jointly celebrated birthdays in October. Tom, in his nineties, called mid-seventies Joe a youngster. But Joe couldn't even made it over to the U.S. side that last celebration so we took Tom over for a visit, along with Joe's cake. Joe was so bad off he couldn't get up from the couch. At least they saw each other one more time.

Joe died in hospital of cancer of the jaw during the winter and was cremated, then brought back to the Flathead to be buried the following year.

Tom Reynolds was in a talkative mood as I drove him north to Joe's funeral.

"He set her up in a love nest, you know."

"Joe Bush?"

"Oh, yes. His girl friend. He had a love nest. His first wife found out about it and went to the bank immediately and cleaned him out."

"Then what happened?"

"Oh, he married her then, but—"

But I never heard the rest for we had arrived at the border amongst the crowds of Canadians and Americans there to attend the pig roast celebration requested by Joe Bush for his memorial service.

Tom and I stayed close to each other, sitting on the huge log out in front of the bar/restaurant, watching the crowd of people, many on the verge of intoxication. All wore extremely casual clothes. Tom was dressed perfectly, in his good red plaid flannel shirt and tan pants. His brown fedora hat and high laced boots gave him the aura of a 1920s outdoorsman. Tom drank only coffee. I had nothing.

Joe's daughter, Arlene, was more than busy, watching over the roasting pig and making arrangements for the caravan of vehicles that would accompany Joe's ashes to the final resting spot on a remote hill to the north, over a rough logging road.

Tom turned to me, after looking around.

"If I had come to this affair, dressed as they are, they would say, 'That old man doesn't have the sense to dress properly.'" Right on, Tom.

It was my first backwoods funeral.

As we got into Arlene's car, Tom sat in front, I, in back with Joe Bush's first wife. Before Arlene hopped in the driver's seat, she thrust a brown plastic urn at me.

"Here, you can hold this."

Thus it was I held Joe Bush in my lap on his last ride.

The lonely skirl of a single bagpipe cut through this part of northwest wilderness, sounding a mournful tribute to the man whose ashes were being scattered along the outside of an old logging area. Joe Bush's grandson, Mark, held the brown urn in both hands, spreading the remains carefully in a long drawn out semicircle so he would have enough to reach to the edge of the tree line.

As Mark finished, there was a slight pause.

"Tom, go ahead," Arlene called to the thin, ninety-four year old gen-tleman, who had told Joe Bush he would have a last beer with him.

I stood there with a semicircle of about seventy people. A few moun-tain peaks showed through the tops of the tallest trees that totally encir-cled us, miles and miles of trees, cutting us off from the real world that seemed centuries away.

Tom, in his stiff-legged gait, brown fedora set firmly on his head, walked over to the line of ashes scattered along the ground, a long thin line of pale beige. Tom set down his six-pack of beer, removed one can, pulled the tab and carefully and slowly poured the beer over the line of ashes. When the can was empty, he replaced the can into the beer pack, walked back to where he had left off, and again, poured another beer all along the thin line. He repeated this four more times, having judged the distance and amount of beer involved perfectly, ending up at the last of Joe's ashes with the final drops of beer. Then Tom walked back to the group of people in the semicircle.

Even though the funeral had started off with some raunchy remarks by Joe's old buddies, Tom had such class that everyone had become silent. The sight of the old gentleman faithfully fulfilling his promise to Joe, was extremely moving.

It was a rough ride back down the rutted and overgrown road to Joe's Place.

Arlene would run it for him now that he was gone.

CHAPTER 11

I was forever grateful Joe and I had sense enough to take the video camera with us to the evening party at Canadian customs.

I can't imagine such a gathering any where in the world, anytime in history, past, present, or future. Never would such an intelligent, lively, wildlife orientated, interacting group of people meet again in these exact circumstances: the grizzly bear trappers from U.S. Fish and Wildlife, the bear study group from Canada and the United States, George, the biologist from Greece, other biologists, Ron, who knew wild but true stories from his early R.C.M.P. days that would curl your hair—all brought together informally in the Canadian log cabin built by the Canadian government to house their customs' staff in the wilderness.

The story was that Canada wanted to outdo the modern facility the United States had built just across the border for their customs inspector. Ergo, the Canadian quarters building was a beautiful log home, totally electrified by a 40,000 watt diesel generator that could have lit up the entire North Fork. (That the R.C.M.P. seized the building after completion and the many stories of "short cuts" taken during its construction is another story for someone else to tell).

So there it was, with full modern electrical conveniences, set in the middle of nowhere. The closest Canadian town was about sixty miles to the north and west, the road even rougher and much more desolate than the North Fork.

After the border closed for the day, and after marvelous food and drink, the crowd in the cabin, some sitting on the floor, called for story time.

I wasn't sure the bear kids had ever heard Ron's UFO story that had been one of my favorites since I first heard it.

"UFO, Ron," I called out.

"Tell us the story, Ron," Irene kidded in a high falsetto voice, egging him on.

"Lemme get another beer first," he said, before settling down on a stool by the kitchen countertop. He began.

I started video taping.

"Okay. One thirty in the morning, up by Prince George, on the hard highway." Ron, a natural exuberant story teller, with his neat Canadian accent, threw himself into the telling.

"What year?" he answered to a question. "About 1973. Chris, you were still in diapers."

Chris, the youngest in the bear study, led the laughs.

Ron continued. "But we were patrolling, heading north and I was driving. Don was taking the passenger seat. It was being one of those late, quiet nights in the late fall, leaning on your elbow and driving and all that."

The audience, settled down and mesmerized by Ron's rich voice and expressive gestures, never moved.

"Don says, 'Oh, look at that!'

"And I said, 'What?'

"He said, 'Well, look at the goddam light!'

"And I said, 'Shit, probably a goddam airplane.' And that's up north, looking directly north.

"He says, 'Oh, shit, look at that!'

"So I straighten up so I'm not behind the dog leg on the car and I could see this light and it was glowing in the sky. It just got over to us—oh, it couldn't be more than a yard over to the left, eh? So—"

"Was it different colors?" Tim interrupted.

"White, just white—and that intense white light, you know, that you see in welding? An intense white blue light.

"Stopped the car, but it came on down and it was really moving. There was no deceleration. It was just stopped. It was in plain view and it had to be maybe 100 feet off the ground. We mentioned taking a couple of shots at it." (Much laughter from the listeners.) "So, anyhow, I get out of the car, turn the engine off and there's no sound. We should have heard it 'cause it wasn't that far away. And then I thought I'd try something.

"So I get on the radio and call the Prince George office and get Baldy Hughes Air Force Base which is the radar station just slightly west of Prince George. The thing couldn't have been much more than forty miles off the highway. So anyhow, they start to scan and the sergeant at Baldy says, 'We see nothing' and I say, 'Well, there's gotta be something' and they say, 'Well, we don't see anything.'

"So while we're standing there, this thing just—no gyration, just straight up.

"But as it's going up, it goes like this." He motions with his hand and finger. "It's got a little gyration now. And we still got Baldy Hughes on the line and he says, 'We got a little bit of interference now.' I say the thing seems to have stopped. Like it was huge, eh? As it went up, it seemed to shrink at that rate of speed. Twice the size of a big star and it had just stopped there.

"When it stopped, this goldurned van pulled up with six or eight railway workers that were working graveyard shift out by Shally on the rail line and they say, 'Did you see that?'"

Ron's voice, throughout this entire telling was full of feeling and he used his hands constantly to accentuate points, arms waving as he described the incident.

"So anyhow, we were watching this thing and the sergeant at Baldy was listening and he said, 'I'm going to get hold of Colorado,' and then he says, 'We've got them on the line and they've run the tape back and he says all they've got is static.' They couldn't run the tape back at Baldy Hughes but in Colorado, it's taped down there, eh? Like they can monitor Baldy Hughes.

"So we're watching it and watching it out there and this thing starts to reclimb, very slowly and it gets almost to the horizon in the east and stops and sits there. This observation takes over a two hour period. We watched it and it never moved from that spot on the horizon. Then—swish—it just totally disappeared over the eastern horizon, right across the sky and the thing just keeps going on at a high rate of speed."

Ron paused for a second and groaned in a low voice, "Then came the paperwork."

Everyone laughed. They all worked for governments!

Tim said, "They told you to forget about it, probably."

"Thought you were nuts?" Irene called out.

"Well, they told us not to say anything about it. But then we had all the goddamn newspapers hounding at the door saying, 'You've seen it. We have all these Canadian National Railroad employees that were with you—eight or nine guys that said they had seen it. You were watching it with them and you were talking with them,' and so forth and so on.

"And of course then they sent the big sheets of paper: what happened, what you saw and so forth. But when it first stopped it was over to our left which would be to the west. You could see around it—you could see the sky around it but there was nothing there—like a ball of light."

"Wonder what it was?" someone asked.

"I don't know but when I looked at it over to the side, you know what it looked like to me when it was off over there? Remember those great big round Gulf emblems they used to have for a sign and they used to light them up? They had to be maybe twelve feet across and they'd put "Gulf" gas, or about that size? But you couldn't see anything. The light had a tendency to pulsate. And then, there was no acceleration. It was just instant. But I'm glad to see this thing in Belgium 'cause it wasn't one or two of 'em. There were six of 'em and they had those two guys that scrambled from the Belgian Air Force and get a video tape of the radar thing on their scope and locked in on 'em."

Irene asked, "They saw a similar thing?"

"Yeah, but actually they saw a big craft with three major big lights on it. A red light came down and the light bounced around and then went back."

I hoped no one would interrupt Ron. He was on a roll. No one could beat his true stories. The atmosphere in the place was perfect.

"**Kitimat!**" sounded from behind the dining room table.

There was a pause, to set the stage for the next story. I don't think Ron's expertise on crowd control was noticed by the group for he was rearing to jump into the next story but patiently waited for the room to settle back down.

Ron started in an official curt police voice:

"One year we had a bear problem. I, myself, killed thirty-five or thirty-six bears. We had one kid walking home from school and a bear ran out between two houses and nailed him onto the bloody ground and put him permanently in a wheelchair. He lost half his head. This was on his way home from school. The bear came out at him.

"Bears were all over. You'd have people running out of their houses 'cause the bears broke into the house.

"Anyhow, across from the Kitimat Gordon Hotel there was a bakery. There was an old night watchman at the hotel by the name of Leo. He phoned the police office one night and said, 'A bear just broke into the bakery!'

"Mitchell went down there and he ran the bear off. The bear did a lot of damage."

By this time, someone had replenished Ron's drink.

"The next night, Leo called back right at shift change. The bear broke into the bakery again. Mitchell said, 'Ron, let's take care of it.'

"We went down to the bakery, he was in front of me, kicked the door open and here was this black bear sitting on his haunches. You know those tubs of pie filling, just like those tubs of ice cream? They're wood and they're about that round and about that high."

Ron demonstrated the size with his arms and hands, sitting like a bear clasping a large tub on his lap, arms wrapped around an imaginary large tub.

Irene, in a questioning voice, teased Ron, "Is all this true?"

Ron nodded, "Yes. The guy who shot that bear is now stationed in Cranbrook.

"Well, this bear's holding it like this," Ron dips his hand into the tub and brings his hand to his mouth like a bear dipping the pie fill out of it.

"And he has his paw in it, like this." Ron even looks like a bear. "Mitchell just opened up with his 30-30. But that place was a mess. It had knocked over everything. Like the bakers rolled all their dough and put it in pans and they had them on those carts."

Tim interrupted, "The bears?"

Everyone hooted.

"Probably! Then when the bakers came in at four or five in the morning, they'd just roll 'em into the big ovens and then start baking. They'd let them rise that period of time. It was kind of humorous the way the bear was setting with this big tub," and Ron demonstrated again, becoming the bear, holding the tub and eating from it.

I didn't want Ron to miss telling the hilarious Indian women story that only he could tell with such fervor and gusto.

"Indian women story, Ron!" I had to shout above the noisy talk that had meanwhile broken out.

"I've never heard the Indian story," Tom said seriously.

Someone asked George, the Greek who spoke very little English, "George, are you following all he's saying?"

"Okay," George answered.

"Okay, Ron. Indian women," I repeated insistently. At this stage of the evening, it could not be missed.

Ron looked around, changing his demeanor and suddenly becoming younger.

"I was just a young man, innocent, and kinda naïve, okay? Actually I thought I had been around quite a bit. Anyhow, we get to Rupert, eh? Prince Rupert. That's where I got stationed. It's Saturday. At Rupert with the fishing fleets in those days, it was something, 'cause the population was 12,000 to 13,000 people and when the fishing fleets came in, this population actually doubled in two days, so you're looking at about 26,000 people.

"You gotta figure the mid-sixties was the last of the big fishing on the west coast. Fishing, since then, has gone.

"But anyhow, you have all these people on the streets and if something happened, like a fight, the hordes of people came out 'cause they all hung around dives we named 'Navajo Junction, Moccasin Square Junction.' Actually, it was Third Avenue, Prince Rupert.

"We're in the office and a call came in. There's a fight down by the Belmont which is down at the bottom of the hill, on Third Avenue where all the bars are.

"We got in the paddy wagon, went down the hill to the bottom. Then we can't even move 'cause there were people all over the streets. You just can't move. You could see a bit of a clearing down about fifty yards along the street.

"We get out, lock the van up and work our way through the crowds. There's an area, a circle of about twelve or fourteen feet. Everybody's standing 'round, yelling and cheering. Here's this Indian woman. She's about 285 pounds and her name was Alice. The other one, she had to be 375 pounds and her name was Mamie. When we get there, they're both naked from the waist up and they've got handfuls of hair, eh? And they're screaming and yelling at one another." Ron changes his voice to accentuate the action.

"Anyhow, Carlson says to me, 'Fontana, take the big one and I'll take the small one.'"

Ron was really playing to the audience here so everyone burst out laughing.

"He gets this one and he just arm twists 'er, runs and hustles her up through the bloody crowd and everyone's booing."

Ron made booing, reverberating sounds and none of us could stop laughing at this point. He enjoyed this story so much and the reaction of his audience, he got better and better, throwing himself into his role.

"He gets up and gets her into the bloody van, eh? And he won't come back to help 'cause he has to watch the van and watch her. Besides, it's a good lesson for me.

"So anyhow, I dragged this Mamie, she's like this, eh?" He acts out a person being dragged under the arms. "So anyhow, I got her under arrest and she's starting to"—Ron makes a grunting sound under his breath, really into it now, arms showing his moves, voice in perfect intonation—"and the crowd was starting to boo and chant, things are getting kinda like, harried. So anyhow, she's just egging the crowd on, you know. They're starting to get a little aggravated. She just goes limp on me and goes through my hands like a sack of soggy shit and when she does that, the whole crowd—everybody on the street—you gotta realize there's gotta be 700—800—1000 people at this particular time watching it." Ron's voice gets higher and louder. "She hits the ground and everyone says, 'Yeaaaa!'

"Well, anyway, I lean over and get 'er and pick her up again—"

We're about hysterical laughing.

"She's not resisting or anything," Tim interrupts.

"No! I get her up and start to move again and the crowd goes 'Boooo. Boooo'—she goes limp again and the crowd goes, 'Yeaaaa. Yeaaaa.' So anyhow, you gotta imagine what this is like. She's 375 pounds. Her breasts hang down to her knees like a pair of goddamn panty hose with a boulder stuck in each one, with stretch marks that make a road map look unsophisticated."

Shrieks of laughter greet his choice of descriptive words.

Ron is now totally wound up. The room is all his. The consummate story teller.

"Anyhow, I try to get her up," he laughed. "I'm getting pissed off but trying not to show it so the crowd doesn't react. So I get down and just got—and just get," he repeats, remembering, "the goddamn—like rolls, eh? I just squeezed it. She gets up," Ron snarls and clenches his teeth, "and then she sort of stands up and starts to walk and I try to push 'er and then she throws her hands in the air and says, 'Look everybody! They're gonna take me back and screw me! Whooo! Whooo!'" Ron's falsetto cries ring out above the laughs. "Anyhow, I get her back to the goddamn van and get her into it and Carlson says, 'Entertaining, isn't it!' I coulda killed him!"

Ron turns serious while we catch our breaths.

"We go down and get back to the police office and wheel both of 'em in there and Jerry's doing the goldurned Alice there and Mrs. Leyton was our matron, so I get Mamie and I'm over here." He points to the side. "Your name? And you must remember, this woman has no teeth"—Ron affects a slurring lisp—"and scraggly hair, and smells to the high heaven and she leans over to me and she says in her slurring lisp, 'My name is Mamie but all the boys call me Sweetlips'.

"She started rubbing against me, you know, and Mrs. Leyton was just laughing and laughing."

Ron looked around at the crowd, reveling in the listeners reaction. Some of us were laughing so hard we were crying.

"After three or four weeks of that summer you couldn't make me blush."

"Nice going, Ron," someone called from the audience.

Nothing could top an evening like that.

If I happened to spend a day at the port, it could be every bit as great.

I'd hear the latest information from the animal study people as they'd pass through, and catch the latest happenings in the North Fork and the park, a touch of civilization for me.

And to take a fast walk with Brig along the airstrip at nearby Moose City was to see the mountains from a totally different perspective.

The Rockies, their higher ramparts often traced with snow, stretched north to south along the eastern margin. Kinnerly, not visible except for its tip from our cabin, hidden as it was by Parke Peak, appeared in full awesome view, especially beautiful to me since it resembled the Matterhorn. The airstrip was sufficiently level so I could walk without fear of tripping or stepping in a hole, attention fixed on this special mountain for the five minutes it was in walking view. The other giants of rock spread south in a line until hidden by closer intervening forests.

The Whitefish range to the west seemed rougher up here along the border, as it continued its way north into the wilds of British Columbia.

This morning, a red-tailed hawk swung low to check us out, then went on about his business. Brig and I walked the entire strip length to the moose ponds beyond, on the watch for the usual inhabitants.

Deer sometimes hung around the edges of the trees on either side of the meadow, ready for a quick escape as they gauged our speed and distance. We inadvertently scared off a flight of ducks once as we appeared up over the grassy bank above the pond. But we had been lucky enough to catch sight of river otters as they cut a swath in the deeper, wider stands of water that slowly flowed to the river.

Today there was nothing, only the wind and the varied smells of the wild, wet place just beyond, some pungent odors cutting through the unbelievably clean fresh air. And, of course, the cutoff wooden bridge to

Airstrip at Moose City, with windsock

nowhere, standing dark and forgotten at the edge of the tall, yellow brown grasses, dried and bending in the breeze. Constructed for some scene or other for the notorious western movie flop, *Heaven's Gate,* it, too, went nowhere, ending abruptly just a few feet out over the water.

To see the ponds from above, from atop the higher, almost sheer hill to the west that overlooked the area, was breathtaking, for the view encompassed a panorama of a twisting, turning array of acres of a morass only a moose could love. The scope of the ponds was not evident to us as we stood on the bank's edge, gazing south at their same level.

On the way back, I noticed again the many piles of moose poop that were scattered all along the strip over a long distance as if the moose had been in a great hurry with no time to stop. Hollows and pressed down areas in the tall grass showed where animals had bedded down.

The airstrip's windsock squeaked as it turned at the vagaries of the wind. Half way down the field it stands, a marker in the midst of the tall grass.

A movement caught my eye to the west of the windsock as I stopped to listen to its fittingly lonely, yet musical sound. A covey of birds, invisible but for the tops of their heads, scurried about in the grasses. Brig paid no attention to them, more intent on the game smells that were right under his nose.

Weather is all encompassing in this wide open stretch of meadow, caught as it is between the two ranges. The winds are usually constant and, especially when they blow in from behind the Whitefish range, can bring an instant change, blotting out the sun with huge roiling black-gray thunderheads. In this season, their moisture content could engulf a person in huge, wet snow flakes for an immediate white-out.

It was marvelous to stand there, buffeted by the winds, in the midst of the snowy wet, the promise of winter around the corner. I'd stop and stick my tongue out to catch the flakes, closing my eyes, and we'd soon be covered with the white. For now, the ground was too warm for it to really stay around.

When we lived full time at the port for a few weeks in late October, the early morning walks along the strip became an exciting lesson in reading animal tracks after a light snow. Rarely were there people around, just the wildlife that roamed along the edges of the meadow during the day or ran the strip in the dark of night.

I never did see a moose, but their tracks, and those of deer, were plentiful. Deer prints sometimes had long scuff marks that showed in the snow, off to the sides or rear as if another animal had chased along after it. I pictured it in my mind: this peaceful daytime meadow becoming a nighttime hunting ground.

There were new tracks out there to try to identify after each snow: coyote, smaller animals. What would it be like to hide out there at night and watch the critters go by? Since we had often found bear scat, the thought was somewhat scary.

And I was mindful of one of the study kid's admonitions from a past summer. For some reason, maybe extra rain or a better growing season, when Brig and I had passed the partially trimmed end of the airstrip, I had found the grasses growing ever higher and higher. Just before the ponds, they reached a good foot over my head. Common sense and an uneasy feeling had made me stop and return to the shorter grassed area. Anything could be hidden in that thick, almost impenetrable stuff, and besides, I knew what the bridge and pond looked like.

I learned later that the two resident adult mountain lions had regularly sunned themselves on the bridge that summer.

Moose City itself, along the northernmost eastern edge of the meadow, consisted of about ten or twelve small dark brown log cabins and outbuildings of ancient vintage. They looked abandoned, scattered along the stretch of land that immediately faced the North Fork of the Flathead River.

The U.S. river access to the north was a buffer just before the U.S./Canada border. A cabin so tiny that it resembled a play house sat alone in the meadow, to the south of the main settlement. The cabin, would hold maybe five people, all standing in place and upright. To the east of it and down a high bank by the river was a patch of sandy beach, almost unknown in this rocky country. A giant fallen tree trunk lay there, shaded by tall cottonwoods, a perfect place to sit and watch the water stream by. Glacier National Park, of course, was on the opposite side of the river.

The Moose City consortium, composed of both local and out-of-state business men, gathered there the first weekend of each August. Some flew in, most left within a few days.

The airstrip was used for years by all the animal study groups as they checked their radio signals by plane. But later, during a policy change, they opted to stay with their pilot rather than those associated with

Moose City and thus were forced to use the strip further south at the Wurtz place.

Moose City was usually deserted but for the rare visitor or owner from Kalispell and some of the study people. Diane was the year round resident caretaker for many years. Most of her field work on the gray wolf was performed while she lived there. Her many graduate students were allowed to stay in the cabins, thus affording the groups close access to the remote areas of the north.

Diane lived in one of the largest, oldest and most famous of the cabins, Madge Cooper's. According to the stories, she had purchased 160 acres, then planned during the sixties to open a restaurant and whore house on the border. Her ambitions never materialized and she sold Moose City to George Ostrom. The land was divided into sixty parcels.

Madge, a diminutive woman, became the centerpiece for many a North Fork story. She was so tiny, she'd drive up the North Fork road, with only her eyes showing over the dash. Her rusted wreck of an old open-sided farm truck still stood aslant a hummock of ground by a tree in back of her cabin.

Although pinpointed on some maps, Moose City was certainly no destination point for the tourists. Nor did anyone who respected the wildlife that made the North Fork area so remarkable want it to become any sort of magnet.

From the very beginning, we tried to interest the nationally recognized environmental groups in the uniqueness of the North Fork, trying in vain to have representatives visit, to see for themselves that the area was special. At that time, the price of the small amount of private land available was reasonable with chunks of acreage for sale.

We watched with worry the slow gradual changes over the years, as new cabins, pinpointed by mailboxes, appeared like dragon's teeth along the road. It was shocking to learn the North Fork had been advertised on a national basis. As the Flathead valley was suddenly discovered and promoted, even the terrible road couldn't stop people from finding this special place of wildlife and beautiful views. Many would travel to the border, looking for land, and ask Joe about any available parcels.

So far, most of the action was south of Trail Creek. When I discovered a wide new dirt lane one morning, suddenly punched through to the east of us, about a half mile south, my fear for the wildlife overwhelmed me. Insidious development was creeping ever north. The cloud of that discovery followed me for weeks, only lessening as the lane's weeds grew high.

The North Fork had been lucky to survive a past serious threat when an exploratory oil well had been drilled on private land to the south of Polebridge. It was an eye-opening event. Half the landowners were enthusiastic about the drilling. They dreamed of riches beyond compare, with oil wells traveling northward to the border, with Moose City becoming a field of oil rigs like the old days in Titusville, Pennsylvania. The North Fork was split, between those who were trying to preserve it versus those who wanted to exploit it for its riches.

A lot of waves were churned up by the oil well. Surrounded by a high chain link fence, with an armed guard, it boded ill for the North Fork in more ways than one. The well came up dry. But the division remained, especially in the perception of wildlife, taken for granted by so many.

Perhaps because of old ideas and stereotyped views, predators were detested by many North Forkers. The grizzly was okay. He could be bragged about, mounted, or converted into a throw rug. Wolves were worthless competitors, mountain lions were fun to hunt and coyotes weren't even considered. They were automatically shot.

For too many of these people who lived in the North Fork, the hat of choice to wear depicted a wolf head, caught in the gun sight of a rifle. Thus, it was as if someone thumbed his nose at the entire Endangered Species Act, and in particular, the protection of such "vermin" as wolves, when Kyran, coordinator of the current study groups, received a wolf mortality radio signal during an aerial overflight.

Its body was found on private land, close to the road. It had been shot. Rewards were offered, rumors of possible suspects surfaced from time to time. No one knew anything, of course. No one was arrested.

A few weeks later, after this incident, Joe and I were driving north to the border in the early morning. We could see a black creature in the middle of the road a good distance ahead. We thought at first it was a small bear. It was a black wolf.

Brig happened to be with us and sounded off, barking like an idiot at his wild cousin. The wolf stood quite still, as if trying to figure out what this beast was that had approached him, with weird noises coming from its belly.

Thrilled, we watched this jet black lanky creature until I remembered the wolf that had been killed.

Lowering the window, I shouted, "Get off the road! Run! Hide, before you get shot!"

The wolf ambled off to the side, disappeared between some trees, then reappeared about ten feet away in his perfect wolf stance, gaunt head lowered, almost mystical eyes peering, staring at us through the underbrush. Oh, what a tremendous, gorgeous creature.

A radio collar hung from his neck. Gleams of sunlight shone off a green ear tag.

It was great. He at least was collared and identified, a degree of protection. He wasn't a nonentity to be disposed of easily. He was known. And he was in a lonely area, north of Mud Lake.

*   *   *

I noticed with consternation that the new neighbor directly to the south of us had strung a one strand electric wire all around his cleared meadow.

He proceeded to bring in two horses and two mules. They quickly grazed their way through the small field. In no time, the mules broke out in search of better pickings. They ended up at our back door early one morning. Still in my nightgown, I went out and shooed them back down our lane. Stupid man, I thought. When Joe went off to the border, the mules were grazing to the side of the lower main lane.

I looked around for them carefully before I took Brig out for his morning walk. They were nowhere in sight. Good, I thought, hoping they had run off to outer Mongolia.

Brig and I had gone about half way down our lane when the mules appeared from nowhere, thundering up to us—huge, clomping around, the largest one particularly interested in Brig. In an instant he had the dog down on his back, holding him there, pressed against the ground with his giant head about as large as Brig. The mule bared his teeth and started to nibble on him. Brig could not move. Terrified, he froze, legs up in the air, the whites of his eyes showing at me, as the mule worried at him. I screamed, shouted and swore, punching and hurting my hands against the gigantic mule bodies that were bouncing and thrashing around us. Both were so tall I couldn't see over their backs. The smaller one hesitated after I grew louder, wilder and more frantic but the larger one kept on pressing and shoving Brig. I had been vainly trying to loosen the leash the whole time, but the mule's head kept butting in the way.

We were fighting, working our way up toward a rail of the fence. I'd be kicked to death with Brig. I finally got his leash unhooked and screamed at him to run, beating at the mule as hard as I could with the metal catch on the leash.

It was as nothing.

Still frozen with fear, the dog couldn't move. The mule proceeded to shove him up, hard, against the fence, batting him with his head. My cries of terror finally penetrated Brig's brain as I screamed at him to "Run"!

He broke out and ran like hell across the field, hit the lane and disappeared from my sight, the two mules close on his heels.

Oh, God. They'll kill him and I won't even be there! I ran up the road as fast as I could, trying to remember if I had left the garage door open.

Could he fit under the back porch? My breath rasped in my throat. My side hurt so bad I could scarcely breathe. Brig would be an unrecognizable bloody pulp.

The two mules appeared at the top of the rise in our lane, side by side, and charged down toward me.

I screamed and waved in a frenzy, jumped up and down and ran back and forth, madder than I had ever been in my life—I would have killed—or been killed. The mules split apart just before they reached me, then pounded up into the overgrown part of the lane, coming back together as a pair after they had passed me, eventually slowing and stopping to feed at the lower common road. I stopped breathing and thinking as I hurried up the lane, afraid of what I might find.

Brig slunk out from under the workbench in the garage. He had squeezed himself into the smallest of areas. The mules had been stymied.

Oh, God, I prayed, taking the dog into the house, checking him for hurts, shaking and furious at the jerk who tried to graze such large beasts in such a small area, and not managing them properly.

Later when I calmed down, I sat on the front porch and watched the mules as they wandered off up the North Fork road. "Go to Canada, you damn wretched animals!" I shouted, hoping they'd never be found.

About two hours later a small truck tore up our lane. The driver leaped out.

"Do you know who those mules belong to?" he shouted to me.

"The jerk down south of us—they almost killed my dog!"

"They're right on a curve on the road way up north. I'm afraid someone will crash into them. You can't see 'em until you're right on them!"

Then he was gone in a cloud of dust as he tore back up the North Fork road.

Then I felt guilty. Someone could get killed if they hit them with their truck or car. But there was nothing I could do.

I waited on the front porch and watched for over an hour before I head the clopping of hoofs from far up the road. The two mules broke into view, side by side, racing fifty miles an hour, right down the middle of the North Fork road, like a phalanx of tanks. They wheeled into the main gate, tore up into their own lane and disappeared. About one minute later, the guy with the small truck came speeding down the road and into the lane as fast as he could safely drive. He had hazed them back with his vehicle.

I hope he shoots them, I thought balefully, hating the creatures who had rampaged throughout the area.

After a few minutes, the small truck reappeared, then turned south, still speeding. I waited about a half hour before I very carefully walked down our lane, without Brig.

The damn mules were peacefully eating in their pasture as if nothing had ever happened.

The neighbor to the south came up from the valley the next morning and took his animals away and I haven't seen them since. He left the electric fence stand the rest of the summer, before finally taking it down. We never heard if the incident had been reported.

I would rather meet up with a grizzly than those blasted mules, mindless, bony and uncontrollable. I heard later from a lot of different sources that some mules kill dogs. That was sure the intent of the ones we met up with. I seriously thought of carrying a gun on my walks if the jerk ever brought them back, but he never did.

*　　　　*　　　　*

Men take their personal problems with them wherever they go. They were just more obvious in the North Fork.

The border had closed for the day. Ron and three men from Great Falls gathered together outside the port with Joe to shoot the breeze while he waited for me to pick him up. The three from Great Falls were going to camp at the river access that night and raft the river the next morning.

A pickup with a camper drove up from the south and parked across from the port. The driver then wandered over to join the group.

He was somewhat strange but they thought maybe he had been drinking a bit. He claimed he was a truck driver from outstate, and, during the ensuing conversation, remarked he had no spare tire. Of course, the guys kidded him, a truck driver with no spare, especially on a road like the North Fork.

I picked up Joe and Ron returned to his Canadian quarters, where his R.C.M.P. past kicked in. Using his scope, he watched as the truck driver stooped down at each of his four tires. Ron assumed he was checking the air.

During the evening, the man from the pickup walked over to the three men camping by the river and told them someone had cut all four of his tires. He asked if he could join them for a while. The man may have been weird but it was possible there was a nut in the area. The campers weren't sure of anything. Maybe he had cut the tires himself. After their visitor left, the three, uneasy, took turns staying awake throughout the night.

Later that same night when some of the study group kids were returning home to Moose City after an evening of volleyball at Polebridge, they saw the pickup camper at Trail Creek. They stopped to give assistance, realized how strange the man was and thought it best to leave.

There were pieces of tire strewn all over the road when Joe drove north the next morning. Tom, of the forest service, drove up and told him there was an abandoned pickup camper sitting down near the Ford Work Center with no tires, apparently driven the ten miles from the border on its rims.

Mary Louise and John, who lived just north of the work center, were going to town that same morning. When Mary Louise answered a knock at the door, it was the driver of the camper, looking for a phone. Mary Louise, kindhearted as always, gave the man a cup of coffee.

They had no phone but since they were about to leave for town, he could ride with them. As they turned the curve by the Ford, there was the pickup with no tires sitting smack in the middle of the road. When their passenger said it was his truck, John told the man they had to get it out of the road before someone would come around the curve and crash into it. But the man had no idea where his keys were.

John walked up to the truck. The interior of the cab had been totally demolished, as if someone had gone berserk inside. Even the foot pedals had been torn off.

Just then Larry and his post and pole crew drove up. Larry was a designated special deputy of the neighborhood watch program, so he radioed for aid. The valley sent up an ambulance, manned by two women medics who took charge and transported the patient, strapped to a gurney, down to a valley hospital. The gentleman, who did have major mental problems, had not only stopped taking his medication, but had thrown it away.

An incident that made everyone more wary.

*   *   *

One boring afternoon at the port, Ron had come over, sat back in Joe's squeeky desk chair, glanced at the typewriter in front of him, and started in.

"It was an afternoon like this. The clerk was busy typing away. An R.C.M.P., thinking of his up-coming pistol qualification, sat back, practicing his aim and trigger pulling by "dry-firing". He was aiming at the round knob on the side of the typewriter carriage.

"Aim. Click.

"Aim. Click.

"Aim. Click.

"Aim. **Kerboom!**

"There had been a bullet in the supposedly empty chambers.

"The R.C.M.P., stunned, ran into his sergeant's adjoining office.

'I just shot a typewriter!'
"The sergeant's reply, 'Did you kill it?'"
Ron swore he wasn't the one.

CHAPTER 12

Not only the wolves favored the Mud Lake area.

There was so much bear activity near Madam Queen's old cabin that Marca used the old bear boards that had come with her property.

Wood had been cut to size for the steps on either side of the back screened-in porch, for a strip under the screen that ran the length of the porch fronting the lake, and for the area immediately underneath the front windows, door and side window. Nails were driven through these boards so about three inches of the sharp ends stuck out the other side. With the flat end of board down on the ground and steps, the nails stuck up in the air, enough to keep any inquisitive beast away.

Always careful to keep a clean area because of the bears, Marca was eager for an early start to town. She put her garbage, well-packed in plastic, in the trunk of her car for its trip to the valley garbage site the next day.

Safe enough, she thought.

But a black bear discovered an open window during the night, climbed in and tore out the back seat to get to the garbage locked in the trunk.

Bears are opportunists where food is concerned, but many have a bent sense of what is edible—or a warped streak of humor. Don and Sue's, just a few miles north of Marca's, were visited twice by black bears of the same ilk and intelligence, probably taught tricks of the trade by their mother. They liked to chew up and destroy automobile tires.

Their uncle, Bob, his cabin situated just before the steep climb to Tom Reynold's, thought he had locked up his new Ford Explorer with its leather cushioned seats. But a bear climbed in a forgotten open window, left paw and claw marks all over the interior, and tore up the expensive upholstery.

Bob was so proud of the bear damage, he stopped by our cabin to show it off. It was the talk of the day when he bragged about the incident to the automobile people back in Iowa. Not many insurance forms list a bear as the cause of damage.

Bob reported catching sight of a young wolverine by their mail box, probably a true sighting since their land holdings extended almost to the border, large and undisturbed. Wolverines were rarely seen. The last lynx was reported to have been trapped up the North Fork a few seasons back. Hunting, poaching, and loss of habitat continue to contribute to the toll of wildlife.

Canada can't be counted on to replenish our losses. The Great Bear Foundation once called Canada the "black hole" for grizzly, so many crossed over from the States, only to disappear. They still can be hunted legally in season. Moose don't always fare well either. Canada once opened a special four day hunt in a district to the north of the North Fork. Over two hundred moose were killed in those few days. Tom Reynolds even commented on the sparse moose population the following summer.

There was once a black bear. How true. He made a nuisance of himself south of Trail Creek, checking cabins for food, heading further north until he broke into the old Wurtz cabin. We had word about the bear for a few days after that incident, then everyone seemed to forget about it. It wasn't 'til later it dawned on me. Of course the bear had disappeared. A perfect example of the code of some on the North Fork: shoot, shovel and shut up. In such a remote area, many felt they could do as they pleased, with impunity. After all, they had been born there and lived that way all their lives.

Grizzly were even hunted legally in Montana until 1991. The feeling, heard over and over in the North Fork, was that hunting helped bears retain their fear of humans. Otherwise, God forbid, human fatalities might occur outside Glacier National Park. A federal judge finally halted the hunting.

The underlying situation was not usually broached in public discussion. But one summer, Don was so concerned he couldn't keep quiet. He knew full well from experience the status of the North Fork.

It was at a Glacier National Park summer meeting at Polebridge, intended to educate and enthuse the tourists by positive informative descriptions of their surroundings. Don sat there, listening to the comments and interaction and finally could keep quiet no longer.

"Do you know that half the people up here in the North Fork want to cut down all the trees and shoot all the animals?"

A stunningly true statement spoken from the heart.

Attending the monthly landowner meetings could be an education in the overall state of affairs in the North Fork. Often, more was learned outside on the porch, listening to conversations before or after the meetings started. There was always time for some locals to deride the study groups and to question their animal safety methods. This from the ones who hunted.

During hot dry seasons, the meetings became a platform for the old timers who took delight in expounding wild and scary possible fire scenarios. The Red Bench fire of 1988 partially justified some of these discussions.

The lightning-caused fire began September 6th, spotted at mid afternoon in the Red Meadow creek drainage. Within four hours, whipped by winds up to thirty miles per hour, it spread eastward toward Glacier National Park and had grown to 2000 acres. A major stand was taken at Polebridge as the fire's path shifted from east to south. The fire was generating its own weather. Forest service crews, county crews, landowners, and others battled to keep homes and Polebridge cabins wet down as the fire swept through. The historic mercantile store, saloon, and many other dwellings were left standing in a blackened field. The unusual bridge that crossed the North Fork of the Flathead River at Polebridge was burned, destroyed completely on the west side. Originally made of logs and poles, it was the source of the name for the ranger station and the small town.

Over 38,500 acres burned, about 9000 on the west side of the river, and the remainder in the park. Twenty-two homes and cabins burned, as well as other outbuildings.

Then the rains came and wet snow finished the fire two weeks later.

The fire up at Tom Reynold's place in August, a few years later, was only three and one half miles to the north of us. The Canadian inspector and Joe's relief at the border noticed the smoke one evening, drove down to Don and Sue's to check, then up to Tom's.

None of them knew anything about it, so the two inspectors returned to the border to radio it in before going back to Tom's. Always at the ready, the two had only one beer in their vehicle. They offered the first drink to Tom, intending to share the single brew three ways. Tom never realized their intent, politely accepted it, and drank the whole can.

He undoubtedly needed it, for the fire was much too close to him. Apparently a trespassing hunter had built a campfire on a stump along a trail up behind the old gentleman's cabin.

A responding plane dropped four loads of retardant, one on each corner, laying it down within ten feet of the designated targets, which really impressed Bob, Don and Sue who were working with rakes and shovels. Twelve to fourteen people from the forest service dug a circle to contain it. The fire was held to three or four acres after two days of hard fighting.

We missed that one since we were down in the valley during Joe's time off. As soon as we returned to our cabin, heard, then saw the helicopter with its bucket, we dashed north to be clued in on the fire. The forest service was still babysitting it because everything was so dry. The helicopter came twice a day to drop water on the spots still smoking.

It was tremendous to stand on the road and watch the helicopter pilot judiciously drop the bucket to scoop up a load of water from the small, irregular slough to the east of the road with scarcely a ripple, then fly off for his drop, wheeling, banking, the pulsating whomp whomp of the blades deafening, surrounding us as we looked skyward from our vantage point between the road and slough.

Bob's words of wisdom:

"Run like hell to keep it (fire) from catching up. If you don't know how to fight a fire, run like hell!"

The ports were of great assistance as locals, fearful of forest fires, dashed to the border in dry spells to have lightning strikes radioed in after electrical storms.

Pity the poor Moose City landowner who had come north for peace, quiet and relaxation. Instead, when he awakened, he found hordes of people setting up a base fire camp to support the fire fighters of the Starvation Ridge fire of 1992.

A dry lightning storm one evening had set four different smokes over in the park on Starvation Ridge. Joe made a run back to the port to call it in but it had already been spotted by the lookouts.

The following day, Tuesday, the clouds of smoke grew in size. We watched late into the night as trees, directly across from us, but over on the park ridge, torched into bright flames like Roman candles, a frightening display to which we had front row seats. Standing at our back door and looking straight through the cabin, the fire was framed by our front door.

Further down the range, the second largest fire would grow, then simmer down. In total, there were five different fires all started by lightning from the same storm. One, close to the flank of one of the mountains, continued to burn naturally until it ran out of fuel.

By Wednesday, the smoke was wide spread from Kintla to Parke Peak. When the wind came up in the afternoon, the Kintla fire billowed into gorgeous, full white clouds, interrupted at times by smaller, dense, greasy-looking black smoke.

The battle was joined.

Large slurry bombers showered bright red retardant over the area, as they made their passes to drop their load. The sun glinted off their wings as they banked to turn for another run, or headed south for refills in the valley.

Helicopters swooped down with water that, when dumped, shone with a huge burst of clean spray against the dark green backdrop of the forest. After they made their drop, they'd sweep around toward Boundary Mountain, make a slow turn, then cross back down toward the valley. At the notch going toward Kintla Lake, the helicopters would turn and fly down behind the line of hills, out of my sight, to lower the canvas bag into Kintla, then reappear a bit further up behind the ridge, circle over the fire, and at times, disappear into the billowing smoke. I'd not breathe until the 'copter flew up, shining in the sun, the pilot deciding the best place to drop his load after instructions from the ground. Two worked the fire all afternoon.

Talk about guts. The pilots made the trip, time after time, about every three minutes, through the dense smoke.

I did nothing that day but watch the constant aerial warfare against the enemy that refused to go away, sometimes using the binoculars that brought the fire fighting too close, then feeling safer after watching minus the glasses, realizing how far away it really was.

The next morning I drove the five miles to the border with the video camera for Joe had said the fire camp was going to be set up at Moose City. As I turned the bend in the road about a minute away from the straight stretch to the border, five vehicles were in a line ahead of me, blocked by a wrecked semi that was carrying supplies north to the fire camp. At four in the morning, it hadn't made the sharp hairpin turn onto the narrow, single lane Colts Creek bridge. It had smashed into the wooden right-hand guard rail and partially dropped off toward the small creek below. A heavy duty wrecker had to come all the way from the valley to haul him out. Joe, earlier, had been able to creep on past to make it to the port.

The open meadow at Moose City was filled with trucks, tents, school buses, trailers and everything needed for the fire fighters. Scott Emmerich, the park ranger stationed at Polebridge, was inside the custom's office when I arrived, explaining the battle plan to Joe, the location of the fires and how they were fighting them, so Joe could pass it on.

Scott took me along when he returned to the fire camp. I learned the caterer had to come all the way from Washington state, because there had been so many fires this season. The garbage from the camp would be collected and safely stashed each night in a metal bear cage, set off to the side, then emptied out and hauled away by truck each morning. Grizzly are attracted to fires because of the easy pickings on the dead insects, any dead animals left in the wake of the fire, or on garbage inadvertently left behind by the fire fighters. The Starvation Ridge fire was slow burning, thus animals would be able to escape.

I got out of the way, onto a slight rise by a tiny cabin at the edge of the trees toward the road, to shoot videos of the camp activity.

A helicopter waited at the far south end of the cordoned-off field, rotor blades turning. Other 'copters were nearby, at the ready. Of various sizes, they would carry the fire fighters to spots where they were needed. Two groups of yellow clad, hard-hatted fighters, most native Americans, with their Pulaskis and other equipment, huddled down to the ground, waiting to file into the 'copters. It didn't take long to load, rise into the air, then turn, flying close overhead. Each 'copter swung up from behind the trees, banked, then flew off into the haze of smoke caught up against the mountains 'til they disappeared.

We were invited to have dinner in the field that evening with the fire fighters. The weather suddenly changed, fast, as we followed the line of people filing along the dropped down side of the catering truck with its high counter: hamburger patty, mashed potatoes with welcome hot, hot gravy, corn, on past the long salad bar of various veggies, sauces, then over to the dessert table, with vanilla wafers poked in mounds of chocolate pudding and beyond, canned peaches in large glass bowls.

By the time we sat down to eat inside the huge dining tent, with double row on row of folding tables and chairs set up on the grass of the airstrip, a great wind that suddenly blew up grew strong enough to suck at the canvas walls, billowing them ferociously in and out. By dessert time, a cold slashing rain pounded hard against the tent, drowning out the conversations of everyone who had come to eat: the native Americans, rangers, support people and yes, the poor Moose City landowner, Jim, who had been caught in the new crowded city that had sprung up so fast.

The wind howled, the temperature fell rapidly, fifteen degrees in less than an hour, then continued to plummet. The rain switched from sleet to half-snow, then back to sleet. A blast of winter in the middle of August had suddenly swooped in from over the Whitefish Range.

We had parked our vehicles at the ports. Together with Ron's relief, his wife, and Arlene, we made a dash for the border, running up the airstrip through the most bitter cold weather I had ever encountered, clad only in light summer clothes. No one had been prepared for this sudden onslaught of unbelievable rough weather. We seemed to make little progress against the hard, cutting, slashing gale.

Shivering uncontrollably, bent over against the wind, my jeans and outer corduroy shirt were soon soaked in front. They'd find our frozen bodies in a bent-over, staggered stance, I thought, expecting ice to form on me any second. It took forever to fight across the usual short distance. I tried to call out through lips too frozen to enunciate the words—my teeth small ice cubes.

Fifteen minutes later we were finally inside the Canadian quarters, electric heat turned high, in borrowed dry Canadian clothes, warm drink in hand, settled down to watch a short environmental film the Canadian inspector had wanted to show us.

I couldn't concentrate, thinking of the cold, wet fire fighters, caught up on Starvation Ridge in this cruel, ugly storm, the helicopters grounded by the weather. Later, the drive to our cabin, slimy and treacherous, did nothing to alleviate my worry over these people who worked one of the most dangerous jobs in the world.

The next morning we awoke to a world blanketed with a heavy wet snow. It had effectively extinguished the fire.

The fire fighters were finally brought down from the snowy ridge by helicopter. A few opted to walk out.

Over the next few days, the North Fork road was filled with a steady stream of trucks, school buses, and finally, a truck loaded with porta-potties, all headed south.

The semi that had wrecked the entire side of Colts Creek bridge didn't attempt a second try. It was parked on the airstrip until it could go north through Canada.

There was one fatality. Budlight, the Canadian relief's aged, fat, and deaf Beagle, was too inquisitive. He just had to go over to investigate all that activity while the fire camp was being established. A truck accidentally backed over him, killing him instantly.

Since the Canadian inspector's tour of duty had some days to run before his break, he sealed Budlight's small body in a plastic bag, then stored him in one of the basement freezers, preserving him for his home funeral and burial.

Almost a week later, Brig and I walked the Moose City airstrip in the warmth of the sun. But for a few ruts, it was as if nothing had been there. The windsock squeaked alone as it swung in the breeze.

A bit of white shone in the midst of a clump of thicker grasses. I stooped down to retrieve it—a scrap of computer paper, smaller than my nail.

Indeed, they had left a clean camp.

*   *   *

Such experiences as we had in the North Fork, events that mattered, influenced and changed us forever.

Great stories can also come from such memories, placing events in a time and place, never to be forgotten, to be repeated over and over within circles of friends, often bringing much laughter in retrospect. Particularly, in the North Fork, was this so, where some became the stuff of legends.

Chris was indelibly etched in my brain as the bear study guy who rescued a gopher from the bottom of their outhouse, using a snare on the end of a pole. His telling of tales was hilarious. He had many, especially of George the Greek.

George really was from Greece, a biologist sent over to work with and learn from the study group so he could set up a similar program in Greece. His English was not too fluent, other than the frequently used word "Okay".

Chris, George and Richard, a Canadian student with the bear study group, were out in the wild and came upon a roaring creek. A large aspen had fallen across it, so Chris and Richard crossed over on it and continued on into the woods. George backed up, refusing to go across. He searched up and down the creek for a log more to his liking.

"So I ended up," Chris explained to a group of us after dinner one night, "going back across our log, holding his hand and bringing him across. We finished work and returned to the creek and log to go back across.

"But George cried out, 'No! No!' He started to look again, up and down the creek, for a different log. Richard and I sat down to wait for him and started to eat our lunch. George picked a spruce, going by size. The one he liked looked like someone spread axle grease all the way across it. This was the one for him—big rocks down below it, water gushing—big drop-off.

"George starts off to shimmy across it laying on his stomach with his arms wrapped around the tree. We hike down to the spot to watch him cross, sitting on the end of the log, eating our sandwiches.

"He's just about in the middle, looks up at us, and all of a sudden— **whoop!** He'd turned over and now is hanging downward by his arms and legs, back toward the water and rocks. He's just hanging there, his eyes like saucers.

"My God, now he did it, I was thinking. If he falls down back first on the rocks, it's a pretty good fall. Hit the rocks—ugh! Paper work!

"I pulled off my boots and socks and got down into the icy water. I'm standing in the water and it was coming down over my back and shoulders. I'm doing this—" Chris raised his arms upward, "and George made it across on my hands to the other side.

"George gets off at the other side. I was mad, shivering cold, but **hot.** George just stands there.

"His comment? 'Oh! My pants are muddy.'

"Then he takes off for the truck."

Chris gave a big grin. "I lost it!"

*   *   *

I finally heard the detailed story of Luke, the grizzly bear, from Chris.

"Luke got shot in '91. The bullet went into the wrist. What we think happened, he turned toward the hunter, one paw up like a hunting dog. The bullet went in the wrist and down the bone toward the elbow and lodged there. He was messed up pretty bad.

"We caught him, doctored it up and tried to disinfect it. It was pretty nasty. We did the best we could, cleaning and sewing his foot up. We never did see him again that season.

"We were pulling into the bear camp early the next year before we saw him again. There was Luke, walking down the road. We got a good chance to see how he walked, which was on the back of his paw. He lay down in the road in front of us, about fifty yards ahead. He just laid there, ate a little bit and ignored us.

"We kinda knew he wasn't going to last too long. As Dave (bear study) said, 'it was hunting season'.

"Sure enough, three days later, hunters in Sage Creek (Canada) stopped us and said, 'You're not going to like us too much. We have something for you.'

"They gave us Luke's radio collar.

"Actually, the collar was dead. So we'd have never gotten that collar back because the battery had died in it. We'd have never known what happened to Luke. When we were watching him on the road, Dave had turned the radio on and couldn't pick up Luke's frequency. We thought we had the wrong signal. It was a good thing the hunter gave us the collar.

"We told him the whole story of Luke's foot, who he was, where his cubby was and so forth, that his name was Luke and made him kind of feel bad a little bit that they shot someone we knew.

"He showed us the hide he'd kept off the bear. I got a good look at the paw. The claws were—betcha they were four inches long at least and almost into a full curl down at the paw, 'cause he never used them on the gravel to wear them down.

"The hunter told us where the body was so we saw his arm bone, could see how the bones healed and could see traces of lead in the bone where he was shot. It was curiosity, to see how he had healed and what the bullet did to him. The paw had become callused on the back side from him walking on it."

Luke meant a lot to all who knew him or heard his story. If animal spirits can come back to where they lived, I hope Luke is wandering around up there in the north country, not hurting, not hungry, just roaming in peace and quiet, smelling the smells and not having to drag his poor foot.

*   *   *

George the Greek became the focus of other stories.

Tom and Harry had been trapping for two months north of the border, trying to catch a mature female grizzly to relocate to the Yaak. They had been catching either males, females not the right age, or black bears.

On this last day, they had trapped a black bear in heat, before successfully capturing the acceptable female grizzly.

Tom took the griz over through the U.S. Customs Port of Roosville so the proper documentation could be processed. Harry returned to the bear camp and was going to pull their trailer down the next day, back into the States.

That night, while Harry was asleep in the trailer, he heard a noise outside. He looked out and there by the window was a big bear determined to get inside the trailer. The bear kept trying to break in.

Harry yelled and shouted but it did no good. The tranquilizer gun and noise shells were outside in the truck. The only weapon he could find was a butcher knife. The bear was trying to get in the entire time. Harry and the bear even came face to face, with only the window glass between them, so he slapped and slammed his hand, hard, on the window a couple of times, hoping to scare him away.

Eventually the bear gave up and Harry went back to bed.

The next morning, as he opened the trailer door to go outside, he looked over and realized George the Greek was sleeping inside his tent just a few feet away.

Asked later if he had heard anything during the night, George replied, "No." Several gashes had been torn in the trailer's side beneath the window. After that, George was required to sleep inside one of the trailers.

The explanation for the attack? Harry's clothes had the scent from the female bear in heat trapped that day. And the aggressive bear was an amorous male.

*   *   *

We always had bears on the brain so when one of the early U.S. Customs inspectors, John, and his wife, Wendy, had dinner at the Canadian quarters, the griz naturally became the center of conversation.

The late l970s and early 1980s must have been a wild time around the border. The bear studies had just begun. The biologists learned mostly by trail and error. Bear bait was kept in fifty gallon drums and left at convenient spots for the scientists, but without much regard for other people in the area. Of course, the grizzlies were drawn to the bait drums, some kept not very far away from the U.S. border station.

John and Wendy were living in the old log customs building, for this was before the new modern one was built.

Wendy described how she carried a gun when she visited the outhouse.

"All I could think of, while I was sitting there, was no one would believe this," she laughed.

She finally complained and the bear bait was moved further away.

We heard the story of a game warden who, along on a trapping/collaring capture, was so excited he trembled as he fell on the tranquilized bear, running both hands over him, a chance of a lifetime for a true grizzly aficionado.

The funny stories continued: one grizzly was trapped and a warden thought all was okay. Then the bear stood up. The snare was dangling only from one claw. He tranquilized it, fast. One legendary bear in the South Fork study dug up eighteen of twenty snares to steal bait unscathed.

Culvert traps weren't always fool proof either. One female expanded herself after capture, bent the culvert cage, dropped the pin and walked off.

*   *   *

Whenever son Steve was able to visit, we saw to it that his days were packed. Of course, we had to check out the loons and leeches at Tepee Lake. Walking further up the dirt lane this time, we were unhappy to find a newly half-formed graveled road to the east of the lake that had been cut through and wound back even deeper into the forest. We turned back, not really wanting to see where it ended. Maggie and Joe opted to travel the easy route along the gravel. Steve and I took the lower, more gloomy and darker lane along the lake, more in keeping with my mood because of the new road discovery. Perhaps we'd be lucky and see more than the resident jack rabbit that hung around by the loon sign. We saw nothing.

Joe was waiting at the car.

"Where's Maggie?"

"She's coming," he replied. "She wanted to stay on the new lane."

She certainly was—racing toward us, feet flying high above the gravel, as if running for her life.

"A grizzly!" she panted. "I came to a Y in the road and there it was!" she half laughed. "He went one way. I went the other!"

To think the only grizzly we saw at Tepee took the easy, more open route, just like a lazy human.

*　　　*　　　*

Joe couldn't participate in some of our neat experiences because of his border work, but we garnered the benefits.

Steve, Maggie and I were invited to visit the bear camp just across the border up in Canada, but on the opposite shore of the North Fork of the Flathead River. The wild stories about how the bear group crossed back and forth to avoid the long way around, over forty-five minutes by road, were intriguing. They had rigged up a crossing with ropes and an old canoe, using it over the years, back and forth, over and over, for business and pleasure, canoeing or sometimes walking. In high water, since the canoe had a hole in it and leaked, they had to paddle fast.

A relief customs inspector canoed over one evening to the camp with a keg of beer for an evening's visit. The canoe capsized on his way back with the empty keg. Since he was more concerned about hanging onto the keg than the canoe, I could imagine the condition of the thing.

We decided to walk across. It would be easy to find a shallow spot since it was a hot mid-August afternoon. The study groups often waded over this time of the year.

Crossing the border, we walked up the road, past the famous wreck of the old wooden bridge that at one time spanned the river to the road on the other side. Now jagged ends of splintered logs and timber ended abruptly at the water's edge, ten feet high in midair. Some poor fellow who didn't know, could easily walk up the gradual ascent to the bridge on a dark moonless night and experience the last thrill of a lifetime.

As the story goes, many years ago the Canadians tried to blow apart an ice jam on the river and succeeded in destroying the bridge, too.

It was always neat to stand right on the edge of the remains, stare into the rush of river below and ponder upon the results of man's good-intentioned follies.

The Canadians had solved the problem by rigging a system slightly downstream from the original bridge. A person wanting to cross had to climb a steep ladder, unlock a padlock with a closely monitored key, and then climb into a small, open two person transport cart that hung from a large cable.

Upon loosening the overhead brake, the cart would freely careen down the slope of cable until it came to a natural stop about midway across the river. Then the operator had to pull upward, hand over hand on the cable, to the other side.

Many weird ways to cross the river, indeed, but for now, we'd take the safer route and wade across, on our own dependable two feet. The three of us found the barely visible path through the woods to the river and came to the study group's crossing with the canoe on shore. Maggie and Steve waded right into the icy river, picking their way carefully over the water-smoothed rocks.

I hesitated. The bottom would be slippery. I remembered the story in the newspaper about the fisherman who had run into the river to escape a grizzly, slipped on the rocks and broke a leg.

The kids were more than half way across. They had no trouble.

C'mon, I ordered myself. You'll never forgive yourself if you don't go now. Never ever another chance like this.

New snow on the mountains

I didn't want to lose out on this adventure of actually crossing the North Fork of the Flathead River on foot. I held my breath and stepped into excruciatingly cold water that swept up over my sneakers, ankles and socks.

I don't think I breathed during the entire crossing. I waded carefully over the uneven rocks, feeling the rush of current almost up to mid shin, not even wanting to think about what it would be like to slip and have to sit down in it. I'd croak. Some have said that hell might be extreme cold. I agree. My feet had no feeling. The sun sparkled so on the water, it was difficult to figure the size of the rocks and thus the unevenness of the bottom. I had a poor reputation for being sure-footed.

The main channel, narrow and fast, was slightly deeper but negotiable to my numbed brain and feet. The kids waited for me on the opposite shore, nonchalant about the whole thing, so of course I was, too, though my heart pounded.

Celine, Bruce's wife, came to greet us as we squished up the path to the camp, the beautiful river their front yard. Their kids, a girl and boy, climbed down out of the trees they had been playing in, and helped take us on a quick tour of the camp, a strange assembly of a shack, trailer, and a few outbuildings, all intertwined and surrounded by forest. Celine served us juice as we sat in metal chairs by the river. I was grateful to feel the warmth of the sun. Celine's French Canadian accent and naturally sophisticated mannerisms made us feel as if we were in a world apart from everything, in a particularly beautiful and isolated country.

She and the children were living in Quebec at the time but stayed with Bruce while he was in the woods with the bears and the kids were out of school. What a great way to live and raise a family.

We talked about pollution of water, looking out on one of the last clean rivers. We discussed the fate of the grizzly, so threatened even in this remote place. Humans had driven it here to its last enclave. Would they make the effort to save it?

Not fair for the bear, I thought. Man thinks only of self. It was a depressingly true thought.

We, sitting here in this beautiful place, so close to being the perfect spot on earth, waxed philosophical as we attempted to solve the environmental problems of the world.

Celine offered to take us back across the river in the canoe when it was time to leave.

"Nah! We'll go back the way we came," we all cried. It would be a fitting end to the afternoon's thought-provoking session.

Again the shock of ice water. We turned and waved good-by, not paying too much attention to where we entered the river. As I waded behind my kids, the water rose to mid-calf, then suddenly up past my knees to mid-thigh. The strong pull of the current dragged at my lower body. It dawned on me I was about to be swept off my feet and carried downstream.

"Steve! Wait up!"

His hand grasped mine and steadied me. I thanked God for his extra height. It was scary as we picked each step very carefully, not really able to see the bottom clearly because of the rush of water and each other's wake. We veered back upstream to a more shallow part, my heart racing like crazy as we finally reached the other side where Maggie waited. We climbed the path through the woods and I couldn't speak 'til we reached the dirt and gravel of the North Fork road.

"Thanks, Steve," I shivered, not just from the wet and cold either.

Nature is uncompromising. It does not tolerate mistakes. I had been lucky.

On the walk back to the border all I could think of was how U.S. and Canadian biologists crossed the river almost daily, in that beat-up canoe, or perhaps wading as we did.

No wonder they all had character.

*   *   *

We happened to walk the lower airstrip one morning before the kids left and discovered bones scattered all over the field. I found the horse skull dragged behind a bush.

It was poor old Goldy, of run-away fame from our horse days who had simply disappeared one day, then found dead of gut torsion and buried on the strip. Coyotes had uncovered and scattered her remains.

I rescued her skull and some of her other bones, scrubbed them clean and bleached them, then painted her head white. I'll mount her on a fittingly decorated piece of wood and hang her on a wall in honor, where she can gaze down on us with her hollow sockets, remembering her days of glory and freedom in the wild fields of the North Fork.

*   *   *

My greatest experience lay just ahead, August 29, 1992. A gorgeous day weather-wise, wonderful in memory. The undercurrent of chill in the air was more pronounced than usual as Brig and I started down our lane about midmorning. The mountains were especially beautiful and my mind was a million miles away.

I was still adrift mentally as we reached our lower lane to turn the bend at our ranch gate.

We saw each other at exactly the same instant.

There, less than fifteen feet away, was a large grizzly, sun shining from behind, illuminating its ears and top of head with a surrounding glistening, golden touch, a most wondrous sight.

The bear rose to its full height. I stood utterly still. Brig pressed his head hard against my thigh. I carefully laid my left hand on the dog's head.

Awe, admiration, wonder—all swept over me. I am sure I said in a low reverent voice, "Oh, you dear beautiful thing!"

The grizzly, tall and healthy looking, wheeled away back into the edging of the underbrush by the field.

I slowly backed up, very sorely tempted to take a few steps forward to see. Was the griz cutting across the field toward the woods? Was he running? Which direction? I wondered if he had a collar on—I couldn't remember.

Common sense made my feet continue backwards, still slowly, holding Brig's leash short and tight. I turned around, finally, and we walked swiftly back to the cabin. I don't know that I even breathed. Higher than a kite, I walked on air with excitement and pure unadulterated joy.

I could do nothing but pace with the adrenaline rush, a grin on my face, before settling down somewhat to type a page of the description of it for Maggie's next letter. That wasn't enough. Brig and I piled into the Blazer and drove to the border to tell Joe.

Not even Ron could lower my exuberance. He treated it matter-of-factly. After all, he'd had to deal with grizzly professionally back in his R.C.M.P. days.

But I loved them. Had all my life. This meeting with the grand beast was a treasured experience.

Fred, assistant to Bruce in the bear study, told Joe later I was lucky the grizzly hadn't charged since the distance was so small and we had surprised each other. Could it have sensed I was no threat?

Not one even asked me if I was scared. They could tell from the way I acted that I was too thrilled with the encounter to feel any fear at all.

CHAPTER 13

It's a strong urge to cut your own greenery for the holidays, a *Currier and Ives* print with thick multigreened forests, fresh snow and high mountains overseeing the fun of it.

October seemed a bit early but a three inch wet snow fell the previous night and threatening, leaden skies overhead hurried me out into the trees behind the corral. Clad in layers of warm clothes, heavy gloves, boots and clutching a saw in one hand, I used the other to steady myself on the trees along the uneven, slippery and suddenly unfriendly route to the area I had previously chosen.

Close to the open track back to the salt, thus easier to drag back to the cabin, the runt of a spruce was scrunched up tight against another larger fir that would grow much better minus its too close neighbor.

Further away from the trail than I thought, it was rough going between the crisscross limbs of downed trees, old stumps, and underbrush weighted down by the heavy, drifted snow. Within the stand of trees as I was, the smell of wet pine was intoxicating.

Stump holes, made to look even with the ground by the snowfall, were dangerous traps. A young logger friend of Ron's relief at the border, who had been working way back in the Canadian timber, accidentally stepped into a deep, snow-hidden hole, bent his leg over other fallen tree limbs, breaking it so severely it had been over a year before he could work again.

In unsure places, I thrust the saw into the white to test its depth.

The fun was just beginning.

The recalcitrant saw knew it was in the hands of a tenderfoot and kept pinching. To stop and look at the surrounding snow and trees only made me feel colder, and work faster and harder. No back woods glamour, no old-fashioned work ethic—just beastly cold with underlying worry.

Nature has been described as cruel and unforgiving. Maybe. To me, it's just there, while we attempt our puny efforts in its midst, hopefully in harmony with its essence. It promises no quarter and gives none. I may have been only fifteen minutes away from the cabin, but given certain circumstances, it could be enough to cause problems since I was alone.

I cut faster. The wind had picked up, sounding first way to the west within the depths of the trees, the heavy rustle coming toward me, louder and more powerful until it swept around me.

Stopping for breath, I had to look over at the mountains. Cold or not, the solitude, the grandeur of the vast panoramic view that surrounded me, the cleanness, wholeness of it, drew me within its very being.

The wonder of it all, a place that nurtured and replenished the human soul. Reflecting on the universal quality and personal appeal of native American beliefs was natural and fitting in these wild and magnificent surroundings.

The snow-capped peaks were blindingly beautiful, for that part of the sky had cleared, traces of clouds hovering about their tops, giving them a windblown tattered appearance. The Canadian mountains to the north had been transformed from their warm weather staid shadowy masses into much wilder snow white pinnacled peaks.

Even as I paused, entranced, the tops of the mountains were losing their identity as their white peaks melded into the clouds. What would it be like to be marooned up there during a fast change in the weather, or storm? No one could last.

Long dark shadows from swift moving clouds passed across the upper swatches of Starvation Ridge, the yellowed larch jagged against the darker, variously greened fir forests. Just below, in our field, only a few aspen had any fluttering yellow leaves remaining on their bared branches.

Beating my cold hands together, I looked over at the notch between the mountains where Kintla Lake was hidden. Then I shivered. Ignorance of the ways of nature can be deadly. A few summers before, an airman had been enticed into swimming in the clean, clear invigorating lake, the air warm, the setting outstandingly beautiful. When he never returned to duty, he was listed A.W.O.L. His body was found a few months later. Hypothermia had claimed him.

Wildlife stay in high country during mild weather, then are forced down with the snows. Thus, hunter success depends on weather, which can be treacherous. A Kalispell hunter took a chance and crossed Trail Creek road in a snowstorm, went over the edge and down 250 feet to the bottom of the drainage. Found by other hunters the next morning, he had broken many bones and lost an eye.

One season, thirty hunters were trapped by a heavy snow twenty kilometers north in Canada. Rescuers snowcatted in to pick up all but a stubborn six who refused to leave. They wanted to hunt. Even as these men forced a second rescue, one shot a moose on the way out. Not a very knowledgeable group for they placed others at risk because of their self-centered conceits.

In a snowstorm, the North Fork road can be a treacherous beast. It quickly turns into a one center track until a driver meets another vehicle coming from the opposite direction and someone is forced to go into deep snow. The ditch awaits the losers in the too quick maneuvers that lead to skidding and spinning out of control. Drivers are on their own. No auto service here! Good fortune shines on the road victim when a good Samaritan with a winch on the front of his truck rounds a corner.

Swirling snow creates whiteouts and covers landmarks, scary as hell at night, especially in a heavy snowfall. Driven hard against the windshield, the white stuff stops wipers, and plugs radiators and air filters.

The road has been transformed into a narrow white tunnel formed by the headlights reflected off the wind-swept flakes that come directly at the driver, sometimes creating an eerie sensation of floating.

The loneliness of the road can be deadly.

Dave, when we first met, told how he had almost broken into our cabin late one October night. After duty at the border, he, his father and the U.S. inspector had gone down into the valley to party, only to discover upon their return the North Fork was in the throes of a strong late fall blizzard. In their attempt to reach the border, they ran off the road south of Trail Creek with ten miles to go. Cabins were deserted, already closed for the winter.

They trudged north, a long harrowing trek indeed, especially when Dave found himself walking in large grizzly bear tracks, so fresh they hadn't filled with snow or been blown away by the wind.

*   *   *

It was total relief when I finally succeeded in cutting the small fir away from its neighbor and dragged it down toward the cabin, leaving it for Joe to cut up.

I'd appreciate the beauty of the mountains from the warmth of the cabin.

*   *   *

Since the Canadian port was occupied twenty-four hours, Bill, the Canadian relief inspector, took care to always bring Joe up-to-date with overnight events.

The gate had been locked at 5 o'clock so Bill changed out of his Canadian customs shirt and headed north into the woods.

"I was driving back much later when a car I hadn't seen before was coming at me, had a couple of nineteen year olds from Victoria in it. He was flicking his high beams at me to stop. I did—let him get out and come to me. I still had my customs cap on but he couldn't see it. He asked me if I had any gas, said he was about out.

"I asked him where he was coming from and he said the States.

"When did you cross the border?

"He said, 'About three'. Well, I'd been there all day and I hadn't seen him. I asked him if he was sure. He says, 'Maybe it was about five.'

"I climbed out of my truck and my official Canadian customs cap was now visible for the first time. They had broken the law by running the border."

The teenager realized he'd been caught. The boy seemed relieved, his gas was low, but his girl friend became quite upset, especially when it was explained to them that, since the pair had only eight dollars with them, Bill could seize their vehicle and let them walk sixty miles to Fernie to get money to pay their fine and retrieve their vehicle.

He didn't, satisfied they'd learned from the scare and left them to nurse their car back to civilization.

People run into trouble going into Canada at this remote crossing because of more restrictive Canadian handgun laws. One U.S. couple drove north, and admitted they had a handgun when questioned by Bill. He told them how sometimes people would return to the U.S. side and hide their gun for safekeeping until they returned.

The couple, from Texas, explained they only wanted to go into Canada a short way and camp overnight. They had brought the handgun, a 9mm, for protection from the bears.

An R.C.M.P., on duty, who happened to be visiting Bill at the time, told them that the pistol was no protection from a bear.

"You're just going to make him mad with that pistol," he explained.

So the couple, heeding their advice, drove back down the North Fork road a short distance into the U.S., still within sight of the Canadians who watched as the man stopped and got out of the car. He walked into the woods, returned to the car, then drove back into Canada.

Bill had a feeling.

"Want to bet he still has the pistol?" he asked the R.C.M.P.

Bill asked them if they still had the handgun. They said no. They had left it in the woods, hidden. He asked them two more times as he started looking through their things. The answer was always no.

The pistol was found inside one of the rolled up sleeping bags.

The events that followed were automatic. The 9mm pistol was seized, never to be returned, and the couple were fined $500 which had to be paid on the spot. If they could not pay, their vehicle would be seized until the fine was paid. The Texans paid the fine and went on into Canada for their overnight stay.

Joe was on the Canadian side when the couple returned, less than an hour later. Stopping when they saw Joe, Bill and the R.C.M.P. standing outside, they explained.

"No hard feelings but we just can't stay in Canada after this."

It was an expensive lie they told. They had paid $495 for the handgun, had not even fired it before turning it over to customs, and had to pay the $500 fine for denying they had it.

During the open season, cars from both directions would drive to the gate during late night hours. At times a belligerent driver would show up after hours, wanting to cross, demanding the gate be unlocked for them. Some even attempted to drive around it. The threat of a $5,000 fine usually ended that. Sometimes other events would end the confrontation.

A Canadian family arrived one early evening to discover the entrance to Canada and home was blocked by the locked gate. The Canadian inspector watched a few minutes as the man investigated the padlock, then walked around looking for a route around the gate.

Ron walked out to tell the man the gate would not be open until the following morning and warned him of the results if he tried to go around the gate. But the man became very belligerent, demanding that the gate be opened for him.

"The situation was getting rather tense and I was starting to wonder if things were going to get physical," Ron said as he was telling the story to Joe the following morning.

"We were really having a good exchange of words. While all of this was going on, I looked beyond his car and watched a black bear come out of the woods just below your building. So I said to the man that he better go and protect his family. He said, 'From what?'

"He turned then, saw the bear, and said, 'Oh, my God!'

"He ran back to his car, turned it around and took off back down the road. Never saw him again."

A new road cut through the field would be created yearly during the closed season by vehicles driven around the east side of the locked gate. Once, the padlock was broken off three weeks before the season opened, discovered by the study kids who reported it. They put one of their own locks on the gate and passed word to Joe under which rock the key was hidden.

Joe went up to the port three days before the 1992 season to get a head start on removing the massive wooden shutters that covered all the windows and doors in off-season. While there, a Canadian vehicle drove up from the south, intending to drive around the gate illegally into Canada.

The three men were obviously shocked when they saw Joe, bringing their utility vehicle to an abrupt halt in the middle of the road. They pretended to go to the river access, then got out to tell Joe they were going to camp there for the three days before the border opened. They left immediately after Joe told them he had radioed their license plate in to the R.C.M.P.

The license plate check enabled the R.C.M.P. and Canadian customs to catch the men with high powered rifles purchased in Kalispell, Montana, and taken north illegally without paying the required duty on them.

Oh, the speed of our government! For three years, Joe had been requesting necessary money for digging a ditch wide and deep enough to prevent almost any vehicle from taking a detour to either side of the gate. Thus it was a great day when it was finally approved, but only for $300. A man with a backhoe who lived a few miles south of the border agreed to do the work.

The new ditch extended into the forest to the west and to a steep hill near the river on the east. The $300 allocated for the project was not enough but the man was kind enough to complete the project free.

The ports were the center of many activities. Locals, fearful of forest fires, dashed to the border in dry spells to have lightening strikes radioed in after electrical storms. Survey teams from the Flathead National Forest used the U.S. port's quarters several times as home base when working in the area.

To me, it was a window on Canadian life to the north, an up-to-date information center of exciting animal study work, and a remote, neat and necessary small arm of the United States Government.

∗ ∗ ∗

One summer a large wooden cross suddenly appeared by the side of the road south of Polebridge. It was soon followed by a great canvas church tent.

Some laughingly remarked it was about time North Forkers got religion. The preacher, Bo Tanner, had come from nowhere, married the daughter of a North Fork landowner and set up his place to preach on his father-in-law's property. We heard rumors about the flare-up of anger over something concerning his pigs and a neighbor's dogs. Bo gained instant fame, however, when someone burned the tent to the ground.

When he later reported cement blocks had been tossed through his cabin windows, local law investigated and set up a covert operation one night to catch the perpetrator. The accounts we later heard were a hilarious mishmash of fumbling around in the dead of night and confusion over who belonged to what shadow and what might be a target.

Bo simply disappeared after he was asked to stop by the sheriff's office to be fingerprinted. He left a bunch of dead animals behind and his truck at the airport. His wife didn't even know what had happened to him. The story became blown-up and famous enough to be picked up by a national television program that, on location, reenacted the past weird goings on, hiring locals for fifty dollars apiece.

Upon further investigation, his wife learned she had been a victim of a bigamist who had married numerous women over the years. No one cared about Bo's real name, and he's been forgotten, except for a laugh now and then when his North Fork name pops up during story time.

*   *   *

How some of the less mentally endowed public found their way north via the North Fork road will forever remain a mystery. "Missing sixty cents of their dollar" was the way one Canadian described these travelers who appeared from nowhere and found themselves in a sort of limbo at the 49th parallel, wanted by no one.

The "bicycle lady" with all her worldly possessions in a plastic bag between the handlebars, crossed the border into Canada, intending to head north, looking for a job. Canadian customs refused her entrance since she had no money, no prospect for work, no specific destination, and refused to give her name. To call her a bit strange was an understatement.

After a second try to get into Canada, and again refused, she pushed her bike down to the river access. When she didn't return right away, Joe checked to make sure she hadn't flung herself into the water. He talked kindly to her and warned her about how dangerous it could be to travel in the semi-wilderness as a bag lady on a bike.

Joe feared for her safety but when he radio contacted law enforcement, they could do nothing since she had committed no crime. She did give Joe her name before she started back down the road.

Later, the ranger in the Bowman Campground, one of the most remote in Glacier National Park, told us how she hung around there for a while, bumming food from campers. Eventually, the lost soul biked down to Polebridge and pestered people to carry her and her bike on down the road. After a few days, someone gave in and loaded her stuff on top of their car and took her south.

CHAPTER 14

Someone in the bear study had mentioned doing CPR on a bear. A black bear, Chris specified later, as we picked his brain.

"Really? How do they do that?"

"You cup your hand over their mouth, like that."

He used Brig and clamped his muzzle shut.

"And you blow. I don't put my mouth on their nose 'cause it's too gross. But open your hands and just blow in their nose. Just make a funnel and blow."

He demonstrated. Brig ran away.

"You grab them by the hair and skin on the sides of their ribs, along their side. Lift up. Straddle them over the top. Lift 'til they come off the ground a little, and kinda drop them, just a little bit. I've had to do it two or three times and have gotten them back every time. It can happen during hibernation, because their metabolism is different. Not as wide a range for the anaesthetic. We hit them with an antidote then. We pull the black bears out of their dens in wintertime, to refit collars, do measurements and so forth."

"Fred Hovey, the Canadian bear researcher, left one morning to go check a grizzly that had hibernated inside the upper part of a tree trunk," I remarked.

Chris said that in the Yaak, a lot of the black bears hibernated in big, hollowed out cedar trees.

Having conversations with someone like Chris who has handled about 250 bears, is almost as good as being there. Given the chance, I'd have been like the warden, all over the tranquilized grizzly.

"How do they smell close up?"

"It's a strange odor, hard to describe. It's sort of a cross between a wet dog and a spicy, almost cinnamon-like smell. It definitely has a spicy flavor to it, but it's unlike any spice I can name.

Chris with a sleeping grizzly

"You learn something after each capture. Look at Tim. Over the years, he's worked hundreds and hundreds of bears and is probably close to the thousand mark.

"Everyone works a bear different. They have their own way of doing things. Things that Dave and I used to do, they're only things Dave and I did. We tattooed in a little bit different spot, the lip and groin. We all share what works best for us. Everyone does it under the lip. A lot of times the lip doesn't turn out real good, so it gives us a double check. We can always look at both of them and get the numbers pretty much right. The groin works real good. The numbers stay better there."

"How do you clean them up if they're hurt?" I asked, remembering how he and Tom had helped poor Luke.

"We try to doctor them up as best we can. You can't always. You don't want to leave a bandage or anything like that. We've had vets come around with us and give us tips on how to work this or that and I've taken a course in vet practices.

"A lot of it is common sense. We've all had to clean 'em out and stitch things up. When adult males fight, they really tear each other up. You get to see some nasty cuts and stuff that they've got from other bears that are infected, other wounds—really gross stuff.

"I caught a black bear one summer, caught it by the hind foot, which is odd. You don't normally catch hind feet. It was a back leg that had already been broken, a compound fracture that was just beginning to heal. Real nasty looking, probably a couple of weeks old, broken, re-broken, it was still fairly loose. It had cuts from the compound fracture we cleaned up as best we could, set the bones, and kinda got things back together the way we thought they ought to be.

"Lo and behold, we caught that bear the next year and he was walking on that leg. There was a big chunk of—you know, the bones had healed and a wad of this and that, but he had movement on it and he could move his paw around so the joints didn't fuse. That makes you feel good when you catch 'em and see them moving around.

"Dave and I had one that had a big cut in her neck. We normally use absorbable sutures. We stitched this bear up on the neck, worked her and let her loose. That night, I was cleaning the drug kit, throwing away wrappers and stuff like that, and this suture package said "mono-fila-ment", which means a non-absorbable nylon type.

"I though, oh my God, how did we ever get this in the drug kit? I went through all the stuff and somehow, we got a package of the wrong type sutures. I felt pretty rotten about that.

"We caught that bear two weeks later, and I pulled the stitches out. It was perfect! The perfect time is ten days to two weeks. Everything had healed perfectly. I snipped 'em all and pulled out each suture. Couldn't ask for anything better.

"Lots of times you go into a trap site and you'll see the bait gone and everything sprung. You won't know what came in, what took it? Lot of times you can't find tracks, but you can find hair. You learn what the different hairs are and what they're like.

"We use dead deer and stuff for bait. You can pick out the deer hair and bend them around. They leave a kink and kind of break in half at the broken mark. But you can take a bear hair and roll it as tight as you want and it won't show a kink or a break. You can tell whether it's a grizzly or a black bear by even one single hair.

"Black bear hair will have uniform color throughout. Grizzly hair will have a white tip. Even a dark grizzly bear will still have a real small white tip. So you can tell from even a small number of hairs what we have coming into the trap.

"After the bear is snared, they'll take out their aggression on whatever is close at hand. Grizzly usually dig a big circle around the tree, just as far as they can. They can churn up the earth like a rotor-tiller went through. They beat up and scatter all the logs and chew on the trees. They can tear a tree up pretty quick. We use a tree at least fourteen inches in diameter as the anchor for the trap. That would be the small end. It's best, if you have a choice, to use a fir or a tougher tree, harder wood. You don't have to worry so much about getting the tree chewed off.

"After the drug's administered the bear's eyes stay open and we keep the blindfolds on 'cause the eyes will be dilated, maybe in direct sunlight. It keeps debris and junk out of their eyes while we're working with them.

"We're always quiet 'cause the drug stimulates their hearing and that makes them come out of the drug faster. So the more quiet you are, the more time you're going to have to work on the animal.

"A couple of times we've had bears wake up on us. We've had to hold 'em down or whatever, until we get things packed up and out. One time, this summer, we had to transport a black bear down the road, to get her away from the other capture, a male. If the male came out of it before the female, he would kill her. Anyway, you have its head on your leg, so it doesn't bounce its head around. You look down and see this tongue and jaw click, or opening up a little bit. The anesthetic wears off from the nose down.

"You have to hold the bear down in the back of the truck until you get to the spot you want to get to, then pull it out of the truck and get going. A couple of times we've had bears wake up and you put a headlock on 'em. With ketemine/roupon, they just wake up and go.

"When you talk about interesting captures, it's always a cub capture, 'cause they're the most dangerous, the most exciting," Chris continued. "Tom and I had John Jacques Camaras, a French biologist, riding along with us for a month to learn how to trap so he could catch bears where he worked in the Pyrenees.

"He was in the middle of the truck between Tom and me as we rode down to check a trap. This was in the North Fork, up Cabin Creek, next to Storm Creek area. The trap was close to the road so we could kind of check it from the truck. Tom was driving, I was in the window seat. We pull up and we had this large black bear. Actually it was one I had caught before. He was 310 pounds which is big for that country and that time of the year.

"We hop out. It's just a black bear. The guns are in the truck. We're kinda wondering around, walk over to it. Boy! That's a big black bear and he was way up in a tree, at the end of his cable. I don't ever remember a bear being that scared, for as big as he was. He's awful scared.

"Then we looked over and saw another little bear, in the snare, back in the woods. Tom said, 'We got another one. A little guy.'

"Tom starts walking back over there, then kinda slows down. And I go, 'Don't you think that little guy looks a little bit grizzlish?'

"Tom stops. '**Get in the truck!**' he shouts.

"And we go barreling back down, right by the male black bear, and we're diving into the truck.

"Oh, my God! 'Cause it was a cub and here we caught it. It was a yearling, not a cub of a year, but a yearling grizzly. This big male black bear that should have been king of the woods, the reason he was up in the tree was mama grizzly was pacing back and forth right behind the yearling that was caught. She had that male black bear scared to death, scared for his life.

"The mother was pacing back and forth, back and forth. We never saw her but we could hear her in the woods, snapping stuff and her jaws popping.

"Went back to camp to get help 'cause it was a pretty dangerous situation; having the male black bear caught, we had a lot to do and yearling cubs are dangerous. Tim Thier was up there at the time 'cause we were actually trapping for a transplant bear for the Cabinets.

"Tim said he'd be down so we drive back.

"We were busy thinking about all we had to do head of us—

"John Jacques says, 'Oh, is beautiful.'

Tom working with grizzly. Note cover to protect face and eyes.

"He's looking at the scenery! He was in the middle and there is a pretty view but he doesn't know what we're getting into! He really hadn't realized what this was about.

"We get up there and got things worked out. Tim came out to help and it was Tom driving, Tim with the jab stick. Tom had the cable cutters and I had the shotgun to cover everyone.

"We back the truck in as close as we can to the bears. We had two jobs.

"Tom leaned out the window and just jabbed the black bear. That was no big deal. He kinda passed out. We idled the truck back and Tim and I jumped out and jab-sticked the little guy, jumped back in the truck and waited for it to go down. Had to jump back out of the truck and get it out of the snare. We keep the cable cutters for that situation, so you don't waste time trying to take it off. You jump out, cut the cable, and throw him over your shoulder and you get out of there.

"We threw both the bears in the back of the truck and went roaring down the road. That was one of our more interesting captures. I have pictures of Tim and me in the back of his pickup truck, with this big black bear and this young grizzly, both piled in the back of the truck.

"I was in the back with a gun and Tim was in the back and we were just holding onto the bears and bouncing down the road, Tom driving. We went down the road about a mile and worked the grizzly and male black bear. We left the black bear there and took the young grizzly back real close to the capture, so its mother could catch back up with it again.

"Capturing a cub is more exciting. You've got mama bear protecting it. Mom is not caught and you don't know where she is, so you've got to get the little guy out of the trap and not let mama get you.

"The worst thing you can do, bear trapping, is catch a cub. That's the most dangerous thing you can do, because you know you've got another bear that's not going to leave. It happened to me about five times, I think."

With tremendous satisfaction, we heard that a North Fork grizzly bear study was scheduled to begin the spring of '93. It would be similar to the successful one conducted over the years in the South Fork that had just recently been completed.

It would take years for all that information to be analyzed, but already it had proved that sows with cubs, particularly shy of humans, had been driven to the highest, most rugged and remote habitat where survival was more difficult for cubs. This information was so vital it was decided to start the North Fork study immediately. A U.S. Fish & Wildlife computer-compiled map of the North Fork identified clearly how private property and development were dividing the usual bear routes to historical feeding grounds.

Finally, we would find out what was happening to our grizzlies, what we could do to help their survival, and thus, by extension, all the rest of the wildlife in the North Fork. We were looking forward to the next season as never before.

But this excitement was tempered by dreadful news. In February, Ron had suffered a stroke and wouldn't be coming back as the Canadian customs inspector. He was a reliable fixture at the Flathead port. We knew he had had a heart attack a few summers before while on duty. But he was indomitable. Still with five days to go on his duty schedule, he lay on the couch that faced the large picture window, eating aspirin, in a position so he could see vehicles crossing the border northward. He'd go outside, do his clearance, then retreat again to the couch.

After that attack, Canadian officials had let him return to the Flathead only with his doctor's permission. Ron always inveigled it out of his long-suffering doctor. Sometimes he'd follow his doctor's orders, most times not.

It was a morning ritual for Ron to have Joe over for morning coffee after opening up, thus a natural way for Joe to check on Ron's general state of health. We were heart-broken, not only for him, but for us, a selfish feeling.

No one else had his mechanical expertise. No one else had his wild early R.C.M.P. experiences. No one else knew and loved the area as he did. His stories would stay with us forever.

Change is constant. But some changes are harder to accept than others. The Flathead was Ron. The two were synonymous.

*   *   *

It didn't help when I'd look toward Crevasse lookout and think of the changes up there.

It took less than a season for the old lookout to be torn down, its remains burned and tossed down the slit in the ground, then blown up. The tiny parking place was expanded with explosive charges. A locked gate at the bottom now prevents any access by the general public.

The study groups could use it, however, for it was the perfect high spot to listen to their radio telemetry signals.

And not just from bears, wolves and ungulates.

A study of mountain lion and wolf interaction in the North Fork, under the direction of Maurice Hornocker began October 1992 with the arrival of Toni, who had over seven and a half years of experience during previous studies in the southwest and Florida's Everglades. To last three to five years, the information gathered was particularly important since none of the wolf reintroduction proposals had considered the effects that it might have on resident lion populations. The North Fork region of forest service and Glacier National Park land was a natural for such a study with its wolves and population of cats.

Tom and Chris with sleeping grizzly. Note clawed tree in back.

Toni, with her long blond braid down her back, was matter-of-fact in her amazing descriptions of how she and her assistants captured and collared the cougars. Using tracking dogs, their leashes snapped onto their belts, they track and tree the cat, then use an adapted 22 rifle as a dart gun. The climber uses a belt and spurs, just as tree climbers do to reach the treed cat.

"Believe it or not," Toni reported, "mountain lions in a tree are timid.

"I'll climb the tree usually opposite of the way the cat may be sitting. If everything's worked the way it's supposed to have when you get up there, the mountain lion is under just enough to maintain it's rigidity with the drug we use. You get a loop over at least one hind foot, if you can, two. With karabiner and a piece of rope, we actually already have two slip loops on this rope. So I will karabiner that rope onto a limb, then slip one noose over one foot, if that's all I can get, or two if I can. That way, if the lion did fall at that point, I'm already secure. He's there. We've got the loops on and tightened. I'll grab the long rope, throw it over the branch, and karabiner onto the end of that. Then to the person on the ground, the darter, I'll go 'Okay, we're ready!' He's got all the slack out, and I'll actually push the lion out of the tree. Then we just lower.

"I'm in the same tree with the cat. The person on the ground is the anchor person with the rope.

"The dogs are always controlled. The minute we get there, we take the dogs off. With some cats, we move the dogs way off. Some others we leave 'em in a little closer. We tie them to a tree with double ended snaps so they're secure. And if the cat jumps, then we don't have dogs running after the cat.

"The Hornocker Institute has to get permission from the park each year before we take the dogs in. We have to go to a vet and get fecal exams done on all of them to make sure they're not carrying some kind of bug. They also all have to have all their shots, which is great. The rule is we don't release on a track unless we know it's absolutely fresh and preferably that we've actually tracked it out and have jumped the lion from a day bed, so that we know what we've got.

"A mountain lion chase can be long," she continued. "The shortest lasted fifteen to twenty minutes. The cats are sprinters; they're not built for long distances. They have small lungs, a sit and wait predator."

Toni gave Maruice Hornocker a lot of the credit, "He and the Craigheads actually developed the radio collar system. No one had ever done grizzly bear research until the Craigheads. Hornocker pioneered the whole technique of how to work with mountain lions."

Communication and education are important aspects of field work. Toni continued, "Getting the information out to the local people is the most important thing. We have to educate. Sometimes it seems like a losing battle. Some have no vision."

What a firsthand education Toni gave me. I listened intently for I knew next to nothing about cougars. Females can weigh up to 100 pounds, while males can range from 140 to 180 pounds.

"What are your personal feelings toward mountain lions?" I asked her.

"There are lots of myths connected to lions. I get excited at handling them, to see them. Afterwards, it's depressing. You work with them in a tree, inspecting them, checking the individual coats and bodies, muscles and so forth. We use quiet voices, then afterwards, it's a let down. I don't like doing it for each individual but I do it for the population."

The cougar is placed on an insulated pad and emergency blanket and assessed for any injuries. Surface abrasions are treated. One person monitors temperature, respiration and pulse at fifteen minute intervals. The lion's breathing is watched carefully and the animal's heart rate is monitored under the "arm". The study people actually carry a stethscope.

"We keep careful track 'cause we are responsible for the cougar. Drugs can act differently, just as in humans. We place ophthalmic ointment in the lion's eyes and then cover the eyes to shield them from sun, snow and our movements."

Adult lions are fitted with radio collars attached with a heavy single layer cotton splice, or a heavy double layer cotton splice. Splices are attached so collars will eventually drop off in the event that a transmitter signal fails or a lion disperses beyond the study area limits.

Lions are marked with a numbered plastic ear tag in one ear and a corresponding number tattooed in the other ear. Sex and age are determined, morphological measurements are taken and a final thorough examination is conducted. Age is determined by tooth wear and body weight. Recovery is always watched until the lion becomes ambulatory.

"Florida inoculates their panthers," Toni explained, "since there are so few and they are endangered."

The statistics from this study are not only of importance but are interesting to anyone who's concerned about wildlife. Lions kill more often because bears and wolves and other animals steal what they kill. So far, interactions of lions with wolves and bears have primarily occurred during the winter or spring. A wolf killed a three/four year old female lion. A two and a half or three and a half year old collared female lion was possibly killed by wolves. A four/five year old male lion was killed by a bear and a two/three month old kitten was killed by wolves near an ungulate carcass. The study has documented instances of wolves feeding on lion kills and of treeing lions.

The lion study is trying to find out who was there first, and how often wolves are usurping lion kills. Cats get bumped from kills easily, by wolves and bears. This knowledge is important since it could affect survivorship of offspring and therefore, conservation, especially since cougar reproduction rate is low.

Many clues are left at kills. Lions are neat and cache in the snow in little volcanoes. They can drag, then cover their kill with sticks or duff, or hair they pluck off carcasses, "hair-feathers". Toni has come across tracks on plucked carcasses but it's been scattered because wolves get a piece and cart it off. Sometimes the lions have a huge dig area or cache, with soil and roots on top. The cover insulates the meat. They have "toilet" areas around a kill where they defecate, then cover it.

Cougars eat everything in their kills. Their rough tongue cleans the bones. Their scat has contained hair, bone and even hoofs.

"Tell me about your bite!" I remembered to ask, having heard it mentioned previously.

"The first cat we captured this season, Jamie went up and he lowered her so we got her on the ground. As we're working, there's a certain way I do things. Putting the collar on is number one. Also, making sure they're okay. Then we start taking measurements. I grew up all these years knowing that when you're working around the mouths, be real careful.

"Well, I was getting teeth measurements with calipers, and sure enough, I had this finger in," (she extended it) "hooked up in between and she just laid down on it. It took probably close to a month to get the finger back to normal. But she cracked from the top through the bottom, through the nail. She went all the way, a good job, to the bone. Cats, bacterial-wise, have the nastiest mouths and claws. I flushed it with needle and syringe. It eventually healed. That's about the only thing I've really had happen. I felt really stupid, more than anything else. I kinda went—" Toni made a face, a grimace, "when it happened."

"She was knocked out?"

"Yeah. But they still maintain a lot of their reflexes. It was just the wrong thing to do."

Biologist Shawn Riley, who wrote Montana's draft cougar plan in '92 stated that thirty years ago, lions might have been considered a threatened species. He wrote that cougars were rare. They've been able to ride out periods of low deer numbers partly because they had the protection of roadless areas. Roadless areas must be maintained, otherwise the west would become like the east, with lots of deer but not enough space for cougars.

People must value wildlife enough to be willing to share their space with a top-level carnivore.

I asked Toni if the thought of losing some of her collared cougars to hunters bothered her.

"There are two cats that travel between here (our cabin) and the park," Toni said quietly. "I worry about them."

Solitary habitats and remote haunts helped protect the cougar. They molded their lives to the environment. That environment is changing, under pressure from development and people. Another growing concern is that the cougar population could be in trouble and no one would realize it. Indeed, an animal of value and beauty.

*   *   *

All the study kids and Joe already knew Bill, a Roosville inspector on the Canadian side and frequent visitor at the Flathead during Ron's days. He reveled in his transfer over to the Flathead to succeed Ron. Young, with sandy-hair, six feet six inches tall and a master of crib and all other board games, he was an avid reader and could be as intimidating as hell when he needed or wanted to be.

Wayne, who alternated with Bill his first year was a gourmet cook and loved to entertain. Many a banquet fit for royalty was hosted in the Canadian quarters that summer.

Some of the best social gatherings in the North Fork were spontaneous. Marge, Joe's relief for his three days off, and her husband, came down to our cabin for coffee after work. Then Wayne, his wife, Cathy, and Cathy's visiting parents stopped in on their way up from Polebridge. When Tom and Tim drove up after a busy day of trapping and collaring grizzly, everyone resettled, crowded about our round kitchen table.

And oh, how the stories flew!

Wayne's group was so wound up and enthused over the wildlife they had just seen coming up the North Fork road in the dark, they couldn't sit still. First a mountain lion had ambled across the road in front of their headlights. They caught sight of a grizzly as he dove into the underbrush to the side. Deer—moose—you name it. The piece de resistance, however, had been a herd of elk they had watched near the river, with a seven point bull elk in charge. They had been lucky enough to see all of them in their short half hour's drive north.

Many travel the road at night and see nothing. Or just miss the sighting of a lifetime as we had while following Maggie in our truck one night as she drove the Blazer up ahead of us. She had the luck to have a great gray owl, a rare northerner and the largest of the owls, rise up from a kill in the road directly in front of her, to swoop up and over the front of the Blazer with a wingspan so large it seemed to blanket the windshield as it rose in the air.

Descriptions of sighting after sighting followed. The very fact that Tim and Tom matter-of-factly related their events of the day was thrilling to us all, especially to the visiting outsiders.

Just about any gathering in the great north has its own never-to-be forgotten stories that stay with the listener forever.

Wayne and Cathy had been at a party one evening. The talk, as usual for the area, turned to bear stories. A girl in the group started to weep silently before she related her experience.

She had been working in the forests in British Columbia as a flagger, directing traffic, keeping the road free of vehicles as a helicopter transported logs over the road during a logging operation.

She took advantage of a lull in the activity to go back into the woods to relieve herself. Suddenly, a blow struck her in the head so hard from behind she hit the ground, face down, teeth and mouth full of dirt from the force of it. As she lay there, a grizzly flipped her over and held her head in his mouth.

Then he left as quickly as he had come. When she staggered out of the woods, covered with blood, the driver of a vehicle stopped, got out and attempted to help her.

Another driver pulled up, took the scene at face value and thought the other driver was attacking the girl. He tried to fight the would-be rescuer off. The helicopter pilot had landed, wondering why the traffic hadn't been stopped, thus holding up the entire operation.

After the incident, further investigation revealed what led to the attack.

Down over the adjacent hill, they found a boat filled with fish, dragged up on shore, left by a careless fisherman. The grizzly, attracted by an easy meal, had been disturbed by the helicopter flying around. He climbed up into the woods to defend his cache of fish, and targeted the unsuspecting girl.

A chilling tale.

With evenings like this, no wonder we all loved the North Fork so. We were living the best of times.

Even the rainbows, symbols of the good life, were spectacular. Once a magnificent rainbow traveled down the length of the mountains in a perpendicular cloud fashion, from Starvation Peak past King Edward, over the empty slot at Kintla, past Parke Mountain, slowly building in intensity of color and size as it hugged the peaks until disappearing into black-gray threatening clouds over the ranges to the south.

The cloud formations were as strikingly grand, some thunderheads blowing up in the sky to the south as white giants, big as the mountains themselves, huge updrafts thrusting high into the atmosphere. Others were whipped into saucer-like shapes, hanging around until the red of the sunset tinged them a light pink.

A gloomy, cloudy, early morning sky would at times be rent by glorious crimson shafts of bright light, shining straight down to illuminate a particularly breathtaking glimpse of mountain, magnificent in the spotlight cast by the hidden rising sun. Later, the same day, the range could barely be seen through the shimmering sun as the clouds lifted. Only in the afternoon as the sun moved, would the intensity and angle of the brightness change so defining shadows could once more delineate the individual and infinite variety of rock mass before us.

The alpine glow that bathed the mountains the few minutes before the sun vanished behind Mt. Thoma was heart stopping. Always, the mountains dominated, presenting quick flashes of superb beauty to our senses even as we walked, talked, worked. And of course, the mountains helped make the weather.

Spring was especially rough on the early arriving hummingbirds. It was worrisome to wonder how they'd survive in a cold, wet rain. A few would find shelter on the antenna wire directly outside our bathroom window, a good spot under the eaves and close to the feeders. I'd slide the window open wider so more heat would escape to them.

Summers flew by, measured first by the early blooming small white, wild strawberry flowers, then the wild roses along the lane and an extensive array of lupine, golden rod, blue bells, and a few glacier lilies. The reds of a carpet of Indian paint brush, from a light faded pink to deep-set crimson, covered the open space to the side of the corral. We were ablaze in a profusion of wild flowers. Butterflies, grasshoppers, weird, unknown insects, and a close hairy jumping relative of the brown recluse spider, made their appearance.

Fall weather changes were more dramatic, rapid and fearsome as harsh winds swept in from all directions, leaving behind foggy clouds clinging to the Livingston front and thickening behind us along the Whitefish range.

Dropping rain or snow, low clouds moved swiftly overhead. There were fewer clear days. Nights, coming earlier, became biting cold. The Columbian Ground squirrels simply disappeared under ground in mid-August, but for the rare one skulking along a trail to one of its burrows with a last mouthful of grass.

Traces of snow on the mountains, left behind by the low clouds made them so especially beautiful it was hard to look away. "New snow on the mountains" was a happy exciting time. Never were the Canadian ones so wonderfully outlined. The snow line moved lower as fall progressed, the weather dominated by the cold and wet sporadic drizzle, soon changing into snow showers. Small piles of shaded wet snow grew larger.

It was time to pick the few surviving Indian paintbrush to place them on Robbie's and Kitty's graves. Kitty had died suddenly of a heart attack that very summer, cut short as he told me in his bossy Siamese fashion, that it was time for all of us to go to bed. Now, with each other's company, he and Robbie could forever enjoy the change of seasons.

The last forlorn leaves fell from the aspen and birch. The larch, in most places a sickly yellow green, looked more bare by the day. During a fall walk a lonely lane to our north could be especially dark, even gloomy. Here the trees grew so tall and thick their crowns formed an overhead canopy. Underneath, Brig and I walked over the resultant thick carpet of brown duff left from decades of autumn's Tamarack needle shedding. It was a quiet, almost cathedral-like stretch, with a few downed tree trunks left in the undergrowth, surely many hundreds of years old before cut and left to decay.

This autumn walk turned into a perfect, almost glorious moment. Just as Brig and I started to climb the hill, the wind came through and blew masses of yellow larch needles down on us, the shafts of sunlight through the thick stand of trees transforming them into a steady shower of bits of gold that rained in magical profusion. Such was the beauty so inherent in this place.

Danger was the other side of the coin. One mistake could be deadly. It was the simplicity and swiftness of it that could be astounding.

Outside on the screened porch of our cabin, barefoot and in my white flannel night shirt, I waved good-by to Joe as he drove past the corner of the cabin and off down the lane for his full day of errands in Kalispell. It was so early and cold I couldn't wait to hop back into bed.

I reached behind me and felt for the doorknob. It wouldn't turn.

Oh dear God! Somehow the door had swung shut and locked behind me.

I raced out into the lane, screaming, waving my arms, but Joe kept driving steadily down the lane, the vehicle's blinking taillights mocking my stupid predicament. I couldn't run fast enough, gave up, and tore back up to the cabin, around the yard to the front porch. Filled with dread, I realized it would only be by chance that Joe would glance back and notice my leaping, frantically waving figure.

The cold wind whipped around me, my wet, half-frozen feet already losing feeling from the mad dash down the rocky, frosty, snow-spotted lane and yard. The brake lights blinked again as Joe turned at the mail boxes and disappeared down the North Fork road.

I was too scared to cry. I was in real trouble.

Always conscious of how alone and far out we were, I made it a point to keep everything locked. Without hope, I pulled at the front screened door.

It was locked, of course, like always.

I ran through the yard to the back door again. Locked. The temperature hovered at thirty-five degrees. There was no one around for five miles. The little high window in the back of the cabin, now inside the add-on porch, would be the cheapest and most logical one to break. It was so high, though, I'd break my neck on the other side, 'cause I'd have to go down head first with nothing to hang on to or stop my fall. After really checking its size, I realized I'd never fit through it. The kitchen window was too small. The bedroom window was split with a metal divider that cut it in half. Again, too small.

That left one of the three large double-paned picture windows. The garage was still locked. No ladder, no crowbar. I'd have to search for a big enough rock to break the glass.

If I could even break it, I thought bitterly, recalling how long it had taken me to initially even break the glass of the picture window we had removed and then replaced because of a broken seal. Using the back of an ax, it had taken many, many hard blows to finally crack it before breaking it into easily transportable pieces for discard in the valley.

All those thoughts flew through my brain in seconds. Beginning to seriously shiver, the idea of my walking barefoot up the North Fork road for five miles in a night shirt, in this weather, scared the hell out of me.

Desperate, I ran to the front again, succeeded in pulling a section of the screen from out of the door mounting, reached through and unhooked the latch.

With real fear, I half-sobbed, then tried the inside wooden door, holding my breath.

The knob turned. It hadn't been locked!

I shook uncontrollably for a long while. Relief? You bet.

How simple a mistake—how dire the consequences could have been.

If the inside door had been locked, it was five miles to the border. I'd have gone down in Canadian and U.S. customs' folklore as the half-frozen woman who had appeared at the stations, barefoot and in her nightie.

Sometimes extreme cold and snow could arrive early in the North Fork. Polebridge could have three feet of snow, yet maybe four feet would fall at Trail Creek. We'd have yet more at our cabin and even deeper on the border.

Not daring to take a chance with the weather, Joe and I would winterize our cabin and move up to the port for the last few days before the border closed for the season. Our truck was all packed, ready to leave, so we made do with what we had, getting rid of leftovers, eating from the pans, a giddy time because we were safe at the port with its electric lights and central heat. No need to worry about the condition of the lane or road except for the final run out to civilization after winterizing the port on that last work day.

The heat would go off at night for we shut the generator down to conserve propane when we'd go to bed. Thus, the cold permeated the entire building in no time, a dead penetrating chill.

I'd retire for the night in long johns, socks, night shirt, big red sweat shirt, and wool gloves. We slept close, Brig producing valuable warmth.

We were in heaven compared to some of Diane's experiences. She was truly amazing. Her comment about the North Fork winters?

"Lots intend to stay up here over the winters, year round. But it usually lasts about three years."

We had heard her hilarious tale of trying to get back to her wolf camp in Canada, in the dead of winter, with her student assistant, a load of supplies and newly laundered clean clothes in the truck. They were stopped by the bad weather. Diane put on all the clean clothes that she could and went to sleep sitting up. (She had the reputation of being able to sleep anywhere and under any conditions). The student assistant was glaring at her when she woke the next morning.

"You slept!" was all he could sputter.

One cold morning at the port, Diane was at the gate at 7 a.m., having made arrangements to go north over Harvey Pass to Fernie, and then on to a place in Alberta for wolf blood samples. She thought she'd be back around 4 p.m. It was snowing. Joe had to go out to the gate with a lighter to heat up the frozen lock so he could open it for her to cross to the Canadian side.

I worried about the snow, the rough lonely road north, the condition of the pass, and all that could possibly happen on such a long trip, over truly rough terrain, and with chancy weather. I worried for both of us, for Diane went blithely on her way, smiling like always. She was back at 4 p.m., mission completed.

She had even stopped for lunch in a restaurant.

CHAPTER 15

Oh, the special feeling that was alive and well in the North Fork during that entire summer of 1993. The very air seemed permeated with the excitement of the good, solid research that was being conducted.

The North Fork was a sort of microcosm, an extraordinary place indeed, where wildlife interaction could be observed with objectivity. After Tim and Tom had trapped and collared the bears, the animals' movements were monitored by Roz and Nancy. The newer coyote and mountain lion research was well underway.

Wendy's coyote study, actually initiated the previous fall, was of particular interest because of the influx of their larger, stronger competitors, the wolves.

Past animal studies had provided a solid foundation. There was Jon, from the early years, making light of how he almost lost his manhood trapping his deer. Mike, with his elk, and Meg, with her moose had also finished their field work, leading to advanced degrees from the University of Montana.

Nutritional studies had been well-documented, adding to the base information. Kyran continued with the monitoring of the ungulates and wolves. He, Toni and Wendy were committed to years of harsh living and working conditions, all in pursuit of Ph.D.s, which necessitated almost as much time on the computer as in the field. Funding for the studies varied. Since the wolf was endangered and the grizzly, threatened, U.S. Fish and Wildlife provided funds and personnel, working through and with the University of Montana. The rest had to scrabble for money from private sources.

Rick Mace, South Fork Grizzly Project leader, stated in a newspaper interview in January 1993 that no one had ever asked the bears. Their project did.

So did the researchers in the North Fork, continuing in the same mode, trapping, collaring and following their animals by telemetry. Understanding how each species lived was a step in saving them, their interactions with each other of particular importance. Only the North Fork had the necessary wildlife for such study.

Tim and Tom trapped between Polebridge and the border from late May through mid June, then pulled their traps because of the heat. Since we had such close contact with the study groups, we heard almost daily updates.

It was great to learn a large healthy male grizzly, collared in Canada, had been named Ron. We wrote to tell human Ron immediately. Still confined to a wheelchair because of his stroke, the news that his name-sake was running around the North Fork, watching out for his interests, would surely cheer him up.

Soon after, Wendy Clark, an assistant to Kyran, told Joe they had trapped and collared a four year old female in the park and named her Joan. What an honor. A wolf had been trapped at the same time. Only twenty feet had separated them.

Wendy Clark always told Joe where Joan was and what she had been up to. Joan hung around a good bit in the woods behind our place. As the study later reported, the four year old female spent the summer in the valley bottom, frequently in close proximity to cabins and developed areas, near the roads, air strip and Ford public camping areas. She was rarely seen and used both sides of the river bottom. Joan regularly traveled back and forth from our place into the park.

Checking the salt blocks one morning, I had found a mess of prints in the soft dark mud: moose, deer, and grizzly prints, about the same size as the ones I had found in the lower lane two years previously, when four year old Lorna had been hanging around. The only complete one was raggedy in the mud, the heel sunk further down in the muck. I found elongated claw marks, about five feet further up from the good print, looking longer because of the slipping and sliding of the bear. Then I wondered when they had been made.

That afternoon, when Joe came home from the border, he told me, "Wendy drove all the way up to tell me to tell you that Joan is around. They got a signal from her back in the woods by our place."

I was exalted! The prints were new, and it was my name sake! I told Marca, who was still at her cabin, and the next morning she came by with her containers of plaster of Paris.

I waited two full days before checking the casts of the prints, for the mud underneath had been pretty wet. I stood there, alone, perplexed. One cast had been flipped out of the muddy print and had landed a couple of feet away. It was in perfect condition. I had a devil of a time digging out the huge moose print for it had set too long. There was only one possibility. Joan had come back, investigated the strange white blobs in the mud, and used her claws to toss the one out and away. I could imagine her flipping and then sniffing at it. I kept looking over my shoulder as I dug, then got out of there. When I made more casts later, my inventory of grizzly prints rose to five, six counting the one I gave Marca.

Grizzly had been around us all our years in the North Fork. We just didn't know them as personally as we did now, as individuals, with names and a history.

Earlier in the season Marca had spotted a sow and cub down Trail Creek. Tom thought it might have been Lorna. They had expected her to have a cub that year (1993).

Lorna, part of the earlier Canadian bear study, was a fourth generation bear, her genealogy of utmost interest and importance to the study. A fifth generation cub would be a treasure. She had hung around the scenes of her childhood mostly between Trail Creek and the border, sometimes appearing further south, then working her way north.

I had always thought it was Lorna that Brig and I had met in our lane, and thus felt extra close to her. Once she had appeared near a cabin where her presence was not appreciated. The owner threatened to shoot her. Post haste, she was trapped and taken across the divide. In no time, Lorna was back, walking down Trail Creek.

The mysterious sow and cub were not seen again. Indeed, no sow with a cub was trapped during the entire time of the North Fork study, a very bad sign.

On the way to the mail box one morning, not ten steps down the lane, Brig raised his head like never before, sniffed the air, again and again, catching a scent powerful enough to make him act weird. I started to whistle and talk in a loud voice to him. Wendy Clark drove up as I stuck the letters in the mail box. I told her how Brig had acted.

The mailbox site was perfect for radio tracking. Researchers could receive signals very clearly. It was one of their favorite listening spots.

Wendy took her reading.

"Joan's up in back of your place," she announced.

Wendy Clark and I usually talked about the state of the world, the fate of the wilderness bill, and, in an attempt to be positive, that perhaps things weren't so bad, that maybe we were just too close to it all. I knew how I had been burned over the last three years, at the cutting edge of environmental attempts in the North Fork.

"You have a grizzly in back of your cabin, so things aren't so bad!" she said as she drove off.

*   *   *

One evening about ten p.m., Bill, Joe and Marca were so engrossed in the movie *Shane* that I was the only one who heard the knocking on our back door. It was almost pitch black outside.

The man asked if we had a phone, which of course, we didn't. He explained he, his son, and son's friend, had decided to bicycle down from Waterton Park, Alberta. He planned to meet his wife, who was driving down, at Apgar in Glacier Park. Now they were afraid they were lost.

They had crossed the border illegally. It was more than bad luck, even sort of funny, that both customs inspectors were in the only lighted cabin for miles around. Clad in light shorts and T-shirts, the three were ill-prepared for the downright cold night. Not only had they sorely misjudged the length of time for their outing, but their lack of preparation was even worse.

The man suddenly found himself and the kids being driven back to the border to possibly be charged with illegal entry into the United States. Joe and Bill explained the seriousness of their transgression and the possible fines involved.

At the port, Joe radioed Immigration to see if they or Border Patrol were interested. Border Patrol declined to make the long trip north from Whitefish and Immigration told Joe to use his own discretion on the matter.

Joe had to decide. Was the man telling the truth? Perhaps it was a quickly made-up story since they were caught.

The account was bolstered by information coming over the radio as Glacier Park's dispatcher called the park ranger near Polebridge. Joe listened.

A Canadian woman was looking for her husband and two boys, on bicycles, coming down from Waterton via the North Fork road. They were to meet at Apgar. Joe notified the dispatcher of the missing trio's location and suggested the woman start driving up the North Fork road to meet them.

Joe and Bill returned the abject, thoroughly scared trio back to our cabin for their bicycles. They would ride down to meet their family, sufficiently frightened by their experience that no further admonition was necessary.

Later, we realized the three hadn't gotten any further than our mail box. They had no lights on their bikes. Since they were probably frozen in their light clothes, they had built a roaring fire that still burned fiercely when Joe and I fell into bed, way past one a.m.

It was well that they did. If they had only known, this adventure story could have been culminated by the fact that Joan, the four year old grizzly who had been hanging around, had walked down our muddy lane to the road that very afternoon, leaving clear, distinct, large foot prints behind.

*   *   *

Always, I worried about the coyotes, not as charismatic as the larger predators, even considered vermin by many and shot on sight any old time. It would be good to know how they were faring in the North Fork.

I learned how smart they could be, walking down our lane once, alone, with the wind in my face. I caught sight of a coyote ahead of me, away to my left, stalking something in the field, a picture of stealth, grace and patience.

I moved forward carefully, just as he was, but kept slightly behind him. By this time, we had both advanced almost to the Y in the lane. Then he saw my movement and instantly melted to the ground. I know of no other way to describe his protective mechanism. He became a light colored rock, immovable. I stood there for at least fifteen minutes, watching closely the coyote, that if I hadn't known better, was just another boulder. Obviously, he would outwait me. I walked away from him backwards, keeping my eyes on him. I turned finally, leaving him in peace.

Since we had a history of coyote neighbors we offered our land for part of the study.

It was natural for Diane to pass on to Wendy not only her vast experience and knowledge of the area and people, but also the idiosyncrasies of setting the smaller, easily opened, well-padded coyote traps. Of course, I hung around, to learn as much as I could.

Finding an ideal spot for trap location was Diane's forte. The left side of our lane was "too green". It would show trampling too much, so she picked a spot just above the ditch on the right-hand side, halfway up the sloping bank, in the shade.

Digging around, she pounded in a piece of rebar to hold the trap in place, then pulled out a wrench to clamp other attachments. She could leave no human scent, so wore work gloves, rubber boots with smooth soles, and knelt on a large piece of cloth, quite dirty from heavy use, a plus.

As Diane worked, she explained how they kept the traps free from scent: they were boiled in large drums in pure water containing no chlorine (no problem in the North Fork!) together with bark. The tannin stained the steel and took away all the smell. The water would turn black. It was a natural non-smelling process, albeit a tedious one.

She set the trap and carefully laid it flat in place, then sifted dirt over it through the sieved end of a coffee can. Diane continued building up the sifted dirt all around the trap until it reached the height she wanted. Then she took a baggie, a hole at one end so it would fit properly, and laid it out over the foot press spring. The sifted dirt would hold the trap properly in place, the baggie would keep the dirt, which she then kept adding, from clogging the trap and spring. Additional dirt, again sifted to keep the rocks out, was spread over the entire trap set.

Diane had put three small sticks in areas outlining the trap. When covered with the dirt, she replaced the sticks with carefully chosen rocks to mark the site. She brushed up the few trampled green plants, tossed some pine needles and other duff over the area, then sprinkled coyote scent about a foot and a half up and in front of the trap so that the coyote, busy sniffing the urine scent, would step on the trap and get caught. His nose and sniffing would be directed ahead of the trap.

She and Wendy showed me the paste in a little jar that looked like liver pate or baby food, identified on the label as "Super range all call for coyotes." They also used liquid from a brown bottle, "Nature's call" or coyote urine, with some skunk in it. Neither smelled the least bit strong or bad.

Satisfied with the lay of the trap, both packed up and went off to set a few more, both wolf and coyote. The wolf traps are not as hard to lay. When the wolf gets trapped, he can pull the trap out of the ground and drag it until the anchor hooks catch in the woods, thus holding him safely, in the shade and away from congestion.

Wendy became a familiar early morning and evening sight, striding off into the woods to her traps, with her huge boots on, ax in one hand, bucket in the other with all her accouterments inside. She checked them faithfully twice a day and went through a veritable hell as she caught mostly gophers, who were attracted by the plastic baggies, or badgers or skunks. One badger was so mean, Diane had to fend him away with a board and their scale while Wendy set him loose. As Wendy described it, "He had a bad attitude."

Skunks presented a different problem, of course. One morning at Marca's cabin, Wendy appeared at the door. Her first words of greeting?

"Do I smell?"

She would dash into the port, obviously in need of a quick shower. We gave her extra old clothing we had, as some of hers became unusable. She became adept at using a box to hold over the trapped skunk until it was safely set free.

Wendy, removing a gopher from a coyote trap

Possibly her worst morning? When she dropped her keys down in the outhouse and caught a skunk all before 7:30 a.m. She had to retrieve her keys with a broom and coat hanger. A hard way to get an education!

Everyone cheered when Wendy finally trapped some coyotes. Thunder, collared at Tepee, had a "star burst" in his one eye, (blind) but other than being a little old, about four or five, was in fine shape, weighing in at about twenty-eight pounds. Although coyotes have a small range, he disappeared for a few days, worrying Wendy. She and Marca traveled various drainages for hours, listening for his signal. Even Kyran couldn't find him during overflights.

Happily, he was finally discovered behind Hornet lookout, alive and well. Jenner, another favorite and quite young, was killed by another coyote after he had transgressed on its territory. Coyotes go for the voice box and wind pipe and that was the end of poor Jenner.

Wendy had good help in '93. Mark and Julie, volunteers from California, learned quickly and performed a multitude of tasks to aid Wendy in her almost insurmountable work of catching these wily creatures, so adaptive and intelligent. Although coyotes can hunt in packs for large game, up here they were apparently loners, forced maybe to be even smarter than the average coyote.

I watched from our front porch, as Mark carefully set a coyote trap in our upper front meadow, by some shade trees, along a favorite route for the critters. Many a time I had seen a grayish back and bushy tail as one trotted along the outside of our pole fence, in front of the cabin.

Mark had just finished sifting the dirt layers. He and Wendy were bent over, close to it—the trap snapped shut and a cloud of fine particles of dirt flew right into their faces. I just had to laugh. Not only was I glad it hadn't happened to me, but Mark and Julie would have good stories to tell in their classrooms in the fall. Especially Mark, playing the macho man, as he ruefully described himself later.

Kyran had received the mortality radio signal from Wendy's second coyote, Jenner. Dead about three days, he was found behind Polebridge. Mark picked up Jenner in a plastic bag so Kryan could do the necropsy. Pretty ripe stuff. He about barfed.

Mark and Julie had parked their personal truck off the road at Trail Creek one day, to save gas. Of course, their truck had California license plates. Someone had written "go home" in the dust on their back window. Wendy happened to drive up on them, two locals with a white horse trailer.

Wendy, because she wasn't catching enough coyotes, finally enlisted the aid of a predator control agent, an expert in coyotes, who had a territory of four or five states. He would be involved with the wolves that would be trapped in Canada for Yellowstone.

Personable, knowledgeable, and all business when he declared our area pretty sterile, he brought home to me how the coyotes were apparently declining. I found I had to wall off what he really did for a living.

He certainly knew his bait. He used cougar and bob cat, ground up, and fermented three years. I could smell the new coyote bait, the minced cat, clear across our field as Brig and I walked up along the side jack fence. I had to hold Brig back.

Thereafter, Wendy caught coyotes.

Coyotes are not tranquilized or ear-tagged when trapped. They are either very submissive or smart, for researchers simply drop a small noose over them before "walking" their fingers up the coyote's back, then grabbing them by the back of their neck, as you would a cat. It usually takes about ten or fifteen minutes to collect their data.

Usually.

Wendy caught two coyotes over in the park in mid October, one male, one female. Wendy Clark helped her by clamping the male coyote's muzzle tightly shut as Wendy measured him. The coyote abruptly pulled away, turned his head around and bit Wendy's left thumb, taking a large chunk out of the tip. They field-dressed the injury and rushed to the port, where Wendy shook Joe totally as she held up a bandaged hand. "A coyote just took part of my finger off!" The well-stocked customs' first aid kit was finally baptized.

I reminded Wendy of the crocodile in *Peter Pan* who had gobbled the pirate's hand off, then forever followed him because the hand had tasted so good. The croc wanted the rest of him. Maybe the coyote would go calling at Wendy's cabin door that winter, smacking his lips, seeking more than just a finger tip taste. She named him Spitfire, and started her rabies shots.

Coyotes became even more special to me when the bear study people reported they had found a coyote den with pups right by a culvert up in Canada. The pups had toys: boxes and other pieces of trash. All babies need toys, especially these pups destined for too short and harsh a life span.

                    *   *   *

Whenever the study kids could arrange an evening off, we'd schedule movie time at our cabin, with pop and popcorn, just like city folks. The running water and other amenities we offered were a real draw, even though the movie *Shenandoah* made Wendy Clark cry.

Our water system, after years of reliable service, almost made me cry a few weeks later when the water flow from the well would hesitate, stop, but then start up again. The flow finally quit totally.

The list of possibilities was scary: bad pump, break in the line, or dry well. I saw dollars flying away. I couldn't stand to go through drilling again, not after three dry holes and $5,000 shot to hell.

Referred by a friend to a man south of us knowledgeable in such things, we were relieved to hear him say he heard the water, that the problem was in the line above the pump for he could hear the water pump up and then fall back into the well.

While we were waiting for the repairs, Joe had to take our five gallon water jugs to the border each morning. He'd bring them back full when he returned from work, then take each one up the stairs to dump in the water tank. At a little over eight pounds per gallon, we figured he hauled about 250 pounds of water up the flight of stairs to the second floor each evening for over a week. I saved every drop of water I could. The driller finally arrived and repaired a defective relief valve. We were in business again.

My housekeeping, what little I had to do, revolved around water. The first thing in the morning, before any water at all was run, I'd stretch out my left hand to the bathroom sink hot water faucet, the right hand to the tub hot water spigot. I had to turn them both on at exactly the same instant, running the water until it was hot, or "gulped". Otherwise, we'd get an infamous "vapor-lock" resulting in no water. When that happened, Joe would open an under-the-floor valve under the hot water tank and bleed off the lower water in the tank, keeping the tub and sink hot water spigots open, until the water flowed freely.

These vapor locks were apparently the result of the interaction between an unpressurized water system, very cold well water in the upstairs tank and the warmer water in the hot water tank.

With experience, we figured if we kept the water tank at least one third full all the time, the cold underground water from the well wouldn't be such a shock to the system and the hot water heater. I'd have to run the hot water every once in a while during the day and we did the morning routine after trips to town. Our vapor locks almost disappeared.

During the time Joe was hauling the water from the port, I had a brain-storm and caught all run-off from the spigots in large pans. Since this simple water saving maneuver added an entire day to our water supply, I continued to do it daily.

I'll never take water for granted.

Never!

Not to the end of my days.

*   *   *

It was a natural grouping for dinner at our cabin one evening, Tom Reynolds, Marca and Uncle Bob. Marca had purchased for an enormous sum, the most infamous historical cabin on the North Fork. She had to hear the tale from Tom himself, since he was the only original source of information still alive. What had happened in that cabin so long ago was indelibly etched within Tom's memory. Bill Cruise had been his friend and responsible for Tom's moving to the North Fork in the late twenties. The old gentleman gave his most animated telling ever to the young, blonde enthralled Marca.

"Your cabin down on Mud Lake? Well, there was a woman that Bill Cruise brought up about 1932. He got acquainted with this woman through *Heart in Hand* love magazine. Sent her the money, seventy dollars, to come out from New York City. I don't know why he brought her out. He said he wanted a housekeeper. Nobody in their right mind would have got acquainted with her 'cause her husband kicked her out for tomcatting around and here he gets her for a housekeeper.

"She stayed with him that winter. That spring her daughter came out. She was pregnant. We called her the Pissant. But her real name, her mother called her Lil or Lillian."

Tom laughed, "Anyway, she was no lily! The last time I saw her was when her mother, Madam Queen, had moved down country to one of the other settlers. Here was the Pissant, half drunk, with a glass in her hand, talking to a cook from the park, trying to get him to be a companion for the night, I think. But I don't know if they ever made it. This would be after the shooting."

Marca's eyes widened, "The shooting?"

"When Madam Queen left Bill and moved over to his neighbor, Ed Peterson, that was when Bill went back to South Dakota, back to his old stamping ground, to his old cabin there. He brooded all winter over this Madam Queen deserting him and going over to his neighbor. He came back pretty hostile.

"Ed Peterson was building that cabin you're in now for Madam Queen. Sold her some acres and built that cabin for her. It was in that cabin Ed shot him.

"Four of the neighbors, one on each corner, hauled in the logs and worked on it. Bill Cruise came around with a six-shooter strapped on him and said, 'I should shoot every one of you off the corner there!' Bill Cruise was just trying to scare them, is all.

"Bill went over to see Madam Queen who was with the other lover, Ed Peterson. I guess they had quite a set-to at the Ed Peterson cabin, from what I heard. Madam Queen was scared Bill Cruise was going to beat her up. He was waiting for her in her cabin.

"She didn't come.

"She ran over through the woods so Bill wouldn't see her, and ran down country to a neighbor, Shorty Waters. She was going to stay there until Ed Peterson came. She'd egged him on to shoot Bill. Ed went over to the cabin while Madam Queen stayed down country. There was a pile of wood, logs, on the porch.

"Ed knocked at the door, then stood back. Bill Cruise came out to see who knocked at the door and Ed shot him. Then he went around the cabin and took another shot at him through the window. And the bullet went through the warming oven of the stove. The bullet's in there some where.

"Bill was hit pretty hard. He bled to death. At the inquest, they took evidence from the killer and claimed it was self-defense. Ed Peterson said he was standing right in front of Bill Cruise and he thought Bill was going to shoot him, so he shot Bill first. But the bullet didn't go right here at all." Tom pointed to his chest. "It went through here and here. It broke a rib and grazed the heart. It showed what Ed Peterson did. It was just plain murder.

"The bullet's either in the logs or between the logs," Tom finished.

"Marca can start looking," Uncle Bob commented.

"Two bullets must be in the logs!" Marca exclaimed.

"One in the warming oven!" Uncle Bob said with fervor.

Tom went on, "Walt Hammer, a neighbor, bought the cabin and used it for a while until he built a nicer one and he bought a better stove."

All the energy seemed to have run out of the old gentleman. Perhaps the unhappy memories about his friend crowded in too close for him.

Marca patted his hand.

Tom continued, "Madam Queen eventually moved in with a man named Jeff who had two uncles that had a cabin near Polebridge on the park side. She stayed with Jeff and the two uncles for a year, and then quit and went down—somewhere—found the pickings too slim, so she came back and married Jeff. But she only stayed another year and that's the last we heard of her."

Tom brightened. "She left! Good-by! Good riddance!"

Joe asked, "You know, Tom, some people think of Madam Queen as one of the pioneers of the North Fork. Do you go along with that? One that settled the North Fork?"

Tom gave a dirty laugh, "No chance! She was a real North Forker, all right, a New Yorker!"

It was a prime evening for Marca, for now she and Tom were bound together by the history of Madam Queen. She was enjoying her best summer ever, helping out the bear study, so involved it would be difficult for her to return to her California teaching.

I was as bad. When I'd hear the light animal study plane, I'd dash out to the corral, look skyward and watch its maneuvering. If the plane swooped low, banked, then flew in low circles, I'd know the study kids were getting a fix on a grizzly, their current concentration. I'd wave furiously if the plane flew over me. Sometimes Dave, the pilot, waggled his wings in return.

The plane would usually fly north, then south the entire swath of the valley, over the broad expanse of Starvation Ridge. Other times, it would disappear behind the trees, toward the Whitefish Range.

This morning, the plane circled three times over the area directly to the north of us, then over, low, in the direction of Mud Lake. They hung around for about twenty minutes, circling, taking fixes of the bears.

Dave, with his Cessna 182, was not only good at tracking, but exceptional at seeing bears from above. The best and most experienced pilot around, he had flown with the wolf, deer, elk, moose studies and previous bear studies.

With the switch box in the plane, and antennae mounted on the wing struts on either side, scanning from one bear to the next, switching back and forth, flying around and lots of sharp turning, the researchers could tell the direction of the signal, and then identify the bear from its specific frequency. Some of the researchers had to wear dramamine patches since the flights could be so rough.

Bear collars weighed less than two pounds and were dark reddish brown in color. With the small packaged transmitter and built-in antenna they also had a safety feature: cotton inserts that would rot out over a certain allotted time, about two years, allowing the collar to drop from the bear. If the signal was in the exact same place more than one time, with a low beat, it had probably been dropped.

Nancy intended to hike into a remote area for a dropped bear collar and asked Dave for a good fix from the air for her. They flew into the middle of a steep-sided canyon that produced a lot of bouncing signals. Dave pointed to an old overgrown and undrivable logging road, identified a clump of trees with a big spruce below the road, where a kind of hillside bisected it, and said the collar was by the tree, but within fifty feet of the road. When she hiked in, there it was, exactly where he said, just slightly downhill.

It wasn't always easy to see a bear from the air. At times, the researchers had to circle and swoop maybe a half dozen times and still not see the animal. A lot depended where the bears were. Shadows could be slanted and appear strange, depending on the season and time of day.

The early part of the study involved testing antenna systems. The smaller H-shaped hand-held antennae were deemed best when tracking on the ground. Researchers were interested in the activity and closeness of the bears to roads, cover, non-cover, and use of riparian areas. And where they were in relation to human developments and other habitat factors.

Some previous indications in other studies suggested that when bears were far away from people they were active during the day and slept at night. When close to people, they became nocturnal. The North Fork study would involve tracking bears twenty-four hours a day to see any change in activity that could be related to human proximity. We'd tease the bleary-eyed researchers when they'd come off one of their surveillance shifts.

We had heard rumors of a large, 500 pound grizzly bear who hadn't denned the previous winter, instead following the wolves to eat what they had left behind. Maybe it had displaced the wolves. He was also eating mountain lion kills. They were hoping to collar it, an interesting capture if they could manage to find him. It would also help the biologists during the winter tracking to know if they were walking up to a carcass that had a grizzly sleeping on top of it.

One overflight provided a raw slice of the natural world not usually witnessed by humans.

Dave and Nancy were flying eastward, homing in on a male grizzly over in the park. They could scarcely believe the scene that suddenly unfolded beneath them.

A pack of seventeen or eighteen wolves was chasing a large, dark grizzly bear. A few wolves ran alongside the bear, others were grouped directly behind it. The rest were strung out in a single file. The wolves closest to the bear bit at its rear legs and hindquarters as they trotted behind and alongside it. The bear would stop every few steps and swat at the wolves. Sometimes the bear turned and charged the wolf that had bitten it. At the same instant, some wolves angled off to chase a grizzly bear cub, then encircled and bit at it.

The mom bear leaped over a log that ran up-slope and scattered the wolves enough to allow the cub to jump up onto the log.

Because of the flight path, Nancy and Dave missed the next action. When they flew over again the cub was out of sight. Some of the pack continued to harass the female bear, biting at her from all sides. Appearing to tire, the bear slumped against the log. The log and thick spruce growing near it, helped protect the bear and forced the wolves to attack her frontally.

When last seen, the bear had left the protection of the log and was moving through the trees, without her cub. The bear and wolf pack headed southward, the wolves still after the bear. All disappeared into the trees.

Four days later, Nancy, together with a ranger, returned on foot to the meadow for any signs indicating the outcome of the battle. They found no sign of bear or wolf remains.

Bears have been known to be treed by wolves. Perhaps the cub had been left in a tree for safety. It was best to think positive.

Nancy dropped by one afternoon to show me a stack of pictures taken by one of their automatic cameras, positioned in a tree along a known animal trail. A heat sensing device triggers the camera, photographing anything that passes by that emits body heat. Some were photos of trees within the camera's range, maybe triggered by the differences in temperature during certain times of the day. There were a few deer, and then, buried among the other pictures, a gorgeous grizzly, pictures of it as it passed through, first head shots as it came into range, full side shots, clearly showing the dark underneath, blond on top, and then his rump as he left the camera's range.

The cameras were an important tool for the research groups in both the North and South Fork bear studies. I had been shocked at the news when some of the South Fork cameras were stolen, probably by those who feared the studies and how it might interfere with their way of life.

Human competition with wildlife can take remarkable forms. Mushroom hunters, commercial and private, overran the North Fork after the fires of '88, setting up tent cities along the streams with resulting pollution. One entrepreneur even sectioned off parts of public forest service land and charged for access before he was caught.

Huckleberry season could turn into a disaster for the same reason, hundreds competing for the berries so necessary for bears in the fall, people so frantic and greedy for money as to literally tear apart the bushes in their haste and search for an easy and quick way to harvest them. Even bear grass was being gathered for export to the Far East.

Diane shattered my appreciation of wildlife photography when, in her matter-of-fact way, she told us how many of those photographs and films of wildlife, a wolf howling in the woods, for instance, were actually posed and taken behind fences of commercial "wildlife" enclosures.

What a downer.

In the interest of science, and trying to put a positive spin on things, my walks now included picking up animal scat. I carried a supply of baggies in my pockets to collect the poop for Wendy's coyote study, before transferring it to a brown lunch bag at the cabin, identifying the place where I found it, time of day and date.

I'd line the brown bags along the screened porch windows, or on the porch table, until Wendy would stop by to collect them.

Someday, I thought, I'll mistakenly give Joe the wrong brown bag, and he'll open his lunch at the port, but it will be coyote or wolf scat.

CHAPTER 16

If the grizzly were center stage, Sven and Olley became the main characters. They played around the North Fork that entire summer of 1993.

Four year old sub-adults, they traveled together, usually between Trail Creek and the border. Nicknamed the Bobbsey Twins, it was a sobriquet that fitted their sibling togetherness. Where one went, the other was sure to follow.

One late afternoon, I picked up Joe after the border closed. For whatever reason, I had left Brig at the cabin. Just as we rounded a curve in the road, about a mile north of our cabin, a gorgeous grizzly, dark brown with golden back and shoulders, strolled out of the underbrush and meandered across the road, directly in front of our vehicle. He proceeded to tear at bushes alongside the road, totally ignoring us. We stopped instantly, watching, transfixed. The bear chomped at the bushes and berries, gradually working down a small slope.

Not two minutes later, another bear, identical in color and size, waltzed across the road in front of us, not even bothering to look at us.

"The Bobbsey Twins!" we both said at the same time. This was the first Joe and I had seen them.

The first bear, half hidden by the bushes, stood tall, looked over the bush he had been feeding on, then became only interested in where his twin was. Head upright, his eyes checked as the second bear crossed in

222

front of the car and made his way up the long bank through the bushes and trees, then northwest.

First bear stood, watching.

Both were healthy looking, with full thick coats, muscles rippling beneath their fur.

They looked medium sized when they walked but it was amazing how large they really were, when they rose to their full height. I could have watched those two prime specimens forever, but Joe was hungry too, and we drove on after twenty minutes or so. A broad smile covered my face for the rest of the evening.

Their magnificence was outstanding. The two were at home in this area, playing and eating. I would carry their image with me forever.

I was careful and extra alert the next morning when I walked, singing to Brig as we kept to the middle of the road.

Many of us saw the twins that fall, even Maggie on her quick vacation to the North Fork a week or so later. They just minded their own business, traveling back and forth, leaving their day bed at Trail Creek, intent only on piling on the pounds before winter hibernation.

Tom and Tim returned to trap in early September. Within the first eight days, they trapped and collared six grizzly, including the twins, who they named Sven and Olley.

The two men surprised us late one fall evening by stopping by the cabin. Afraid they had already left the North Fork, I had wanted to talk to them about grizzlies before they went over to the Yaak.

"Sorry to be so late," Tim apologized, explaining how they had just finished cleaning up after a particularly long day.

"Our schedules are decided by the bears," Tom grinned.

Tim started off with an explanation of a cubby.

"It's just to trap bears," Tim began. "Traditionally used to capture bears. We get logs about six feet long and we pile 'em on top of each other so they'll make a *V* at the base of a tree. The sides of the cubby are about three or four feet high, with an opening about four feet across at the wide part. You just pile up the logs, sticks, whatever, in place at the apex. You put some bait in the back of the cubby, the snare in front. It sort of helps funnel the bears into one spot so when they go get the bait, they run into the snare attached to the tree.

"The snare is a quarter inch cable actually in two parts. One is the cable with a loop on a swivel that tightens up on a bear's foot. It's activated by a spring like a big safety pin that's closer to the ground. The loop on the snare is put around the spring and you try to set everything up so the bear steps in one spot only. When it does, it's in the loop and depresses the spring. Then when the spring goes up, it tightens the loop on the bear's wrist. The bear will pull back and it locks in place. The spring falls off when the bear tightens it up. Pretty simple.

"We check the traps once a day, sometimes twice, depending where they are. Every day for sure. We wouldn't ever dream of leaving them more than a day without checking them."

I asked Tim if they ever caught the same bear twice.

"Oh, yeah. We caught a bear just yesterday we caught three weeks ago. We've been trying not to recapture some of these bears. But we've caught one or two we didn't want to. We find some bears that don't care. It's worth it to them to get the bait. Some get caught eight or nine times.

"You've worked with grizzlies so long you'd know. How smart are they?"

"They're definitely smart; depends in what sort of context," Tim said. "They can figure things out real quick as far as snares and what people are doing. They're definitely very smart."

We talked about size.

"The biggest one I've ever handled was Sugar Ray, down south of here, in the South Fork. About 650 pounds. But there was another bear that was caught over on the east side, by Augusta, that was killing cattle. Chuck Johnson and I had just returned from Harvey Pass (Canada) in 1978 in the springtime. That bear, in the spring, weighed over 600. He was probably the biggest bear I've ever encountered."

Spring weight, I knew, is the time of year when bears weigh the least, right after they come out of denning. One small sub-adult that denned north of us lost 140 pounds in the den, or one third his weight.

"Sugar Ray was in a trap. We had to tranquilize him, put a collar and all on him."

"What kind of tranquilizers do you use?"

Tim explained, "We use two different kinds but the main one is called Telazol. It was developed back in the seventies for handling bears. It's probably the best drug available. You have a very broad latitude. Sometimes weight is difficult to estimate and therefore it can be hard to maintain the state of unconsciousness. When the bear starts to come around, it's fairly slow.

"There's another drug we sometimes use, a drug combination, Ketamine/Roupon (Xylazine hydrochloride). These are two drugs together. You have to be more careful 'cause they can work pretty fast. It's dangerous."

I found out later from Tom that Telazol is used on dogs and cats by vets and it's a preferred drug for bears, so predictable they don't need a snare. With the other, he said the bears can jump up on you even with the snare on.

According to Tom, "There are two different ways to tranquilize bears. For the large, more aggressive ones, we use the capture gun which has a charge that goes off and pushes the drug all the way down into the bear. We use a jab stick with a big metal syringe on the smaller ones and inject them with that."

I asked how they trapped the twins, the favorite bears of the neighborhood.

"We caught 'em in a cubby at a trail set. We typically put two snares at the same site in case two animals traveling together come into the area. If we'd only have one snare, we'd just catch one, and the other one would be there defending it, be it a sibling, offspring or whatever. We artificially created a trail."

Tom laughed, "It's kind of an interesting story. We walked up to the two bears, one on the left and one on the right. The one on the right was a lot more aggressive. The one on the left we thought was small and mellow, so we decided we'd dart that one and jab stick the other. We estimated the one we darted at 300–325 pounds so darted for that weight. We go to jab stick the other one. The bear's kinda laying on his back, like this"—Tom threw himself back into the couch, "With its arms out like this"—he extended his arms—"And Tim comes to his side. The bear just rolls over and charges Tim, actually rushes right into the jab stick and tranquilizes himself."

Tim explained, "That one was a little bigger than 250 pounds. The bigger one we figured was 350. Sven turned out to be 325 and was the aggressive one.

"We thought it was a mother with a two year old offspring but it was two males, about four years old. It's possible they were three."

"Do you still take a tooth out of each one?" I asked.

"We can get a general idea of how old they are from that. To get a precise age, you need to remove a very small tooth—you can hardly see it—and send it to a lab where they decalcify it, and use a microtome to cut off real thin slices, put them under a microscope and count the rings, just like a tree, to get the precise age."

"What about hibernation? Tell us about the griz that didn't hibernate last winter. Joe and I heard he followed and ate wolf or lion kills, easy pickings for him."

"I really don't know too much about that one. Grizzly bears will be up much later in the fall than black bears. If you go to a grizzly bear den in the winter time, they are apt to be much more aware of what's going on than black bears. They usually build their dens in higher elevations, at about six thousand feet on a steep slope. The dens are easier to dig again. Grizzly pick remote sites and dig into a slope, steep because they are more inaccessible. They aren't dummies.

"They usually use mouthfuls of bear grass to line and make this big nest, sometimes using tree boughs or branches off bushes that are easy to get. They are much more likely to be alert. The fact that they stay up later and get up earlier in the spring—they're more prone to be out than a black bear."

"Would Sven and Olley den together?"

Tim said they could.

"That would be a heck of a den," Tom laughed.

My favorite "what if" with Sven and Olley was what if a person who didn't know of the twins, spied the one, thought that was it, but then had the second one amble up? Sort of neat but probably an instant heart attack.

"What's the wildest bear you've ever captured? The one that's given you the most trouble, hard to catch?" I asked Tim.

"The most exciting capture? Memorable? In 1977, my second year working with bears—I was with Terry down in the South Fork of the Flathead. We had caught a couple of big males in the spring time. It was about the first of June.

"We had been in camp since the middle of April. There was still some snow. Anyhow, we recaptured one of these males. He was about 400 pounds or so. We were using Ketamine/Roupon, the first year we were using it on bears. We had done about fifteen or twenty black bears. Thought we knew how well it worked, on black bears anyhow, and we thought we'd use it on the smaller grizzly bears. As far as I know, this is the first time the stuff had ever been used on a grizzly. So we caught this 400 pound male in a snare probably 200 feet up a hill from our truck.

"We went up there and darted the bear. Got him out fine. We didn't have much to do with him since he was already tagged and collared. We wanted to see how this particular grizzly would recover. What we didn't know then was this drug can put an animal from a tranquilized state into a natural sleep, so he can sleep it off. When they wake up, they can be rearin' to go. That's what happened to this guy.

"We were sitting there, watching and waiting for him to come out of it, and then we decided to get up. He never moved. We put all our gear back on the truck and we sat off to the side, about eighty feet away, waiting for him to get up, for we had more snares to check. We were getting impatient, so we'd get these little sticks and flip 'em at this bear, trying to get him to at least move so we could leave. Several of the sticks had landed on his back.

"Being very young and foolish, I told Terry I was going to go over there and take those sticks off his back. He didn't think it was a good idea. I said, well, even if the bear did wake up, he'd do what black bears do. They wouldn't go very far very fast. No big deal.

"I walked over there. The bear was leaning up against a tree. I sort of came from behind the tree. I had a stick in my hand to use to flip the sticks off the bear's back.

"And the second I touched that bear's back, he jerked his head up.

"Terry yelled at me, 'He's got his head up! Get out of there!' But by that time I was already running!"

Tim's sober voice made us all laugh. It was okay to laugh. He obviously made it. He was here, sixteen years later, telling us about it!

He went on, "I took off down the hill and the bear's right behind me, Terry yelling, 'Get going! He's right behind you!' I was booking as fast as I could for the truck. I could hear the bear crashing behind me. It was almost like in the movies, where you're being chased and fall? Twice, I fell on the way down to the truck! I did a complete roll on both of them and I know I was on my feet in a second, running again. When I hit the road, the door on the driver's side of the truck was facing me. I looked over my shoulder and the grizzly was right behind me. I knew if I went to get in the truck on the driver's side, he'd nail me. So I ran around the front of the truck and jumped in the passenger's side. Just as I slammed the door shut, he was right off the window—could have touched him!

"I just had the door shut—I had made it—when I heard **A-KA-BOOM**—the shotgun going off, and the bear sort of weaved a little bit.

"I thought, 'Oh, no! Just when I'm safe he shoots the bear.' The bear wobbled a bit, turned and ran off down the hill. I waited for a little bit to make sure the bear was gone and I got out of the truck.

"Terry was in the back of the truck and he was laughing. I thought he had lost his marbles. The shotgun was laying out on the road but about ten feet behind the truck. What happened was when I took off running down the hill, the bear hot on my heels, Terry ran down the hill parallel to us. And the bear never even looked at him."

"He was just after you?"

"Yeah. And both times when I fell, the bear was literally over the top of me, ready to come down, and I was able to roll out and I was safe. And I guess each time Terry was in a split second of shooting the bear at that point. Why he didn't, I don't know. He should have, really. When Terry hit the road, he jumped in the back of the truck, thinking that I could drive off and be all right. When he jumped in the back of the truck, he dropped the shotgun and it went off accidentally. Then I found out it had blown a hole in the box right behind me. I came very close to being killed twice in ten seconds."

We couldn't help laughing—it was so funny.

Tim kept right on, laughing too. "When you look back on it now, it **was** bad. Terry dropped the gun and it went off and blew a hole in our wooden equipment box and the recoil kicked the gun out of the truck. That's why the gun way laying there. I was sort of shook up. My shirt was in tatters from falling. I had ripped it up. I took if off and threw it away. It was useless. And I had a couple of big cuts and scratches on my stomach.

"But anyway, we started going through the equipment box, wondering what the hell we blew apart, because we had receivers in there, bear collars and drugs in a kit. I started taking stuff out, piece by piece, looking it all over and everything was okay. It turned out the charge—we were using double ought buck—the charge went through the side of the box and right into the bottom left hand corner, where four two by fours came together. It took the full shot right there, so it didn't hurt anything. We were lucky. We went back to camp and I had a beer and tried to relax. We had more snares to check, which was fine. We did it all—caught a black bear that afternoon that looked fine.

"I've been handling bears ever since. That was the closest one."

"I would think your most exciting bear capture was the first you ever did. It would have caused you to go sky-high," Joe said.

"The first griz I ever touched was the Giefer grizzly," Tim remarked.

"Really?" We had heard so much about this famous grizzly who had even made the pages of *Readers Digest*. Dubbed by the media as the "bear of the century", we were listening to someone who had actually worked with him.

Tim continued, "I was there the day they brought him up to the North Fork. Jonkel, all those other guys, it was neat. The first grizzly I had ever handled."

"He came up the North Fork from somewhere else?" Joe asked.

"Yeah. That's a long story. He ended up being in *Boone and Crockett*, shot in the Wigwam (Canada). A man from Pennsylvania shot him."

"Which is too bad," I said.

"Yes and no. He broke into over fifty cabins up here. He was no dummy. What do you do when this guy—?" Tim's voice trailed off.

"I had heard from some that the Giefer loved soda crackers. He was always in cupboards looking for them," Joe remarked.

"Soda crackers and jello." Tim went on. "He liked jello. He broke into different cabins up Trail Creek. He could open up cupboard doors. He never ripped a cupboard door off. He was very delicate in that respect. He'd always come in through the door and there'd be one big paw print. He'd whack it a good one and it'd fly open and he'd come in and rummage around the kitchen. He'd exit out the window. He'd break the windows once he was inside. He was first caught in 1975 up in the

Middle Fork in Giefer Creek. Actually he was caught in a subdivision that was sort of started and partly owned by George Ostrom. At that time George owned the *Hungry Horse News*. A retired game warden caught the griz there at Giefer Creek and removed him to the South Fork of the Flathead. In the early summer of '76 he showed up again in Giefer Creek and hit cabins. It took a while but they caught him again. Brought him up here to the North Fork.

"It was just pure luck on our part. We met this caravan of trucks coming up with this culvert trap. We stopped to talk to them and asked if it would be okay to put a collar on him and they said fine. We had been seeing a lot of griz and Chuck said there were a lot of bears where they had planned to release him. Why don't we turn him loose in Whale Creek? It might not be so competitive for him. So we went to the head of Whale Creek instead and drugged and collared him up there.

"A lot of people thought he was a research bear and that being trapped and collared was what made him do the cabins. But that had started long before he came up here.

"The only cabin he broke into that someone was in, was Tom Reynold's. Tom turned the light on and the bear ran out. He didn't want anything to do with people."

"Just wanted their jello and crackers," Joe said. "The Giefer was smart and Tom was lucky."

Tim continued, "We were told if we had a chance to shoot it, to do it. There was one shot they thought was the Giefer but it wasn't. They took that one down to Polebridge and were showing it off. Someone else took a look at it and saw it didn't have a tag."

"Marca's cabin was broken into by him," Joe mentioned.

"Actually, that was another bear, one time when it was broken into," Tim stated. "I remembered seeing the big paw print on the door."

How stories run rampant in the North Fork and grow over the years. But maybe if I had been around then, every bear would have been the Giefer, too.

Tim continued with the Giefer. "When you go up to Marca's cabin down by Forman's, there's an old barn along there. Two of the guys I worked with spent a couple of nights up in that barn. They had bait outside and were waiting for the bear to show up and they were going to shoot it from the barn. He never showed up."

"He was a wise old bear," Joe remarked.

"Yeah," Tim answered. "He spent his days up on Thoma and then came down at night and raided cabins on Trail Creek."

I gave a deep sigh as I remembered how ten years later I had sat alone, on the Thoma Trail, with a short stick for protection while the kids tried for the top. Do bears leave their spirits behind in places they were fond of? That was rather a neat thought.

Joe brought me back to reality. "How old was he supposed to be?"

"I'm trying to remember," Tim said. "I think he was fourteen but I can't be sure. He was killed in the spring of 1977. I'm pretty sure his skull might be listed in *Crockett*. I think they estimated him to weigh 550 pounds or something on that scale."

We turned to more mundane things about grizzly. I asked Tim about Sven and Olley's day bed on Trail Creek.

One evening a neighbor and I had noticed huge piles of bear poop not a quarter of a mile into Trail Creek from the main North Fork road. The scat was part of a large circle, one edge smack along the smaller forest service road. We had been puzzled for we discovered piles and piles of it further from the road, back in the trees.

The barn near Mud Lake where many grizzlies were caught

"We refer to it as a day bed," Tim explained. "They can be used anytime as opposed to a den. You could inadvertently walk up on them."

"And they poop around the day bed?"

"Yes."

Joe said, "Like a bird's nest. They poop outside. Don't foul your own nest."

Tim continued, "Sometimes the bears use the same bed for days and days, leaving scats around."

"How deep is their sleep?" I asked.

"Bears sleep soundly but they still have their senses about them."

"How long do they sleep at a time?"

"With bears, it depends if they're around human developments or out in wilderness areas. It seems like bears that aren't around people, they aren't active at night. They'll sleep all night. About an hour after sunset until about an hour before sunrise, they're out. But in areas where they forage around people, you see a lot more nighttime activity. They rest generally during the day."

I remembered the bear Tim and Tom had been observing one time and how it disappeared right before their eyes.

Tim explained, "It was a female we hadn't collared at that point, up here in the North Fork, down by Tepee Creek. We had been doing traps, resetting snares, putting more bait out.

"Tom was working on a cubby and I looked up and saw this bear. It came up to about eighty yards, stopped, and sat down. It started to feed on berries. I told Tom to hurry up on the cubby. Then the bear got up and we went back to the truck, saw the bear as it walked right up to the trail-set behind this big larch and she disappeared behind this large tree."

Tom interrupted, "Three feet across."

Tim went on, "At least, probably more than four. It was a big tree. It walked behind the tree and never came out. Where did this bear go?" Tim gesticulated with his hands.

"All of a sudden we saw it come across this little gully. We thought it was two bears at first. It came back across, went over to the trail-set again and then—we had the lid up on the bait can in our truck. You could tell the bear could smell the bait. She started walking through these small trees and came within fifty feet of the truck. We thought, well, this is just getting too close.

"I stepped out of the truck and yelled at it. As soon as I moved, she just disappeared into thin air. We sat there and waited for over a half hour, maybe forty minutes and never saw her again. The last we saw her she was fifty feet away. When we came back the next morning, we had her caught, three or four years old, about 240 pounds or so."

"Where do you get your bait?" I asked.

"That's Tom's job."

"My vacation!" Tom laughed.

I remembered with what glee Tom had me look in the bait can one time when he was parked out back of our cabin. Knowing he was expecting me to turn up my nose at the wretched, rotten smelling, bloodied muck, I sniffed it with nonchalance.

"Not too bad, not bad at all!" I laughed. Tom explained that they collected bait as disparate as carrion from the Bison Range and road kill.

We could have talked grizzly all night, but these guys had to move on the next morning. Their trapping for this season in the North Fork was over.

You couldn't ask for a better team.

*   *   *

Surely Tom Reynolds knew about the Bobbsey twins. But he could be casually indifferent to animal sightings. I had particularly warned him about a mountain lion that he had seen a few times, hanging around his place. I feared the lion sensed his frailty. But he just shrugged it off.

Tom caught the bad flu about once a year, always in the fall. Some blamed his illness on his water supply. He had rigged together an open system that led from the spring high on the hill behind his cabin, and with a hose, brought the water closer. Leaves clogged it sometimes and small critters could easily get into it, then die and pollute the water. During the winter, he had to melt snow.

In the summer of 1992 he got sick right after the Starvation Ridge fire, feeling dizzy and short of breath. When he appeared at the border with Becky during one of her mail days, he looked ghastly.

Ron had thought he was going into congestive heart failure. I didn't believe him.

"I had exactly the same symptoms before I went in to have my arteries reamed," Ron had explained, "dizzy, short of breath," but then he laughed broadly, "and felt like a million dollars when they were through!"

I had dismissed his comments. Tom would live to be a hundred.

Becky brought him up to the border for his last lunch of this season. He looked wonderful, his old self, quite agile and happy, and ate the lasagna right up. We had a wonderful time.

"How do you like my coffee, Tom?" Joe asked.

"Lousy," Tom said, laughing. He never had thought much of Joe's coffee.

"Joan made this," Joe commented.

"It's wonderful coffee," Tom laughed as we all roared.

Tom was under the weather in November, and we blamed his water supply. Becky observed him closely each time he came down his hill for the mail. I sent him up potato soup, which he loved, about three times. And when he snapped out of it, we thought maybe he wasn't eating enough, even though Don and Sue had left him enough food for the winter to feed an army. We made plans to send him up some home cooking throughout the winter, to keep his appetite in good shape. Becky would take it up on her mail route days each Tuesday and Friday.

It was time to winterize our cabin and go to the valley. Down there we'd leave his soup and other goodies on the front seat of Becky's truck as she was inside the post office sorting mail on her North Fork mail days. She'd then deliver them to Tom. When Tom began to look poorly again, Becky told him not to make the trip down to his mail box. She would walk or snowshoe in and take him his mail, supplies and whatever else he needed. She could check and see how he was at the same time.

I used to be scared to death over the years that Tom would fall on his steep hill and not be able to get up. We all wanted him to have his wish, to live out the remainder of his days in his own cabin. Of course, we all worried about him.

Sue called us from Illinois one Saturday in mid-December. She was sending Tom a feather bed. It was arranged that John from the hostel in Polebridge would take it up to Tom after UPS delivery, since he was the closest and had a snowmobile.

I called Roz and Tom, old friends of Tom, who lived deep in the woods off Whale Creek. Their radio phone was a godsend in such a situation. I explained how Sue was worried about the new wood stove they had gotten Tom during the summer. Maybe he wasn't using it properly even through they had checked him out with it over and over.

Roz and Tom snowshoed up to Tom's cabin to check. The old gentleman's cabin was chilly so the couple built up a good wood fire, and spent that Sunday afternoon visiting with Tom. He seemed to be doing fine, even though he had a slight head cold.

Becky snowshoed up Tom's hill that next Tuesday, bringing him his Christmas cards, packages and even vitamins.

The instant she entered his cabin she felt the cold. When she opened the inner door all she heard was his labored breathing. Tom was in his back room, in bed, half sitting up, watching his clock.

It was obvious he had been waiting for her. She held him in her arms as he tried and tried to tell her something. But she couldn't understand him.

Becky and Tom

Then Tom died.

He had hung on to his thread of life until his dear Becky had arrived. Becky sat with him, grief-stricken, then got his Bible and read a psalm.

It was so wonderful and fitting that Tom died in his own bed, being held by Becky, his truest friend for all those many years. She knew how he wanted to die, and he had his wish because of her.

A neighbor south of Polebridge came up Tom's hill fifteen minutes later, on his snowmobile, so Becky was saved the practical decisions of how to notify the authorities and get Tom's body down off his hill. Taken by sled, then by vehicle, Tom went down the North Fork road for the last time.

CHAPTER 17

All twelve grizzly bears that were radiocollared in the U.S. portion of the North Fork drainage, plus one female griz collared in Canada by Canadian researchers in 1993, were located in their dens in the U.S. during a January overflight. Sven and Olley had denned together, safe for the winter.

We took for granted the 1994 season would be as great as the previous year.

Joan ran around, very active, between the park, where she mated with Olley and lost her collar. Recollared, she and Olley hung around Trail Creek and points north.

Lydia was seen off and on, the best sighting near the cabin of Mary Louise and John. Roz drove up to our cabin around 2 p.m. one day to report that Grace, a three year old sub-adult, was out back somewhere. Her signal was steady and slow, a sign she was asleep. I pictured her back in there, during the heat of the day, comfortable within the shade of the forest.

The research took a sad turn when signals from Sylvia's radio collar led biologists to her body. A three year old sub-adult, she was discovered dead on a road near Coal Creek, around a bend and out of sight from the main North Fork road. When initially collared, the biologists discovered the grizzly had a genetic defect. Three of the claws had sort of fused together on the front left paw. Claws are usually attached to bone, but the bone was missing in her deformed paw.

Her body was taken straight to Bozeman for examination and X-ray. Her stomach was full of cow parsnip. She was covered with tooth marks. She had a noticeable hole in the middle of the front of her head that resembled a bullet hole, but the necropsy showed it had been made by a tooth. (When a tooth or bite goes down and in, and then retracts, it takes bone up with it.)

Sylvia had been whacked about so fiercely, apparently by a larger grizzly, that she had suffered broken ribs and back, and been chewed on the left forearm. Her deformed claws were missing. She was not lactating and probably had no cub. Severely mauled, she only weighed 200 pounds.

Bears have no territory but larger grizzlies may not be tolerant of other bears in their area. Evidence at the scene indicated Sylvia had been attacked in another area, then traveled some distance before she died.

The season worsened. The levels of mortality grew.

It was especially heartbreaking to learn of the death of one of the twins in Canada up along Sage Creek. The bear had given an inactive signal and the overflight revealed his bloody body lying there. The Canadian game warden was there at the scene in less than two hours, a remarkable feat considering the distances involved.

The twin had been on a gut pile of a deer, and had pulled underbrush and duff on it from all around, burying his prize. There was a camouflaged hunter's cap in the gut pile, with silver hair in it. From that point the stories vary.

One reported two men drove up, one with silver hair, probably to take away the carcass, or skin it. Other hunters in the area knew of "silver hair" and said he had killed grizzlies before. We heard the culprit had gotten away with the shooting, then later heard that he had been caught and fined.

The twin was nevertheless dead. He had done nothing wrong. The hunter apparently claimed self-defense, the usual ploy. Who can speak for the animals, especially a dead one? The twin had ranged on both sides of the border and the park. He had never shown signs of aggression toward humans during all those months of '93 and '94. A good bear, he was in a remote area, on a gut pile, doing his own normal thing.

But a human had found him and killed him.

By January of 1995, as many as eight grizzly bears, maybe even more, were lost in the North Fork drainage in that single season of '94, including six of the fourteen bears that were being tracked. The twin was not counted, since he had been illegally killed in Canada.

Ninko was the name of the bear whose collar was discovered ten miles up Hay Creek. It looked like the collar had just been tossed off the bridge into the creek. There was no trace of the bear. The Wedge brothers simply had vanished.

Informants had related reports of two other illegal kills of uncollared grizzly bears in the North Fork area, all by hunters. No trace of the bears was found. The losses were shocking to everyone. No grizzly had raided homes or barns. They were just killed.

Poaching is alive and well. As far as I was concerned, human interaction with the bears did nothing but kill them. Consider this: no one would have known of the level of mortality except for the radiocollars. Who knows how many grizzlies have been poached in the North Fork over the years?

∗   ∗   ∗

Tom had been cremated immediately after his death and his ashes kept in the mortuary in town. Don and Sue planned his service all winter, figuring the best time would be during the following mid-summer so everyone that wanted to attend, could.

His ashes had been placed in a small golden urn. We gathered for the memorial on the North Fork road, down at the bottom of his lane.

There must have been over fifty people who made the steep climb behind the kilted bagpiper who had come all the way from Fernie in British Columbia.

Don carried Tom's ashes as he followed behind the piper, going the same way Tom had hiked all those years. We followed silently. Tom was placed in a small grave in a particularly beautiful spot in his side yard. The sound of the bagpiper was hauntingly beautiful. As is the custom up there, people stepped forth to talk about Tom and what he had meant to them personally.

Wendy, whose husband, John, had been so close to Tom all the years he had been customs inspector, led off. She said such neat great things that it made it easier for everyone else to follow.

I wasn't sure if I should, or could speak.

"Tom was at our place for dinner one evening last year. We had Uncle Bob and Marca, too. Marca, a cute young blonde, had been sitting close to Tom all evening, concentrating mightily on his story of Madam Queen, since she now owned the Madam's cabin.

"Suddenly, Marca asked, 'How old are you, Tom?'

"Very seriously, the old gentleman replied, 'I'm sixty-five.'"

That was my favorite "Tom Reynolds" story and it made me feel better as I told it to the group.

More spoke. We all stood there, feeling the serenity and beauty of the place as an afternoon sun filtered through the trees. What a fitting spot for dear old Tom to be laid to rest. Suddenly, a single, long, strong gust of wind swept through the surrounding trees.

Everyone spoke their thoughts aloud as one.

"It's Tom saying good by to us."

With Tom's death, the heart went out of the North Fork as far as I was concerned.

We had over six hours of videos of Tom, being himself, as he recounted stories of his life in the North Fork, a firsthand account of the "good old days", including murder, arson and poaching. We gave a copy to the Montana Historical Society. What a great way for this grand old gentleman to be remembered.

Diane, meanwhile, had decided to go for her Ph.D. in genetics, dispersal, and habitat selection of colonizing wolves in the Central Rockies. A marvelous decision, for who knew more about wolves than Diane? She had been working on the Wolf Ecology Project since April, 1979.

The DNA of the wolf shot just outside of Yellowstone in autumn, 1992, was very similar to the DNA of wolves born in Glacier National Park, suggesting the Yellowstone wolf had naturally dispersed from the park area. An important point. Naturally dispersing wolves would have the protection of the Endangered Species Act. As it stands now, the Yellowstone wolves are deemed nonessential experimental, and can be killed under certain circumstances.

At one of the evening gatherings Diane and Wendy had for a group of their students, Diane laughed when I mentioned, with sincerity, that she could be considered the mother of all wolves. She knew she had been called a lot of other things by wolf haters.

The campfire burned low. We seemed to be the only ones in the world as the sun disappeared behind the hills. The cold swept in. Only some forest and a steep embankment separated us from the rush of Trail Creek. Together with the sound of the water, a wolf howl or two would have been ideal. But we really didn't need to hear the wolves. Their presence was thick in the informal interaction going on between Diane, Wendy, and the dozen or so students that had come for these classes from all over the U.S., young people who would go back home, forever changed by their learning experiences in the North Fork, taking with them and spreading the truth about wolves, that they are predictable and afraid of humans, even timid.

The darkness of night made the surroundings even more wild as the discussion continued: how the popularization of hybrid wolves gave the pure wolf a bad reputation. Hybrids were the "in" thing to own and were increasingly in the news because of their volatile nature. It was bad enough that some people still carried around in them the beliefs set forth from the folklore of old, but any misunderstandings caused by the hybrids were perhaps worse.

Wolves that get by and disperse on their own are shy and smart, traits that need to be passed on to their pups. They can't be tamed. This needs to be thoroughly understood. Always, objectivity in research was stressed by Diane and Wendy to the students. Researchers can't cross the line to advocacy. They can't lose their credibility.

I wanted to be an advocate for all wildlife. I wished everyone had access, not only to the information being passed around the campfire, but to the feeling of being one with the wild, as close to nature as we who were gathered there were, to be understanding about the plight of the wild creatures, their needs and importance to humans.

Then suddenly, the routines of everyone on the North Fork were totally disrupted by one of the most dreaded events in a forest environment, fire.

A wild, deep front passed overhead without a lick of moisture during one of the driest, hottest summers we had ever experienced in the North Fork.

Unbelievably low, massive, swirling black clouds, interlaced with intense lightning, seemed to originate just before they swarmed over the mountains behind us one night, gained in electrical activity, and gathered strength, rampaging over onto Starvation Ridge, rumbling through in such a wide swath the blinding lightning lit up the entire front range.

The space between King Edward, Starvation Peak and other peaks to the north in Canada, became explosive bright lightning strike alleys. Later, we learned at least 651 lightning strikes had been recorded on forest service land that night. The sneaky fire bided its time, lurking in the tinder-dry trees until it exploded the late afternoon of August 14, 1994, shooting a thick cloud of gray/white smoke boiling instantly into the sky, blotting out everything.

At the time Wendy and Marca had been out checking coyote traps, and seeing the smoke, high-tailed it up our lane while Joe was still at the border. Talk about breaking news! Over Wendy's radio we could hear Joe talking to Scott, who would send someone up to Moose City.

Joe had spotted another fire northwest of the main one, a smaller smoke. Wendy and Marca sped off in their government truck. Marca, so concerned that I had no vehicle, drove her Honda back and left it for me in case I needed to get out. I gathered important papers in preparation for a quick evacuation.

The next morning, the smoke pall from the fire extended clear to the north as far as I could see. Wendy raced up our lane, describing how a tremendously heavy wind, accompanied by rain, had blown through Moose City about one in the morning, truly scaring her. Canadian planes, scooping water from Kintla Lake, had already been over the fire with their drops that morning. It was the beginning of a long, depressing, hot, smoke-filled summer and fall.

Canada helped fight the Starvation Creek fire, burning just north of Kintla Lake, from the very beginning. They had the heavy equipment and wanted to prevent it from spreading north of the border into Canada. Over 150 fire fighters battled hard to keep the flames from destroying the historic Kishenehn patrol cabin near the Canadian boundary.

Both Canada and the U.S. were given full twenty-four hour access back and forth across the border. When the two inspectors asked their supervisors for guidance, their instructions were to "open the gate wide!" An agreement had been reached between the two countries a few years before on mutual aid in fighting forest fires. No one wanted the fire to go anywhere.

So when the Canadian and Glacier Park fire officials were briefing Bill and Joe about what all had to be taken across the border, and when, or hauled back and forth, both inspectors nodded yes over and over, or "fine, that's fine. No problem." Then a Glacier official said a large truck full of explosives would be going up.

Bill's facial expression changed to a frown and he paused a minute, before he said, "Fine. Go ahead."

Later he admitted to Joe how worried he was. "What if that thing would blow under my canopy?"

The Canadians had a large valuable commercial tract of trees they were trying to save, so an all-out effort was made. A three mile fire break was bulldozed along the cutline on the Canadian side with large fuel drums spaced along it, filled, connected, and then the 9,100 pounds of explosives necessary for the backfire were added. It blew sky high, sending a column of smoke at least 25,000 feet into the air, clearly visible down in the valley. Only the fire fighters who set it off, saw and heard the tremendous successful explosion that blazed over 600 acres for the backfire.

Scott, the North Fork park ranger, and another fire fighter stopped at Arlene's on the way south, after the explosives had been set off. They had stayed around to observe the aftermath.

Hot, dirty and exhausted, in full fire fighting regalia, Scott had seen our parked vehicles and came in to bring us up-to-date on the fire. His big grin showed through the grime, for he had walked into a reunion of the bear study kids. Irene had set it up, then almost hadn't been allowed through the roads in British Columbia because of the proximity of the fire. Wendy Clark, Kyran, Bruce, even Chris, who had driven clear across from eastern Montana—the room was packed with people and good food.

Scott was in the middle of a piece of cherry pie, probably the first food he'd had all day, when his radio sounded off. He had to leave. A bunch of drunks were trashing Bowman campground.

*   *   *

Knowledge conquers fear. Thus, during the fires, the agencies kept the North Fork residents up-to-date on their every plan and action by bulletins and meetings.

The Interagency Team and a member of the Incident Command Team from Idaho were present for one such fire meeting, hosted by the park, down at the fire cache at the ranger station near Polebridge. They explained the entire scenario before opening the meeting to questions from the audience. Invaluable information was being gathered from the prescribed natural fire being allowed to burn further south in the park. Named the Howling Fire because wolves were heard howling when the fire first started, it was being studied and used as a model for the nation since it was one of the few fires let burn since the '88 Yellowstone fire.

A gutsy decision but backed by science. Fire is a natural part of any ecosystem, necessary to maintain biodiversity. Prescribed fires had been ignited up the North Fork for two autumns. The Howling Fire, naturally started by lightning earlier in the summer, let burn, would mimic natural fires that had been suppressed over the past fifty years. This area of the park, more wet, became an outdoor natural laboratory. Information gathered from it would help develop a national fire prediction model.

The team dispelled my concerns. They knew what they were doing as they brought us up-to-date on everything we needed to know about wildfires. Fuel type counts. Old stands of lodgepoles open the surface fuels to the wind. Dry surface fuels, dead and down, are ready to burn. Surface fires throw out embers, some to die out in the greenstory, others to catch. Fires "candle-out" on trees. A running fire can hit into things, "bumping", sometimes reaching 3000 degrees in temperature in the front.

A fire has been described by fighters, "like a freight train coming at you", with an incredible noise, a snapping, popping, and roar of a fire being driven by winds.

Typically, they fight fourteen hours a day, coping with exhaustion, dehydration, smoke, and dead trees that have dropped to the forest floor. I remembered how dangerous standing trees could be. During the Red Bench Fire one fire fighter from Idaho was killed when a tree fell into a group of five fire fighters standing by a truck on Red Meadow road. Spruce have no tap root and topple over easily after burning out near their base. This one had given no sign of its lethal condition.

It was mind boggling to hear how fire specialists checked the humidity of the trees each morning, measuring, analyzing, figuring the path the Howling Fire would probably take. As these specialists said, pay now or pay later. And it was cleaning out beetle-killed trees in the park that had been a fire threat for years. I felt proud. We were in excellent hands with these Interagency fire fighters.

They knew the risks. The member of the Incident Command Team from Idaho had a friend killed in the firestorm on King Mountain, Colorado, that very July. He described how, from that tragedy that snuffed out the lives of fourteen fire fighters, new guidelines were already being developed, reevaluating the fighter's safety gear among other things.

The individual emergency fire shelters, made of aluminum foil and fiberglass, would incorporate heavier flooring so they wouldn't blow away. They were investigating light-weight breathing devices—all this passed on to us with a quiet intelligence in a "can do" atmosphere.

Thus it was like a bucket of cold water in our faces when a North Fork landowner, known for his nasty disposition and mouth, stood to rant and rave, complaining about the prescribed Howling Fire.

His stance? "Why were they allowing good timber to burn in the national park when loggers weren't allowed to cut it?"

I felt shamed.

*   *   *

The question and answer session after the meeting, touched on fire retardant, a favorite subject of mine since third daughter had, unbeknownst to me, fought fires in Colorado one summer while working as a volunteer with the forest service. She had described it as red snot, heavy and capable of knocking a person down. Used to pre-treat an area, it has been described by the fire specialists as mud-like, a heavy cream, or slick-snot, slowing the fire down.

A slurry plane, usually a C-130, can hold 2000-3000 gallons of the stuff which contains a fertilizer, dimonium sulfate, iron oxide for color, and a thickening gum that makes the glop twice as dense as molasses. Then it's mixed with quantities of water and pumped into the plane tanks. It is easily visible from the ground, and exciting to watch being dumped from the air.

Why do fire fighters do such a horrid, dangerous job? Certainly not the pay, although a steady working fire fighter can make about $10,000 over a long, busy season. Some have said it's the excitement and comradery. The work attracts many college students.

Then there was Scott, who did it because it was part of his job, which he loved. Using his previous position, a U.S. customs special agent, to get a foot in the door, he was the ideal park ranger. We all knew how lucky we were to have him in the North Fork.

*　　　　*　　　　*

The successful backfire along the border's cutline and well-planned fire fighting tactics successfully steered the Starvation Creek fire to run in a northeast direction. It threatened nothing but high country that was in sore need of an ecological burn.

It was a maddening late summer and fall, the same thing day after day. Smoke, over the mountains and Starvation Ridge, against the rise of the deep red sun, gradually infiltrated west, in our direction, until by midmorning I was unable to see the road or even our gate.

The smoke would grow thicker until about three in the afternoon when the wind changed and came from the west. The stiff winds fanned the fire but blew the smoke on our side away, hiding the fire until dark when the red was visible again, like a huge banked furnace, all ready to grow the next day after a sleeping night. The red eyes glared over at us each night, mean looking devils. The next morning the cycle started all over again, as the flames on our end worked eastward toward Kintla.

Never had I paid so close attention to the direction of the winds, as shown by our flag. I was lucky enough to be facing the mountains during a fairly clear day when a huge pillar of smoke rose high into the sky, filling the entire space between King Edward and Starvation Peak in Canada, as the slowly creeping flames reached a new source of fuel along the Kishenehn Ridge. What a legacy we had presented to Canada.

During the nights, it was as if strings of Christmas tree lights had been strung out over the flanks of the two mountains as the fire burned upward, into a dead end. Watching and timing how long and which way the fires crept on became a nightly event. The fire burned in Canada, then crossed back over the lower ramparts of Boundary Mountain, and on and on. Spectacular, mesmerizing, yet awful.

At night the brilliant deep-set stars seemed somehow incongruous with the fire spread out under them, a strange juxtaposition of cold night sky and the gaping wound of fire. Torching trees added to the stark beauty.

But it got to me. I remember sitting on the front concrete steps of the Canadian quarters one afternoon watching two yellow utility trucks head down to the U.S. from Canada, back-ends piled high with gray fire hose, fire fighters dead tired, faces drawn with exhaustion, yet able to smile and wave as they passed.

Starvation Creek fire as seen from our yard

It was cloudy. A few sprinkles of rain struck my upturned face. Oh, God. Please let it truly rain, I prayed. But it was only the wet of my tears that ran down my cheeks. The bit of rain had evaporated in the dry air.

The fire may have been controlled, but the smoke continued. No rain, and a ninety-five degree temperature made the fire danger extremely high in the Flathead.

Smoke from the 54,000 acre fire in Washington poured over us and into the valley, adding to the misery. The forest service had three rangers on duty, checking the roads and trails for campfires. They found more than they should have, for as one ranger, who stopped to talk to us at our mailbox said, there was always that small percentage of nitwits that had to have a campfire for the effect, even though it was ninety-five degrees out and the forest, a tinderbox.

The fire managers had hoped for the "August Singularity" which typically arrives between August 22 and September 10, bringing precipitation, cooler temperatures, and sometimes wind. It was capable of ending the fire season or extending it.

But it never came through that summer.

The Starvation Creek fire burned 4,834 acres, including 880 in Canada. The 1994 fire season, a long, drawn out affair, ended by snow, could be considered a success. Some fires were squashed, others grew and burned within the allotted natural boundaries.

As the saying goes, the government pours dollars on a forest fire, mother nature puts it out.

Right smack in the middle of all the turmoil surrounding the fire fighting, the Canadian fire camp suddenly ran out of toilet paper. Lucky them. Arlene just happened to have enough at her bar/restaurant compound to carry them over.

*   *   *

With no special destination in mind, Brig and I headed north along the road, savoring the peace and quiet that had returned after the exodus of summer traffic. We turned into the gated two track lane that passed through thick trees, then more open spaces before it reached the Y by Mud Lake.

It was one of our favorite walks because of all the evidence wildlife usually left behind. Today there was nothing much. So far, no scat, no prints left within the old tire ruts that held the rain.

This day I felt an absence of the wildlife. Sadness crept over me. This area would be nothing but scenery if the animals disappeared. They were the true inhabitants, the dispensers of the almost spiritual feeling that was an innate part of the wild. Humans, including myself, were the intruders.

I continued on down the lane, really dispirited, fearing most of the bears, wolves, mountain lions and coyotes had fled this area because of all the human activity.

Smoke from the Starvation Creek fire still hovered over points in the park. Only a heavy snow would truly extinguish the hot spots. The layer of cold in the breeze promised that would be soon.

About a half mile into the lane, I thought I heard something. We stood quietly, listening.

A wolf called, far off to the right, near the river.

I stood there, absorbing the sound. The wolf howled twice more. Brig nervously peered into the trees.

Oh, what a temptation! The desire to howl back had grabbed me other times, but there had always been someone around. Even now I had to overcome my feelings of embarrassment.

Dolt. No one was around. No one would know but Brig. He already knew all my secrets. I cupped my hands around my mouth and gave a howl somewhat weak, not nearly loud enough.

I heard the wolf again.

Now I gave a mighty howl, clear and high. What a feeling! I was a partner with the wolf. He howled two more times.

I howled back again, then again. Had that last howl from the wolf been a little closer? This area was known to be one of their favorite haunts.

The wolf howled one more time. So did I. Then silence.

I was really wound up. After all these thirteen years of being up here, seeing wolves, hearing them, talking about them, defending them, I had finally spoken to one.

Exhilarated, I walked on, my depression totally lifted.

Dry hard earth broke the long deep ruts ahead into two wet sections.

I checked the sides by the underbrush. There it was, a faint but discernable grizzly print. Fresh. Made some time after the rain two days ago. Two large piles of pretty recent bear scat were scattered further along the lane.

As I transferred the bear spray from my jeans into a shirt pocket, Brig caught my excitement and held himself at attention, looking ahead. I talked loudly to him, keeping a tight hold on his leash as I tried to clap my hands, then whistled *Greensleeves* as always, to let the bears know we were around.

We continued on to the Y. The weathered wreck of the small barn stood to the side. It was special now that I knew many of the grizzly had been trapped and collared right here the early spring, summer and fall of '93.

I poked my head inside, eyes gradually adjusting to the gloom. The partially collapsed sections of lower stalls stood out a lighter gray from the dark interior. I could imagine how the bear guys must have felt as they stayed inside, awaiting the grizzly.

We turned to return the way we had come. I just had to see the bear print again. Not five minutes later, the loon from Mud Lake flew over, low, filling the air with its resounding hauntingly strange cry. I took a deep breath, trying to inhale the sound of it, to remember it forever. To be at this place, this day, this instant—to see, hear, smell and remember all of this.

I found the print again, but had to turn to face the same way as going in, to catch the light on it so it could be seen more clearly.

I stood there studying it, trying to judge the size of the bear from its track. Tim, Tom, Harry or Chris could have. Not me.

When I turned to guide Brig along the edging so he wouldn't destroy the print, a small gray bird with a flash of white tore by my right ear like a bullet. And right on its tail feathers was an immature red-tailed hawk.

The bird, with a flurry of noise sped into the safety of the trees. The hawk swerved to barely miss me, wheeled away and passed back close over my head.

My cup runneth over.

CHAPTER 18

We really needed a special social event after the turmoil of the smoke-filled summer and early fall. Diane and Wendy planned well. I was on the inside, looking out through the old torn screen and shadowed window of Madge Cooper's rustic cabin, now crowded with the guests Wendy and Diane had invited over for one of Ralph's Cajun dinners.

Never inside a Moose City cabin before, the history inherent in this venerable dwelling was accentuated by the monstrous, shiny, metal antique wood cook stove that separated the small back kitchen from the front living/dining area. A narrow staircase along the back kitchen wall led to the second floor sleeping quarters.

Ralph had cooked his specialty on a small propane camp stove set on top of the old-fashioned one, a sort of incongruous sight.

Wendy was going to live in the Cooper cabin during the coming winter and the next few years while tracking her collared coyotes. Ralph, her husband of just a few months, would be leaving within the week. The conversation turned to the strange individuals who had, somehow or other, found the North Fork road: the lone suspicious looking transient with no pack, who we had seen walking north on the road at eleven o'clock the previous night, the misfits that turned up at the border that Bill and Joe described with utter candor. Diane repeated she was never afraid of the animals when she was alone in the wilds, just the humans.

The "doll man" was one I'd never want to run into. We'd heard bits and pieces about him over the years from the study kids as they'd mention him in an off-hand way in the midst of other stories. The fact that he spiked dolls' heads to the trees that surrounded his camp deep in the wilds was enough for me. Thank God he was way up in Canada.

We didn't want Ralph to get even more nervous about leaving Wendy so Diane came to the rescue. She'd describe the most extraordinary adventures in a matter-of-fact, even self-deprecating manner which added to the fun.

Now she related how she and a student assistant were out in the wilds of British Columbia, in the Wigwam, where a lot of her wolf study trapping had taken place. The jaws of a wolf trap are offset so they don't fully close, but in this case, the trapped wolf had some blood on its paw. Diane and her helper immediately went to work, tranquilizing the animal with a jab stick, collaring it, then checking its temperature, weight, fixing its hurts, and on through the regular biological routine.

The two were involved with their tranquilized animal, when a rather large grizzly bear appeared on the scene, attracted by the blood scent on the wolf's paw.

The action that followed was wild. The grizzly was after the unconscious wolf. Diane made lots of noise, hollering, shouting, trying to scare off the griz while her student ran for the jeep to get all of them out of harm's way, including the poor wolf who was a helpless choice morsel for the bear because of them.

The student couldn't get the jeep to start.

He tried and tried, all the while Diane was running around, trying to keep the bear away. The bear advanced even closer.

In desperation, she began to half drag, half carry the immobile wolf toward the jeep. Finally, the jeep started and the student wheeled over to Diane, who managed to manhandle the wolf, a dead weight, into the front seat. They took off fast in their escape, the wolf in Diane's arms, its head and upper body sticking out past Diane into the back seat. Diane's

big old love of a gangly dog, Max, was in the back and didn't particularly like the idea of the wolf being in such proximity, especially after it
snapped at him.

They drove far enough away for the wolf to be safe, laid it in the
shade of a tree, in a peaceful spot, and watched the animal finish coming out of his stupor, then walk away.

Just an ordinary occurrence for Diane.

Someone lit the candles in the cabin, casting spooky shadows.

"Madge Cooper was found dead right here in her cabin," Diane mentioned casually. "In the kitchen. With a piece of wood in her hands to
feed the fire. Natural causes. She was in her seventies."

Diane had always had peaceful, uneventful stays while she lived there
but when one of her male graduate students had tried to live in Madge's
cabin for a while, he abruptly left—couldn't stay in it with all the weird
events and things that went bump in the night.

Marilyn's ghost story soon followed, related by Bill.

Marilyn, a grade school teacher in Cranbrook, British Columbia, had
been out to the Flathead to visit her husband, Ron, during one of his
scheduled tours of duty on the Canadian custom's side. Very matter-of-
fact and not prone to an overactive imagination, she was in the quarters
living room one night, on the couch reading. Ron had already gone to bed.

She looked up and in the hall that led back to the bedrooms saw the
glow of a cigarette and the outline of a man. When Marilyn got up, the
man turned and walked to the other end of the hall, past the bedrooms
and laundry room, to the outside door that opened to the garage. He
disappeared as he walked through the closed door.

Marilyn woke up Ron, who said she was seeing things. She eventually
told Arlene who wasn't supposed to tell anyone of the incident. But, of
course, she did. After that, strange noises were not taken for granted any
more, especially after one Canadian customs relief, during his stay in
the quarters, woke up suddenly as he was being pressed down on the
bed by something that could not be seen.

It was true there had been some unnatural and violent deaths in the area. The unidentified transient had wondered down into the Flathead and eventually was found in an abandoned cabin, starved to death. Years before, a park ranger shot himself at the Kishenehn Patrol station, perhaps a victim of the remoteness of his assignment.

The Canadians seemed to think the ghost in the Canadian quarters was the Canadian customs inspector who killed himself long ago when the station was located on the opposite side of the river, before the bridge was accidentally blown up. His body was brought back through the States. Maybe he didn't approve.

Most around the table that night, after all the convincing stories, were of the opinion that some might be more receptive to "hauntings" than others.

It's easy to half believe in spirits and spooks when you leave a festive gathering and go driving out into the totality of blackness that can be the North Fork road on a moonless night. It's like sitting in a black box with the only light in the world coming from the vehicle's headlights and green glow from the dash.

Joe was too slow opening up our cabin on our return. I dashed in utter darkness across the corral and bridge to the outhouse, snatched open the door and—instantly visualized the slumped-over ghastly effigy of a tramp that had been propped up inside an old outhouse in one of those damn wild west tourist towns.

My heart thumped out of my chest. Why was I stupid enough to think the "doll man" couldn't travel?

*   *   *

Trapping and collaring wildlife is certainly not mundane work. But mom nature can make the process harder to deal with.

Diane, Wendy, and Caitlin, an assistant, checked one of the wolf traps early the next spring, on a wet, cold morning. The trap was located ¾ of a mile beyond the forest service gate at Tepee Lake. The bushes by the trap were shaking so they knew they had one, and went back to their truck, parked at the gate, for their work kit.

They had captured a thin two year old black female wolf. Working in the pouring rain, they tranquilized, collared, and weighed her, checked her mouth (she had a broken tooth), and verified her general physical well-being.

The wolf's temperature started to go down, down, ever further down. The women became quite concerned. They placed Max's old army blanket under the wolf, but her temperature continued to spiral downward. She was becoming hypothermic. They could conceivably have lost her.

Catlin hurried back to the truck to start the engine, heater and fan, to warm up the vehicle. Wendy and Diane wrapped the wolf in the blanket. Diane took the front end, Wendy the rear. Still in the pouring rain, the two carried the wolf the ¾ of a mile back to the truck. The wolf had weighed in at eighty-two pounds, so they were forced to stop at times to rest and catch their breath.

Finally making it back to the truck, they were able to lift the wolf onto the truck seat. Then they used a tape measure to wrap around its muzzle, but they did not tie it.

The wolf was still way too cold, and not receiving enough warmth from the truck's cold seat. So Diane and Wendy climbed into the truck and held the wolf across their laps.

The wolf's temperature remained too low.

The human procedure for hypothermia is warm, bare skin against cold skin. So the two removed their shirts and hugged and cuddled the animal, giving it their body heat.

Good results. The wolf gave a long sigh. When they turned the heater off, they heard another sound—the wolf growled. When Wendy took its temperature again, the animal passed gas. The wolf was warming up and coming out of it, then shook the tape off her muzzle.

Wendy got out of the truck. Diane was still wrapped around the wolf. She and the wolf flailed around and both fell out of the truck together.

The woozy wolf stood up, very wobbly, stood still a bit, then staggered off, looking back at them with her icy wolf eyes, like "what's been going on here?"

The wolf was okay. They had collared her as soon as they had anesthetized her, so everything had been accomplished that should have been.

Both women ached all over the next day from carrying the wolf down to the truck. When Diane washed her clothes, her bra had black wolf hair in it.

The wolf hadn't been in the trap very long before they found her, so they figured she may have had an adverse reaction to the drug, just as some humans have reactions.

All three took such good care—just as a mom would. Diane told of this event one night after showing us slides from her Romanian trip of the previous year. She was at her best, hilarious gestures, expressions, and all. We had tears rolling down our cheeks by the time she finished.

You can hug a tree, you can even hug a bear, but not everyone can cuddle a real live wild wolf.

It's also a small world.

During her six weeks stay in Romania, Diane had worked hard, at their invitation, to educate them in the trapping of wolves.

Sheep wandered everywhere. Not only did the herders take her traps, but she caught more sheep-herding dogs than wolves. Diane did succeed in trapping the first wolf ever caught in that country.

Guess who popped up out in the middle of nowhere to visit her while in Romania?

George, the Greek.

*   *   *

It continued to be a cold, wet spring. Canadian weather forecasts were so detailed and accurate I never bothered with U.S. reports. Unsettled weather over Medicine Hat, Lethbridge, Calgary, or in the foot hills, always meant rain for us.

Thus, the one I heard early one morning over CBC radio gave me pause. Torrential, steady, unrelenting rain was the gist of it. A feeling of dread came over me at the somber tone of the forecast. We were apparently in for it.

The heavy pounding downpour started two days later, a Tuesday morning, briefly changed to wet snow, then back to rain. We drove down to Kalispell, as planned, for our son, Joe and his family, had seen nothing but rain over their few vacation days. At least we could take them to a choice Charles Russell western art gallery.

The North Fork of the Flathead River was the highest we had ever seen it, ever. When we started back up north in late afternoon, leafed trees were bent completely over, touching the road, giving it a tunnel effect. Many had split or were downed. Apparently a very heavy wet snow had hit the entire lower area, then melted. Further north, we drove through a mile or so of a couple of inches of snow that eventually petered out.

Crazy weather for early June, even up here.

The heavy, incessant rain continued to pour with relentless force on into Tuesday night. Listening to the furious drumming on the roof was more than just worrisome. This was no ordinary rain.

The ground squished underfoot the next morning, totally saturated. Our new outhouse had filled with water. Dirt and rocks had been pushed up against the back of it with such force it had half caved in.

Mike, a neighbor to the south of Trail Creek sped up our drive. A bedrock of common sense, his dark and gloomy countenance scared me. I thought someone had died.

He recommended that Joe go to the border immediately. The river had flooded over to the customs station and Bill sounded like he wanted Joe to see what had happened.

Joe returned about an hour later to take us up so we could see the havoc for ourselves. It was the only way to comprehend the magnitude of the devastation. Over eleven inches of rain had fallen to the north in Canada and it all rampaged down into the Flathead River. The swiftness, force, and power of the water as it burst out of its normal channel could not be grasped immediately. It hit the gut and mind in a shock wave of disbelief. In reaction, we were quiet with awe in the presence of the natural disaster.

A stretch of flowing water, at least a city block wide, with a rapid, strong current through the center churned across the road between us and the two ports. The customs' buildings stood isolated, surrounded by the flood waters.

The entire area was a moving lake flowing relentlessly over to the river.

We made our way slowly beyond the trees and out into Moose City and the cabins.

The river's high water edge on the park side was way up into the trees. On this Moose City side, the water ate away at the black dirt of what now constituted the west bank. The rush of water quickly undermined the edges. Every so often, huge chunks of earth flomped into the water. Some of the Moose City cabins and outbuildings had already gone into the river. Heartsick, we learned one of the first had been Madge Cooper's old place.

No wonder Mike had looked so shaken when he had come to give the flood message to Joe that morning. He and Kyran had been inside the Cooper cabin during its last minutes, in a futile attempt to rescue some of Wendy's belongings as it shook and trembled, increasingly unsteady before it took its final slide into the river.

The surviving cabins stood forlorn, as if waiting their turn to be destroyed by the wide, angry river heading inexorably south on its rampage.

I took steps backward, further into the meadow as a large chunk of field dropped in. A dangerous place to walk because of the rapid, random undercutting.

Huge mature fir trees coursed down from Canada, swept past us, crowns first, pointed projectiles shooting full force down river, their tangled mass of roots thrusting out of the swirling water.

Large hunks of timber passed by. It took a few seconds to identify them as the partial remains of the blown-up Canadian bridge north of the ports.

A smaller log cabin tilted end first and slid into the water, sank a bit, up-surged, then floated directly toward us. As it came down river, the light from behind shone through the top windows, the shifting shadows inside resembling an imaginary rider. I wondered what it would be like to be inside it, on its journey to destruction. Not a chance for anyone, especially when the entire floor separated and slid out gracefully from under the cabin just as it floated past us. The log cabin, not missing a beat, upper part still intact, sunk a bit, rose, sort of gave a half turn during the loss of its floor, straightened, then disappeared around the bend in the river. The glorious range of mountains, capped with snow, was a backdrop of aching beauty to the devastation played out before us.

Returning the next afternoon, we were able to drive through the standing water in the road between the two ports. The Canadian freezers had floated in their basement yesterday. Today, they stood drying out in the garage, manhandled there with the help of a U.S. couple en route to Alaska who had been stranded on the Canadian side for two days.

A high line of debris marked the flood's earlier reach. Now the river flowed where the road to Arlene's restaurant had been. It had changed its bed, racing several hundred feet to the west of its previous channel.

We carefully picked our way through the woods and mud toward the rear of the group of outbuildings and restaurant, climbing over downed masses of trees, gullied sand, silt and rocks. The muck sucked at our shoes, making walking difficult. The river had sent out a mighty arm of flood that joined the rush of water that poured down from the hills behind, all encircling the ports as it raced onward to the river. The far bank toward the east had been transformed into a rocky shoal where twisted remains of trees had run aground. A green roof perched there, high and dry, wreckage from the bear camp.

There was not one tree left standing near the river. The woods we had hiked through on the visit to the bear camp several years before, all gone. It was left so bare by the scouring river on both sides, we could clearly see the distant bear camp trailer.

The landmark old wooden bridge, wrecked originally by explosives, was totally gone, swept away together with the gigantic logjam woodpile that had been alongside its base on this west side. No more setting off fireworks from the bridge's derelict wreck, no more picking a careful way to the edge of it to gaze down into the river.

The metal wire cage of the goofy death-defying river-crossing trolley system was a smashed piece of junk, tangled in a massive pile of debris.

Metal wreckage from outbuildings in back of the restaurant had been heaped into piles by the flood waters. Debris was scattered over the cabin's front porch that now presented an unobstructed view of the river, racing past not fifteen feet away.

Bill immediately decided to throw a party, mainly to cook up and eat the thawed freezer food. There the details emerged.

Wendy had parked the old government truck at Moose City and driven her own car that fateful day. She and Diane were working out of temporary housing by the park entrance at Polebridge, thus on the east side of the river. Two years of detailed coyote materials for her doctorate were safe. The search had already started down along the river banks, turning up her pictures, books, and pieces of other personal items.

Madge Cooper's cabin roof was found along the bank about a mile to the south, half buried and entangled in trees, underbrush, sand, rocks and other debris. The second floor had somehow survived the wild river ride. Wendy's wedding rings and other valuables were found still in a box on top of the wrecked dresser. Madge Cooper's old rusted truck survived just beyond the reach of the river.

The tiny cabin set way back in the meadow was now river front property. No beach, no cottonwoods, all stripped clean away.

Within two days the section of river to the north of the Canadian port was forming its own brand new rocky bank in place of the soft black dirt, an amazing sight of nature repairing itself. Kyran said it best. The Flathead is a wild and scenic river, unrestrained by the machinations of man. The rains came down with such force and speed that the river did its own natural thing with raw power, rising rapidly, then receding almost as fast and rebuilding its new course.

Moose City lost about five acres of land and seven buildings, two of them outhouses. Cooper's cabin had been its oldest building, built by Frank Clute around 1912, and set back about 150 feet from the water's edge, during this rampage no distance at all. A valuable, historic cabin, gone.

Polebridge, to the south, was inundated. The historic mercantile was in standing water, as was most of the tiny hamlet. The hostel and other cabins had about two feet of water inside. The river's rush had provided one big flush for all the lost outhouses. Propane tanks and cords of next winter's firewood floated away down river.

Both customs' buildings received damage. Restricted to the quarter's basement in Canada, flood waters totally ruined all the wall insulation.

On the U.S. side, railroad ties that had delineated the road lanes, floated away. Mud was everywhere, even in the garage and generator room which had flooded. Thus, there was no generator, no electricity, no water pump, no clean water, no toilet use, no lights, and no radio connection to the outside world. Both wells were possibly contaminated.

The border was effectively closed, for with the road gone to the north, there was no place to go.

Ironic. The fires of the previous summer had crossed north over the border and devastated acres of Canadian forests. Now, the rains had come down from Canada and flood waters swept into the U.S. I don't know if that could be called a fair exchange or not.

Madge Cooper's great antique stove? Rubble on the river bottom.

Most of the numerous bridges up in Canada that crossed the many small and large creeks, all feeding into the North Fork of the Flathead, had been torn away, with no easy replacement money available. Not much activity would be going on up in British Columbia between the border, Morrisey and Fernie, although the old Cabin Creek Road could be temporarily used.

Chris and Tom were driving up the North Fork road the day after the flood had swept through. Scheduled to trap grizzly bears in Canada and planning to stay at their old bear camp, they didn't know it had been demolished.

As they rounded a corner, they saw a parked pickup with Florida plates. Seven people, five kids and two adults, were standing along the road, filming with a video camera.

"They flagged us down," Chris told us.

"They shouted, 'Hey, bear here! We've got a grizzly bear right here!'

"I got out of our truck and about twenty-five yards away, there's a grizzly bear in the brush. There are little kids standing out there! I couldn't believe it. I had to pull "Ranger Rick" on them. Had my U.S. Fish & Wildlife uniform shirt on. Told them to get back in the truck and get going, that they weren't doing anybody or anything any good."

Arriving at the border, Chris and Tom stood silent at waters edge, before going north to stare across the river at the wrecked camp. As they said immediately upon seeing and hearing of the magnitude of destruction, it was the best possible news for the grizzlies. A gladsome event for the animals. Roads closed in one fell swoop by good old, all knowing mom nature.

And lo, the griz returned to the river bottoms to feed on the drowned gophers and other delicacies.

Tom and Chris left to continue with their mission, looking for some of the elusive Cabinet Mountain grizzlies. An arduous undertaking indeed, for they trapped from horses, riding their trails for over nine hours a day, time which didn't include the stops to check the traps.

There were none found.

They caught no grizzly on the Canadian side of the Yaak. As Chris described it, they were two grizzly bear biologists who hadn't caught a grizzly yet that season.

A black bear, waiting for his turn to be collared

Eventually they trapped five grizzlies in the Selkirks in Canada and had a grand total of sixty-five to seventy captures for the summer, mostly black bears.

*   *   *

Tepee Lake still has loons but I wonder for how long. A modern, expensive log home, replete with solar system and many outbuildings, was constructed at the south end. A second monstrous log lodge, with huge timbers of ancient forest caliber, took over two years to build. Its front view encompasses a clear-cut that extends to a few trees down by the lake.

The original narrow turnoff to the lake from the forest service road has been widened to almost the width of the North Fork main road. Gigantic slash piles decorate the edges. The road ends at a locked gate.

Other lots are for sale around the lake. Heaps of trash, plastics, shards of metal, and other filthy-looking remnants of past road work and logging operations are piled near the road junction, together with an old trailer and rusted wreck of a truck. It looks even more ugly because of the forest setting.

Marca wanted just a few huckleberries from along Trail Creek and asked me to go with her for company. I don't pick huckleberries any more. Better the bears have them. On the wild shelf of land above the creek and springs were many paths among the bushes, doubled in width and powdery from the footsteps of crowds that had invaded the spot. Of course, Marca found no berries. Neither would the bears.

I stooped to pick up an empty beer bottle that had been tossed in the underbrush, intending to add it to our garbage at the cabin. I'd have needed a huge sack for the 100 or more empty brown bottles I found hidden within and under the brush.

A new lane was cut through the forest down from the junction near Marca's historic cabin. Another cabin would soon be built. Land around Mud Lake was for sale at exorbitant prices. Rights-of-way had been granted to any potential buyers. The route would have to pass the old small barn where the grizzlies had been trapped and collared in '93.

Later, I walked down the overgrown airstrip at Moose City, puzzled at the quiet. Something was missing. Then I realized the windsock wasn't sending forth its comforting squeak as it moved in the breeze. I finally found it, rotted through at its base, down on the ground, hidden by the tall grass of the meadow.

Somehow, seeing the tall slender hewn tree trunk, with its torn and stained white plastic windsock down on the ground, bothered me. A lot.

I stood there, remembering Tom Reynolds and his tales of the early North Fork. It was easy to imagine what it must have been like.

Now, I just wanted to see it as it was when we first discovered it.

*   *   *

I found the tracks down our lane, and I exalted.

A grizzly had traveled through that very morning.

I was careful to keep Brig from disturbing them. We followed the prints, north past the haunts of the Bobbsey Twins, on past the turn to Mud Lake. I was sure the bear would head into the forest there. But it didn't.

On and on the tracks went. Brig and I trudged alongside them, north, over four miles.

Finally, I stopped. The tracks disappeared in the distance, ahead of us. The bear had gone on and on and on. I'd have followed him forever.

The grizzly is being forced into ever smaller and less suitable habitat. Only at night will he pass through, traveling silently like a ghost, through lands that were once his, attempting to follow his old historic travel corridors to faintly remembered favorite feeding grounds.

His presence will be obliterated, just as his tracks are destroyed by the rush of man and his traffic.

Oh, Lord, I love the bears.

EPILOGUE

Blessed are the naïve for they have no sense, attempting the near impossible for often minuscule gains.

Such were we when we attempted to preserve the nature of the North Fork. To try to keep it as it was became a sharp skirmish in the larger battle that would eventually overwhelm the entire Flathead valley.

From the very beginning, we tried to interest the nationally recognized environmental groups in the uniqueness of the North Fork, trying in vain to have representatives visit, to see for themselves that the area was special. At that time, the price of the small amount of private land available was reasonable, with chunks of acreage for sale.

Just setting there, the area became a perfect target for change and development. We watched with dismay the slow gradual day to day changes that became noticeable to others only in the long run. As the Flathead valley was suddenly "discovered" and promoted, even the terrible road couldn't stop people from finding this special place of wildlife and beautiful views.

Overnight, it seemed, we counted over 100 lanes that cut off from the main North Fork road. Land prices shot up, and it deteriorated into a rush that has placed the very being of the North Fork at risk.

All this, a far cry from the old days when there was little activity in the North Fork, with few residents to disturb each other.

In the 1880s, a geological survey described squatter and homestead claims in the area. The infamous road was built in the 1920s from Columbia Falls to Big Creek. During the depression, the Civilian Conservation Corps (CCC) built or improved the road clear to the Canadian border. When we became landowners in the early 1980s, everything seemed blessedly behind the times.

That feeling also encompassed the local philosophy with land, neighbors, strangers, laws and government. About two generations from frontier living, people were used to setting their own rules and answering only to themselves. Anxiety and narrow-mindedness also played a major role in local perceptions. We had been warned that as long as a person didn't cross the old timers, they would be tolerated. Otherwise, don't make waves.

In 1986, a few North Fork landowners saw a need to put some sort of control on growth. A North Fork Land Use Planning Committee of North Fork landowners was created by the county commissioners, with permission to create a North Fork Land Use Plan by the landowners themselves which the county would approve and include in the county's master plan.

The county plan itself was loose, non-binding with no mandatory compliance, and so was the North Fork land use plan that was created by the landowners. Internal differences grew within the committee, composed mostly of the old guard, who, for some strange reason, had the votes necessary to "run the show".

Results from a survey sent to all landowners asked for protection of crucial wildlife habitat, a meaningful comprehensive plan for the area, and minimum lot sizes.

But the approved plan was worthless, asking only for volunteer participation from the landowners.

Land subdivision continued, with more homes on smaller tracts of land. Wildlife corridors were ignored. The truly wild land north of Trail Creek was eventually invaded with lanes bulldozed into prime habitat.

The l986 land use plan called for a review in l991, and Joe and I participated as members of the Land Use Planning Committee. Another survey was prepared for all landowners and the response was outstanding, with a little over thirty-eight percent return, much higher than the county-wide response some time later that pertained to a better county-wide plan. The l991 review included good subjects and did not just ask for volunteer participation. But the weak and unenforceable county plan made the North Fork update nearly worthless.

There have been other efforts to protect the North Fork, some official, others originated by private citizens. The state's Flathead Basin Commission focused on the North Fork with a steering committee created solely for that subject. Its final recommendations were excellent, but nothing has come of it.

The Flathead Transboundary Council was created by a group of concerned private citizens, both Canadian and U.S. Their goal was the establishment of an International Conservation Reserve that would include both sides of the border. With an outstanding group of Canadian and U.S. professionals from many fields as its scientific board, it was a bold and noble venture. It was doomed from the beginning because of lack of the necessary monies and organizational outreach. The political climate of the area finished it.

About three percent of the North Fork consists of private lands, four percent state lands, the remaining, federal. There are many levels of government and agencies involved with the North Fork, each with its own management objective: the U.S. Department of Interior (Glacier National Park); the U.S. Department of Agriculture (Forest Service/National Forest); the state of Montana (state forests and state fish and game); and the local Flathead County. Unfortunately, what is best for the North Fork is lost to discrete, often politically polarized issues. Agencies guard their bureaucracies.

Direct threats from Canada continue to hover within fifty miles of the border. Coal-fired power plants are on the British Columbia agenda, as is carbon dioxide development, ready to go, just to the north, in the midst of prime grizzly habitat.

In the early eighties, the proposal of a coal mine to be located on Cabin Creek, a tributary of the Flathead River in British Columbia, profoundly disturbed the sense of serenity downstream, so much so that the International Joint Commission was requested by the governments of the United States and Canada in December 1985 to examine and report on the implications of the matter.

The mine proposal, as it was defined and understood at that time, was not recommended or approved. But economic climates change. The proposal has been resurrected. Waterton and Glacier Parks, regardless of the designation as "The Crown of the Continent" would be at risk, as would be the North Fork of the Flathead river, even though it is part of the U.S. Wild and Scenic River system.

The continuous threats have given birth to various conservation and environmental organizations that continue to struggle to preserve the North Fork area. Etched in my memory is a statement Dr. Bruce McLellan made during one of the early annual bear meetings: he didn't see wilds in the North Fork. He saw mail boxes along the road.

Dan Vincent, Regional Fish and Game Supervisor, once stated in the Kalispell *Daily Interlake*, that when it was a question between human safety and wildlife, wildlife were going to lose every time. People move into outlying neighborhoods (like the North Fork) without knowing grizzly bears and cougars have always prowled there. When they find out, they often want the animals gone.

Does a landowner have absolute and unlimited right to change the essential natural character of his land which injures the rights of others?

Do individual land owners of limited environmental resources have a duty to preserve them unchanged for future generations?

Does the fact that a landowner thinks he has paid for these rights mean he is entitled to them?

Television ads for farm chemicals blurt out each spring that their ultimate responsibility is to the land. Should not that be the responsibility of us all? Quality of life is related directly to the quality of the environment. The grizzly does not know that the tasty gray moths he feasts on in the fall, in high rocky regions, originate in the pesticide-laced Midwest agricultural plains. He is an innocent.

Is there a responsibility for someone to assure the preservation of the natural scenic and aesthetic values of the North Fork and other wilderness? Aren't these resources the common property of all the people, including generations yet to come? Is government expected to assert the prior claim of society as a whole? Should not the government, even at the lowest level, have a responsibility to create and enforce laws and regulations necessary for the good and welfare of the state and its citizens as a whole? Land use plans, zoning, health regulations, even building permits should be included in those laws for the protection of the public at large from those who are unscrupulous and think only of themselves.

How wonderful it would be if agencies and others would plan a strategy to restore the damaged portions of the North Fork, de-emphasize timber production as the primary purpose of the area, and come up with a management plan from a conservation viewpoint and basis, with well-defined, enforceable guide-lines.

Advertising agencies are well aware of the fact that wildlife sells. Witness the gorgeous wolf running in the "wild" to introduce weed killer. The grizzly sells everything from sofas to food to window glass. At one time, a live cougar, tethered with collar and chain, was the come-on for a valley bar in Columbia Falls. How pitiful. Why can't man extend his innate feelings to the real thing? Surely, humans can get their act together to manage and protect wildlife and habitat. Each and everyone of us must get involved and speak for the wildlife.

Hope springs eternal.

*   *   *

There was Montana Governor Mark Racicot's letter to the Helena office of the Fish and Wildlife Service, in which he expressed the state's **official opposition** to the continued reintroduction of wolves into Yellowstone and central Idaho because of the burden those wolves would likely place on Montana. Racicot's solution: to not only stop the reintroduction, but to provide Montana with federal assurance that Montana could **independently** downlist and delist wolves—to "decouple" Montana and Wyoming and Idaho with respect to wolf recovery, thus allowing Montana to be "more in control of wolf management." (From "Crying Wolf in Yellowstone" by Tom Skeele, printed in the January 19, 1996 edition of the *Bozeman Daily Chronicle.*)

*   *   *

Charles Russell, the renowned cowboy artist, was asked to address a Montana booster meeting shortly before his death in Great Falls in 1926. The old man was horrified to hear himself introduced as a "pioneer".

Misty-eyed, he roared:

"In my book, a pioneer is a man who comes to a virgin country, traps off all the fur, kills off all the wild meat, cuts down all the trees, grazes off all the grass, plows the roots up and strings ten million miles of bob wire. A pioneer destroys things and calls it civilization. I wish to God that this country was just like it was when I first saw it, and that none of you folks were here at all!" Charles Russell (From *Three Hundred Years of American Painting,* Time Inc, N.Y.)

And on and on it goes—.
Who speaks for the animals?

Of note....

Wolves dispersed north into Canada from Montana did not fare too well.

Diane had seven radio dollars returned from Glacier Park wolves that were shot—three in British Columbia and four in Alberta. About ninety-five percent of the wolf population in southern Alberta was terminated in 1995.

The wolf population near the North Fork of the Flathead River has decreased from three packs to one since the 1980s. Radiocollars have been found, pierced by bullets.

Mountain lions were not collared during the winter of 1995-96. Toni continued to monitor fourteen radiocollared lions going into the winter season. Two lions starved to death. Because of lack of funds, the project shut down in May of 1996. She is now lead field scientist of the Yellowstone Cougar Project.

Wendy Clark is now a biologist with the forest service along the Rocky mountain front.

Tim is a Montana Fish and Wildlife biologist for the region that includes the North Fork.

Chris and Tom are involved with grizzly reintroduction into the Bitterroots. They continue to visit Ron in Cranbrook, British Columbia. Though still confined to a wheelchair, his high spirits see him through continued therapy.

Dr. Bruce McLellan, still working with grizzly in Canada, near Banff, is concerned about grizzly genetic lines, since they are living in isolated pockets because of habitat loss.

Kryan, Diane and Wendy received their doctorates. All three are in prime positions to further the survival and dispersal of wildlife, so critical to our environment

Senior citizen coyote, Thunder, surely passed on his longevity to his progeny. Long may they roam the North Fork, true survivors.

CPSIA information can be obtained
at www.ICGtesting.com
Printed in the USA
FSHW012042240720
72473FS